Daniel S. Hamilton

D0916039

Jousting With
The New York Times
1961-2014:
Worldviews in Radical Conflict

"A priest and former editor tangles with
The Times Editorial Board
on its religion-related editorials."

Manufactured by CreateSpace
An Amazon Company for the St. John Fisher Foundation
New York, U.S.A.

Dedication

To

Most Rev. William F. Murphy, S.T.D.

In gratitude for his faithful service
as Bishop Ordinary of
the Diocese of Rockville Centre,
Long Island, New York
2001-2015

TABLE OF CONTENTS

The letters here deal mainly with whether some form of public (tax) aid should be given to students in non-profit independent, including religiously affiliated, schools or to their parents. The Times views aid a violation of the wall of separation between Church and States established by the First Amendment to the Federal Constitution. Letters dispute such unfounded interpretations and their unjust discriminating consequences; aid to religiously affiliated higher education; prayer in public schools, theologians dissenting from Catholic teachings.

Issues continue from Section I through all other sections; issues arisen or becoming especially contentious are women's reproductive rights, a euphemism for access to abortion; embryonic stem cell research-destruction; human cloning; alleged punishment of divorced/invalidly remarried Catholics; priestly ordination of women.

All previous issues continue with more or less intensity; embryonic stem-cell research-destruction; abortion-provider access restrictions; reproductive rights; homosexual activity declared a right; domestic partnerships; frequent, vigorous editorial support for legalizing same-sex marriage; vigorous reproductive rights editorials; vouchers for independent school students debated.

Editorials in favor of legalizing same-sex marriage

continue, Health and Human Services Mandate imposing "neutral" paid (by employers) insurance for all FDA-approved contraceptives, sterilization and potentially abortifacient drugs; religious objections disregarded; religious and other units dispute in court such imposition or its extent. Equal Access relevance disputed.

Introduction

<u>The New York Times</u> is arguably the most important daily newspaper in the United States and in the entire world. Its staff of reporters, photographers, news analysts, reviewers, editors and support personnel cover important events occurring daily world-wide. The Times's diversified, multiple features, special sections and on-line availability respond to readers with the same broad spectrum of needs and interests. Times reporters are dependably diligent in getting all the relevant facts of a story, putting them together in a logical, clear, understandable whole for the reader to absorb without tedium and with assurance that the writer's personal views or the paper's known ideological position will not get in the way of objectivity and truth.

Editorials, opinion pieces, commentaries and news analyses, especially the first two, present a different picture; here the views of the writer or writers enter in or, more likely, predominate. Often we may hear, "The Times says..." as of an authority when the editor or chosen editorial board writers give their views on particular subjects, institutions of government or social problems.

In editorials on basic societal issues, we encounter the paper's worldview, its philosophy of human nature, the ideology that informs all its positions, its value system, the ethical and moral standards to which it adheres and urges its readers to accept.

The basic philosophy of The Times must be described as relativist secularism: Agnostic man is the measure of all things; pragmatic reason linked to the evolving conclusions of natural science is the final rule and guide of life. Such a philosophy contrasts radically with a worldview that accepts the existence of a Creator God, a natural moral law of which God is the author, which man can know and to which he is subject, with or without a claim of divine revelation as an additional source and support.

The two diverse worldviews are not always in open opposition. Reason, intuition, common sense and human experience sometimes unite in a common response. Opposition to the death penalty and torture are examples. Support for universal education, universal health services, justice and peace efforts are others.

Opposing Worldviews

But there are some issues where the two views radically clash. Among these are natural law convictions about God's total dominion over man as distinguished from man's complete autonomy or dominion over himself: For the one, man's personal rights are limited as a child of God; for the other, they are virtually unlimited. Areas where the two views especially clash are those of human life, human sexuality, marriage, the family and religious freedom. I think it is fair to say that The Times editorial board is distrustful of religion, particularly ones that make dogmatic or absolute claims. It is in this context that the letters to The Times contained in this volume (published or unpublished originally by The Times) were written; namely, from an intellectual culture quite different from that of The Times but overwhelmingly present and influential in our civilization and in our country past and present. These opposing worldviews or basic philosophies are evident in the metaphysical, anthropological, and ethical principles underlying the pertinent religion-related editorials, frequently dealing with the subject areas mentioned, and the letters written to challenge their point of view.

It is also true that many additional editorial subjects have ethical dimensions or that rely partially or wholly on ethical principles, but that the solutions advocated for particular problems, unlike the principles themselves, are patient of different morally acceptable solutions rather than only one. Defense measures, immigration and environmental issues are examples. Thus, there is no basic for a clash but only the presentation of reasonably different viewpoints.

Yes, but when there is a clash, for one worldview, the Creator God, who is sovereign and has dominion over man, with the natural moral law accessible to reason and the Ten Commandments (basically, excepting the Sabbath, an expression of the natural moral law) are the final criteria. For the other, all this is hypothetical, useful but not something decisive or absolute. Rather, man is the measure of all things; he is autonomous over himself and collectively over the universe. Natural evolving science is the final gauge of progress. For both, however, in a democratic society, sovereignty and dominion are expressed in the civil order ultimately only by the democratic vote. Although civil law can't impose a theistic or a secularistic moral order, it can allow a culture gradually to slip into one or reinforce the other. Both are, in effect, "religions" or basic world views.

This fundamental philosophy of the world and of human life embraced and projected by The Times, found explicitly or implicitly in its editorials and opinion pages is not the principal philosophy of past or present American society or, arguably, even of that portion which The Times specifically serves. For more than fifty years I have written these letters to contest this secularistic orientation exhibited by The Times's editorial-board.

In recent years the board has manifested this outlook in a prolonged unrelenting advocacy of same-sex marriage with no significantly opposed letters or op-ed essays admitted. Other principled views on these issues are labelled bigoted, anti-woman and anti-equality. The board has continuously asserted "reproductive rights" understood as unlimited access to abortion, condoned the destruction of human embryos for therapeutic purposes, advocated the manufacture of new human beings, of sex education as a "how-to" procedure for teens to avoid pregnancy or how to deal with it in fact, without any review and inclusion of moral standards held by parents. It has pushed to exempt centers specializing in abortion from medical safeguards required for other surgeries; and has labored vigorously in efforts to make the homosexual union a civil right and the moral equivalent of marriage; its unqualified support for persons who, having been conceived and born as a male or as a female, later declare themselves to be of the other gender emotionally or physically or both ways, and then seeking additional civil rights and protections lest they suffer any disadvantage in society for having deliberately and freely made that choice. Earlier in time and ongoing the board opposed allowing taxpaying parents to benefit in some significant way from mandated educational taxation when they exercise their natural moral and civil right to choose religiously affiliated schools for their children.

Yes, a different worldview: suspicion of religion is evident in their thinking that the only acceptable, in effect, the only constitutionally approved or approvable freedom for religion should be worship conducted in worship halls, religious instruction in such halls or their equivalent and services for one's fellow believers. Introductory prayers, even by majority consent, at public meetings should be disallowed.

This different worldview, gives short shrift to traditional religion apparently because of the absolute norms (vs. relativistic, evolving norms) and fixed positions that some religions maintain. The overwhelming vote of the people or majority supreme court decisions, when dissenting from The Times's view, are labelled bad, unhelpful, shortsighted, bigoted or a new obstacle to progress and freedom.

Editorials, Op-Eds, Letters and the Political Process

Citizens have a moral obligation to take part in the political process, above all, to vote. If we don't, an alien philosophy, an ideology destructive of the values upon which our nation was founded and holds dear can begin to take hold of our national outlook, our jurisprudences and our educational institutions. Secularism can shrink or obliterate the fundamental truths and generous freedoms associated with our nation's beginnings.

Among various instruments contributing to and constituting the political process, newspapers with their editorials and letters to the editor are one way of keeping in focus the truths and freedoms we hold dear. People with a strong sense of responsibility should use the letters instrument liberally.

Religious differences in a democratic pluralist society can and should be composed, not compromised, not one or the other excluded. Atheism, agnosticism and the ethical frameworks tied to them are religion-equivalents. Reasonable people based securely on "respect for conscience" can find the ways to preserve our nation's traditions, to respect them, while respecting one another and the beliefs or non-beliefs of each. We do not need to exclude or suppress our beliefs or cease to act in accord with them when we enter the public forum. In some areas, to be sure, where no accommodation can be made we must hold to principles and to binding moral norms. Even then, respect is never lost for those who (theists, agnostics or atheists) lose by the vote or court decisions in a democratic society, their fundamental rights being guaranteed.

A losing vote or a negative court verdict cannot necessarily be construed as a negative moral judgment on the cause or its proponents at that point. Above all, it doesn't dispense its adherents from their convictions as to the truth and the obligation to uphold it. Citizens must keep witnessing and acting in accord with the truth as they know it. That's the responsible and the American way.

I hope, dear reader, the letters published here will encourage you to make your views known to the editor and thus engage with him or her and their associates in an intelligent reflection on the news and on the great issues of the day, and in this way also take part in the political process for the common good of our nation.

Msgr. Daniel S. Hamilton, Pastor Emeritus
Our Lady of Perpetual Help Church
Lindenhurst, New York 11757

Notes

1. Letters actually published by The Times are clearly identified as such by the date of publication being placed next to the date of submission at the head of the letter. Letters published here for the first time have only the date of submission. Most published letters were shortened, by Times editors, as it is said, for space requirements. The NYT-published letters have a Times-editor heading. All other headings are the author's own.

2. Although many, indeed, most of the letters, whether originally published or unpublished, are critical of certain Times editorial positions in the time period mentioned, the flip side of that criticism is a needed tribute willingly given to all the journalists of The Times who pursue their journalistic vocation with strict integrity.

3. Diocese of Rockville Centre, Long Island, positions I held at the time of my writing the letters are, with the relevant dates: Professor, St. Pius X Preparatory Seminary, Uniondale, NY 1961-68; Director, diocesan Bureau of Public Information, 1968-85: Columnist, The Long Island

<u>Catholic</u>, 1962-85; editor, <u>The Long Island Catholic</u>, 1975-85; Pastor of Our Lady of Perpetual Help Church, Lindenhurst, NY: 1985-2007; Pastor Emeritus 2007. The author is a member of the Catholic Theological Society of America and Canada and of the Fellowship of Catholic Scholars.

SECTION I: 1961-1990

July 19, 1961   Pub. NYT July 27, 1961
Catholic opposition is seen as exercise of freedom as citizens

Editor: What is really "outrageous" about the defeat of the school-aid bill is that Catholic educators and legislators have been branded by successive editorials in The Times as *tibétes noires* of this unfortunate climax. This reflects the consistent inability of The Times to see the discriminatory character of aid to public schools alone.

I like to suppose that the position of The Times is one carefully thought out and sincerely held as the best defense of traditional American principles. What is more distasteful here is the implication that the convictions of forty-five million Americans who see the implications of democracy, of free choice in education, and of the bearing of the church-state principle in a different light are in some way fighting against the best interest of the country.

The Catholic community asserts the uniqueness of the educational process, its compulsory character and its ultimate control by the parent. Comparisons with such things as public transportation, parks, etc., are therefore, irrelevant. It asserts that free choice in education is guaranteed by the Supreme Court. The United States does not espouse the single school system in theory or in practice. It asserts the positive necessity, as far as Catholics are concerned, for religiously oriented education. This involves systematic instruction in religion and moral values in a school setting. It asserts its refusal to acknowledge as just and equitable any aid system which makes the free choice of such a religiously oriented education a practical impossibility.

The Times has asserted on another occasion that "freedom for nonpublic education is surely not equivalent to a promise of public funds." If this freedom is not a guarantee of equal treatment then it is not a real freedom at all but only a tolerated deviation from what is to be considered the uniquely legitimate norm – namely, attendance at a public nonreligious school. To this conclusion the Catholic community is unalterably opposed.

Admittedly, the issues in aid to education are complicated. The rights of all must be protected and the best interests of the commonwealth served. No one wants to be in a position of seemingly obstructing the interests of the country.

But surely it is facile to suppose that those who, in the exercise of their freedom as citizens, follow the dictates of their conscience as to a religiously oriented education for their children and suffer an enormous financial disability thereby, are unjustifiably opposed to that which will perpetuate their servitude for years to come.

June 18, 1963   Pub. NYT June 28, 1963
Court's concept of neutrality in religious matters questioned

Editor: The Supreme Court's decision together with Justice Stewart's dissent, on school prayers and Bible reading has served to give only bolder expression to the yet unsolved antimony:

In religious matters the state must scrupulously be neutral; but what are the precise conditions of this neutrality? Does it mean the exclusion of all religious expression and instruction apart from, in the Court's words, "comparative religion or the history of religion and its relationship to the advancement of civilization"? Or is Justice Stewart right when he observes that one is faced, actually, with a violation of neutrality when a "compulsory state educational system so structures a child's life that… religious exercises [or religious instruction] are held to be an impermissible activity in schools [and] religion is placed at an artificial and state-created disadvantage"?

Is genuine neutrality that which permits religious exercises and instruction for those who want them or that which excludes them for all? Are there no practical ways of implementing such a choice, of providing equally unembarrassing alternatives for those who want such religious expression and those who do not?

While striking down what it judged a legal requirement for religious exercises – and therefore an establishment, the Court has at the same time made the debatable twofold assumption that specifically religious expression and learning belong to the home and the church alone and that secular education can actually be isolated from all religious bases and premises. Millions of American parents, who hold the prior inalienable right in the education of their children, will admit neither of these premises.

Despite its own disclaimer, the Court, in holding a concept of "neutrality-by-exclusion," has canonized an ethos favoring the secular humanist view of life.

October 7, 1964   Pub. NYT. Oct. 15, 1964
On Ecumenism

Editor: Your otherwise clear-sighted editorial of Oct. 7 "On Ecumenism," dealing with the *aggiornamento* within the Roman Catholic Church, contains one serious error: "Before Pope John was elected in 1958 it would have been fanciful to think of the Roman Catholic Church recognizing the possibility of merit or salvation outside the Catholic fold…"

On the contrary, the Catholic Church has consistently taught the possibility of merit and salvation for those outside its visible unity – namely, for non-Catholic Christians and for those of other religions. Indeed it is and has been Catholic teaching that God gives sufficient graces to all men to be saved. Basic to Catholic teaching has been the recognition that countless millions have belonged by at least desire and longing to the salvation community which is the church, although in good faith they neither recognized it as such not therefore entered its visible unity.

Ironically, the Catholic position on this universality of God's salvific will (as the subject is called in dogmatic theology) has been much more liberal than the classical protestant position. Most recent and most startling in a long series of statements (through many centuries) by the teaching church was the excommunication, in 1949, of a priest who taught the doctrine you wrongly assume to have been characteristic of the Catholic Church before 1958.

To protect the unborn

Editor: Your "Aborting an Amendment" editorial (June 17) continues to overlook the data from genetics, embryology and fetology which lead to the conclusion that "to terminate pregnancy voluntarily" is but a euphemism for "to kill an unborn human being." Precisely for this reason, supporters of a human life amendment cannot agree that abortion is a "private" matter between a woman and her physician.

Yeshiva University's Rabbi J. Irwin Bleich made this point eloquently at the recent Congressional hearings when he said: "No individual may justifiably take the life of another, other than in the process of self-defense. Fetal life, as a form of human life, is entitled to the self-same safeguards and protection which society accords to all its members. Abortion is not a private matter between a woman and her physician. It impinges upon the most fundamental right of a third party…the unborn baby's right to life. It is precisely because the human baby is defenseless and unable to defend its rights that society has an obligation to guarantee the fetus protection under the law."

Supporters of a human life amendment advocate no return to a "double standard under which the wealthy would continue to obtain abortions and the poor would be victimized." They advocate a single standard which would simultaneously protect the innocent unborn, whether belonging to the rich or the poor, encourage responsible parenthood and premarital chastity and assure adequate social services for the (pregnant) poor.

May 27, 1975   Pub. NYT June 17, 1975
The Children's Rights

Editor: In *Meek vs. Pittenger* the Supreme Court has forced many citizens, Chief Justice Burger tells us (news story May 20) to choose between the free exercise of religion, entitling them and often impelling them to choose church- or synagogue-related schools for their children, and the equal protection of the laws, which should guarantee to all children remedial assistance financed by their parents' taxes. But neither the children who attend such schools nor their parents may both constitutional guarantees together, according to the present decision of the Court.

Certain children are denied these benefits, in the words and with the emphasis of Justice Burger, "only *because* they attend a Lutheran, Catholic or other church-sponsored school," a principle of discrimination which, the Justice continues, "does not simply tilt the Constitution against religion; it literally turns the religion clause on its head.

Calling the current decision a "gross violation of the Fourteenth Amendment rights,: the Chief Justice expresses the "hope that, at some future date, the Court will come to a more enlightened and tolerant view of the First Amendment's guarantee of free exercise of religion, thus eliminating the denial of equal protection to children in church-sponsored schools, and take a more realistic view that carefully limited aid to children is not a step toward establishing a state religion…"

To the Chief Justice's view and to that of his fellow dissenters, Justices Rehnquist and White, one can only respond, Amen! But how long will it take the present Court majority to shed its rigidly secularist approach to church-related schools? And when the day of liberation comes, will there be only a few survivors to set free?

April 17, 1978   Pub. NYT April 27, 1978
Of tuition, taxes and equal justice for all

Editor: Your April 14 editorial "Tuition Credits Fail Every Time" rejects such credits because, first, they include help for the very wealthy, who don't need it. This obligation, more theoretical, you admit, than practical, can easily be overcome by putting an income eligibility ceiling on tuition-paying parents. Congress can take a look at this program as often as it likes.

Objecting that such credits will hurt public schools, however, reveals your persistent failure to recognize that parents are gravely hurt by a system of double taxation which effectively denies their natural and constitutional right to choose nonpublic, often religious oriented, schools for their children.   Such parents, moreover, want no "subsidy," only a just share in the taxes they have already paid for education.

Both public and nonpublic schools serve the common good in this community. For more than a century, Federal and state governments have done just about everything possible to discourage parents from choosing nonpublic schools. These schools have significantly declined over the past decade.

If providing a minimum degree of justice and equity for tax-paying and tuition-paying nonpublic school parents is now considered a threat to public schools, our framework of values has become distorted. Since when is securing justice for a minority a threat to anybody or anything?

If taxpayers want, for example, systems of transportation, garbage collection or recreation other than that provided by public funds, including their own taxes, they ought personally to pay for them.

But schools are different. They are surrogates for parents and inculcators of values. Both our common-law tradition and the US Supreme Court (Pierce vs. Society of

Sisters, 1925) uphold the right of parents to choose the schools their children will attend. When they must educate their children but can benefit from their school taxes only if they choose a state-operated school, their natural and constitutional right is severely impeded.

Fortunately, this injustice, nonexistent in other Western democracies, meets growing criticism today throughout the United States. Perhaps even The Times will ultimately grasp this point about inhibiting a fundamental right of citizens and finally pass the test on equal justice for all.

June 13, 1978   Pub. NYT June 26, 1978
Of school taxes, tuition costs and a 'burdened' right

Editor: Max J. Rubin, in two recent letters, vehemently opposed tuition tax credits for parents of nonpublic-school children.

In response to a private letter Mr. Rubin objects that private schools do not have to keep the disruptive and deficient. He ought to examine performance on this issue, rather than state an abstract principle. Many non-profit, non-segregated schools – like the Catholic schools of the metropolitan New York area – do keep the disruptive and deficient. If they had the resources of public schools, they'd be uniformly able and happy to keep proportionately at least as many such kids as public schools do.

Mr. Rubin fears that if the tuition tax credit idea is once accepted, public pressure will make the amount of the credit grow. Is he afraid of the democratic process? Shouldn't we all be concerned about what is just, about what respect for basic human rights demands? The Universal Declaration of Human Rights states (Article 26, par. 3): "Parents have a prior right to choose the kind of education that shall be given to their children."

But the former Board of Education president verges on the ridiculous when, attempting to rebut the free-exercise-of-religion argument for giving tuition tax credits, he says, if that argument were accepted, "then it is equally incumbent upon the government to grant public aid to churches and synagogues which are in financial need in order to 'guarantee the free exercise of religion.'" How silly!

It is not compulsory in this country to attend church or synagogue; no one pays a tax in behalf of a church or synagogue. But sending your children to school is compulsory; paying school taxes, directly or indirectly, is compulsory.

The right to choose the school your child will attend is a natural and constitutionally guaranteed right. Yet this right is grievously burdened in the United States when parents choose a nonpublic, often religiously oriented school for their children. As a result of that choice they derive virtually no benefit from their school taxes. This is an unjust policy.

Tuition tax credits are a sign that a democratic society recognizes and is determined to right a wrong, the wrong that you must pay school taxes but can benefit from them only in a state-operated school.

Dec. 31, 1979 Pub. NYT Jan. 7, 1980
What the Catholic Church did and did not do to Hans Küng

Editor: In a Dec. 28 letter, four clergymen and one lay woman identifying themselves as American Episcopalians severely criticized the Holy See for withdrawing canonical mission – a technical phrase denoting authorization to teach Catholic doctrines and theology in the Church's name – from the Rev. Hans Küng. The writers view this "silencing" of Father Küng as a blow to ecumenism and "offensive to the conscience of Western culture."

Although it is debatable whether such a small group can speak for the "conscience of Western culture," it is certain that Father Küng has not been silenced. He can teach, lecture, write and publish no less than before, though not now from a seat on a Catholic theological faculty requiring canonical mission. He is no longer authorized to teach in the Church's name precisely because for a long period of time in his published works he has rejected important elements of the Church's teaching.

In reference to theology and scientific method, the writers appear to view theology as a natural science in which scientific method is applied just as in any other natural science. If they are so convinced, they stand opposed to virtually the entire Christian world.

Theology is the science of God's revealed word, the "faith once delivered to the saints"- a phrase the writers dislike though it is taken from the New Testament Letter of Jude, verse 3. God's word may be more deeply understood and even formulated anew in concepts better suited to a particular age, but it may not be evacuated of its constant meaning. The theologian's scientific study takes place within, not apart from. The living tradition of the Spirit-guided Church where pastors (bishops) finally and collectively judge whether particular understandings authentically present God's word.

Withdrawing Father Küng's privilege of canonical mission should not be misunderstood as silencing, assailing, condemning, banning or suspending him.

Although he may no longer teach in a Catholic faculty that requires canonical mission, he may teach elsewhere. Unlike Archbishop Lefebvre, he has not been suspended from the priestly ministry. Church authority does not question Father Küng's sincerity, learning or scholarly contributions. But it does judge important points in his teaching, about which he has refused to dialogue, incompatible with the faith of the Church, incompatible with the truth of God's word.

Though some Reformation Church Christians may be attracted to particular positions of Father Küng, ecumenism would be ill served if such positions were confused with the authentic teaching of the Catholic Church. It is to be hoped that this theologian of great personal dynamism and charm, who has spoken powerfully to so many, will re-examine his theological method and situate it firmly within the communion of the Church he has ably served for a quarter of a century.

Sept. 22, 1980   Pub. NYT October 8, 1980
Segregation rights? Euthanasia rights?

Editor: You fault Cardinal Medeiros of Boston for directly involving himself as a church leader in an election campaign ("The Archbishop and Abortion," editorial Sept. 19). It's acceptable, you hold, for religious leaders to preach and to teach, but not in such a way that this activity reflects, even indirectly, on political candidates.

What would you say if the issue, instead of "abortion rights," were slavery rights, segregation rights, euthanasia rights, sterilization-of-the-weak rights or genocide-of-the-Jews rights? But, you reply, no political candidate is supporting any such enormity or the funding thereof! At the moment, no; in the past, yes. Governments have claimed or upheld such rights; politicians; even sincerely, have supported such positions.

The difficulty now, to be sure, is that you do not recognize abortion, the direct killing of an innocent unborn child, as the most violent oppression of the weak our world has ever known. You do not turn in revulsion when that new, living human being – defenseless, unseen and unheard in his mother's womb, but our neighbor – is by a surgeon's scalpel or burned to death by a saline solution.

If you would take a step to appreciate Cardinal Medeiros's position, treat your entire editorial staff, in small groups, to an abortion experience. Get close up and watch what happens. Then reassess you're your judgment as to whether Cardinal Medeiros is "using the pulpit to intimidate congregations into voting the church's way," or, rather, prophetically alerting moral conscience to its obligation in light of the most violent oppression of the weak the world has ever known.

May 20, 1981   Pub. NYT May 31, 1981
What must human life do to prove personhood?

Editor: Soma Golden performs a useful service in pointing out that biomedical scientists uniformly hold that a new human life begins when the sperm and egg unite to form a zygote, the earliest form of the human species, at conception (Editorial Notebook May 18).

The important question in the abortion debate, Miss Golden rightly adds, concerns the "value of this life from its earliest moments" or, put another way, "When does the fetus become a person?" It's unfortunate, however, that she appeals to Aristotle's outmoded biology for an answer and misunderstands Catholic teaching, which, though it has at all times rejected direct abortion, has never decided the issue of ensoulment.

Those who question whether the new human life is a person imply that the fetus, or "little one," must be able to do something to qualify as a person. Is he producing heartbeats or brain waves (about three to four weeks)? Is he responding to sensory stimuli (about six weeks)? Or growing hair on his head (about 16 weeks)? Or able to live outside the womb (about 28 weeks and constantly decreasing)? Or is an even longer period - does baby talk and socialize adequately? - needed to qualify for the dignity of personhood?

Clearly, speculators invoke a variety of contradictory biological, philosophical, psychological and sociological criteria to answer their question.

What reason is there, however, for denying the little one the dignity of personhood right from his or her beginning, from conception? Nobody can offer any compelling reason. Despite agreement that the conceptus is a new, unique member of the human species, the problem seems to be that the little one is so small and helpless.

Those who want to deny personhood (or "full life," in Miss Golden's phrase) to the new human life, not those who affirm it, are the ones who invoke a host of unverifiable and debatable opinions about personhood. Given their doubt, even perplexity, about when personhood "happens," you'd think they would want to preserve innocent human life from direct attack at every age of its development, since he who chooses to kill what may be a person chooses to kill a person.

Alas, that's not the case. Logic goes out the window in most discussions of abortion, of human life and personhood.

August 30, 1982   Pub. NYT Sept. 9, 1982
Tuition tax credits help repair a civil right

Editor: When in your Aug. 28 editorial "Tuition Credits and Civil Rights" you designate as the larger issue your view that such "credits would subsidize institutions that by their nature violate the crucial premise that publicly financed services should be universally available," you misconstrue the nature of a tax credit.

Taxpayers currently get Federal tax credits for promoting a variety of national objectives - installing energy-saving devices in their homes, investing in certain types of business, hiring employees under WIN programs, hiring individuals of specially targeted groups, and so forth.

These services, for which taxpayers receive credit, are not universally available; they benefit, in the main, particular persons. The tax credit, however, recognizes that those providing the services are meeting a national priority, even though the particular program is neither government-controlled nor open to everybody. Individuals, not institutions, get the credits.

As your editorial headline asserts, however, tuition tax credits do indeed constitute a civil rights issue. Given the unique nature of education, which distinguishes it from other public services, the civil rights issue concerns the right of taxpayer/parents, compelled by law to educate their children and to pay school taxes, to choose their children's schools without simultaneously being deprived of all benefits from the taxes they must pay. This parental right to choose schools is guaranteed by the Constitution (Pierce vs. Society of Sisters, 1925).

International human rights covenants, moreover, confirm this right: "Parents have a prior right to choose the kind of education that shall be given to their children" (U.N. Universal Declaration of Human Rights, Article 26, No. 13).

"The States parties to the present Covenant undertake to have respect for the liberty of parents, and, when applicable, legal guardians to choose for their children schools, other than those established by the public authorities, which conform to such minimum educational standards as may be laid down or approved by the States and to ensure the religious and moral education of their children in conformity with their own convictions" (International Covenant on Economic, Social and Cultural

Rights, Article 13.3).

The Helsinki Final Act (VII) pledges its signatories, including the United States, to implement the fundamental rights and freedoms cited in these covenants.

Your designation of schools as "an essential municipal service" and of tuition tax credits as encouraging "educational separatism" reveals to me a basic conviction, in opposition to these human rights covenants, that all schools should be state-operated.

Most Western democracies protect the right of parental choice in education by observing some form of distributive justice toward taxpaying parents who choose "schools other than those established by the public authorities."

May 20, 1985   Pub. NYT June 1, 1985

As the Church sees it

Editor: Your readers should know that neither the Gospels nor other contemporary data provide any foundation for the imaginative hypotheses of Professor Maccoby about the supposed identity of Jesus and Barabbas or the alleged elaborate concoction of the Gospel writers. Indeed, the Gospels do not present Jesus as a "rebel against Judaism," but as the one who confirmed, while drawing to its divinely intended fulfillment, the religious teaching of the law and the prophets; the one who personally embodied Israel's messianic hope, and the one who, being the unique Son of the Father, gave His life, the life of the incarnate God-man, as a sacrifice for Israel and the nations.

Whatever the compromised status of the Jerusalem high priest at the time, Jesus is clearly condemned for His alleged blasphemy - Matthew 26:65-66; Mark 14:61ff.; Luke 22:66ff.; John 10:33, 19:7 - that is, for making Himself out somehow to be equal to the God of Israel. The Gospels testify that certain Pharisees as well as certain

Sadducees rejected Jesus' religious claims.

Professor Maccoby brings forth no evidence to prove his assertions that Jesus and Barabbas are one; that a religious conflict, as defined, played no part in Jesus' condemnation, or that Jesus presented Himself merely as a human Messiah bent on setting up an earthly messianic kingdom.

May 2, 1986   **Licit and illicit dissent**

Editor: Sister Jeannine Gramick asserts in her letter published May 1 defending the Rev. Charles E. Curran that "Catholics possess a legitimate right to dissent from noninfallible Church teachings." Although some theologians hold this opinion, the authentic teaching of the Catholic Church nowhere endorses it. Rather, all authentic sources of Catholic doctrine affirm that Catholics have an obligation to give religious submission of will and mind to authoritative doctrinal and moral teaching proposed by the Church's magisterium, even when such authoritative teaching is not solemnly defined and therefore not certainly infallible.

Father Curran and some other theologians often cite a brief section on "licit theological dissent" in the U.S. Bishops' 1968 Pastoral letter "Human Life in Our Day" as providing the basis for their position on dissent. This section of the1968 Pastoral clearly intends, however, to sanction no more than a speculative theological dissent on noninfallible teachings; that is, a dissent of theologians that, while putting forward reasons for revision in a specific authentic teaching, recognizes that such a teaching "remains binding and carries with it a moral certitude..." (from the Pastoral).

On the authentic Church teachings currently in dispute, however, Father Curran and some other theologians do not merely put forward dissenting theological hypotheses for discussion and debate; they propose their positions, which contradict various binding Church teachings, as sufficiently certain to be accepted in theory and pursued in practice. They promote, in other words, a "rival doctrine." Moreover, in certain instances, they actively combat those binding authentic teachings, which can no longer be fairly described as only "received teaching," since the Church's teaching office has vigorously, frequently and in great detail re-affirmed them over the last twenty years.

When theologians mandated to teach in the Church's name publicly contradict and combat binding Church teaching, Church authority acts with integrity and consistently in refusing to continue them as officially deputized Church teachers. The Holy See does not question Father Curran's personal integrity, scientific competence or piety. At issue is his contradiction of binding Church teaching.

In the event that the Holy See withdraws Father Curran's canonical mandate to teach theology, he can still teach theology in institutions where teachers of theology require no canonical mandate; he can put forth verbally and in writing whatever positions that, as a result of his theological research, he believes to be true; and he may and must act, in practice, like every other person, in accord with his upright and certain conscience. But he will no longer be authorized to teach in the Church's name when at the same time he contradicts several of its binding teachings.

Church authority has the obligation both to safeguard its own sacred mission and to respect a scholar's professional integrity and personal freedom. The proposed action of the Holy See fulfills this obligation.

September 13, 1986   Catholic officials and the law

Editor: Your Sept. 13 editorial "Who May Speak to Catholics" allows a "dilemma of Catholic politicians: How they can swear to uphold the law and the rights of others when, as with abortion, those rights contradict Catholic teaching?

This dilemma doesn't exist. An officer of government, whatever his religious faith, ethical convictions or lack of either or both, must uphold – in the sense of act in accord with – the law. Otherwise he must resign. But he is not required to enlarge the effect of a law that he judges immoral or to refrain from urging and working for its repeal in accord with the democratic process.

What would you think of a South African government leader who, though he publically affirmed that apartheid is immoral, worked to enlarge its effect by using his executive power to continue particular applications of apartheid not required by law? And wouldn't you be expecting him, in the light of his publically declared ethical convictions, to be the former course of action and refrained from the latter, wouldn't you think of him as a phony?

Now let's take a U.S. government leader, state or federal, who publically declares his ethical conviction that abortion is the immoral killing of innocent unborn human beings. What would you think of him if, at the very same time, he works to enlarge the effect of the permissive abortion law by continuing the financing of Medicaid elective abortions, a step the US Supreme Court has ruled that no state is required take or to continue? And wouldn't you be expecting that politician, in the light of his publically declared ethical convictions, to be urging and working for the repeal of laws he judges radically violative of human rights? And if he continued to pursue the former course of action and refrained from the latter, wouldn't you think of him as a phoney?

The co-called dilemma of the Catholic politician is a creature of straw conjured up by confused editors and by politicians who want to smell like a rose when they should be calling the fumigator. The Catholic politician, like every other politician, swears to uphold the law and does uphold the law – or gets out. Lamentably, you have misconceived and misstated the issue.

Nov. 8, 1986   Pub. NYT Nov. 21, 1986
Holy See's letter respects homosexuals

Editor: David M. Wertheimer (letter Nov. 8), in commenting on the Holy See's recent Letter to the Bishops of the Catholic Church on the Pastoral Care of Homosexual Persons, alleges that the letter's "general attitude and specific language endanger both the emotional and physical safety of the entire gay community."

It would seem Mr. Wertheimer has not read the text of this 4,000-word letter addressed to Catholic bishops about confusions and distortions that have developed in some areas of the Church about homosexual activity. On his specific concern, the document reads:

"It is deplorable that homosexual persons have been and are the object of violent malice in speech or in action. Such treatment deserves condemnation from the Church's Pastors wherever it occurs. It reveals a kind of disregard for others which endangers the most fundamental principles of a healthy society. The intrinsic dignity of each person must always be respected in word, in action and in law" (Section 10).

"The human person, made in the image and likeness of God, can hardly be adequately described by a reductionist reference to his or her sexual orientation.

Everyone living on the face of the earth has personal problems and difficulties, but challenges to growth, strengths, talents and gifts as well. Today the Church provides a badly needed context for the care of the human person when she refuses to consider the person as a 'heterosexual' or a 'homosexual' and insists that every person has a fundamental identity: the creature of God, and by grace, His child and heir to eternal life" (Section 16).

Those who disagree with the ethical norms on homosexual activity taught by the Catholic Church (and by most other Christian communions and Orthodox Judaism) will not welcome this letter, addressed, it must be emphasized, to bishops of the Catholic Church about the church's own teaching and pastoral programs.

But disagreement with the ethical norms will surely be used by no responsible person to misrepresent or distort the letter's teaching about that respect for personal dignity due all persons, including those engaging in homosexual or in any other activity judged wrongful and both personally and socially harmful by criteria based in human reason and in God's Word.

December 5, 1986
Holding to an ethical norm implies no disrespect

Editor: In criticizing the Holy See's Letter on the Pastoral Care of Homosexual Persons and my letter printed Nov. 21, Bert Hansen (letter Dec. 4) regrettably passes over the former document's explicit and categorical condemnation of "violent malice in speech or in action" against homosexual persons as endangering "the most fundamental principles of a healthy society" and its equally decisive affirmation of the "intrinsic dignity of each person which must always be respected in word, in action and in law" to dwell on one sentence which, in Mr. Hansen's interpretation, designates "civil-rights legislation" as "a cause of increased anti-gay violence and implies thereby that civil libertarians are more to blame than bigots for encouraging such attacks."

Mr. Hansen's sharp criticism, voiced, also, by some others, deserves to be met head on.

Homosexually active persons have the same natural and civil rights as all other persons; and these rights, the Holy See's Letter emphatically states, must be scrupulously protected. But a moral right and, consequently, a legitimate civil right cannot be founded on an activity that is objectively wrongful and both personally and socially harmful. Homosexual relations is such an activity.

It is true that some citizens judge homosexual relations moral and they opt for legislation giving protection to persons precisely insofar as they are practitioners of homosexual activity. It is equally true that other citizens, a majority in our society at present, judge homosexual relations to be morally wrongful and socially harmful. Such citizens conclude that a legitimate civil right cannot be founded upon such a practice.

Mr. Hansen apparently holds the former position; the Letter of the Holy See, clearly, the latter. Those who hold the former position logically view legal measures to protect homosexual activity as "civil rights" legislation and it opponents as "civil libertarians." Those who hold the latter position regard such measures as permitting and approving morally wrongful and societally harmful behavior. They view promoters of such legislation as profoundly mistaken about the true good of the human person and of society. Thus one man's civil libertarian is another man's assailant on public morality and the social good.

The Holy See's Letter categorically condemns any violence in word or in action against homosexually active persons. Its criticism of civil legislation that would give special protection to homosexual behavior is fully consistent with this position and no disparagement of authentic civil-rights legislation or of its proponents. Whether legislation giving protection to homosexual behavior causes an increase in "irrational reactions," as the Letter asserts, is, of course, a matter of opinion that must stand the test of a sociological gathering of facts. But the Letter implies nothing about the relative force of bigots and lobbyists for this legislation in prompting such attacks.

November 19, 1987
Authentic dialogue presumes differences

Editor: Some Jewish religious leaders have voiced profound distress at Cardinal Ratzinger's statement (Cardinal's views Assailed by Jews, 11/18) that in the Jewish/Catholic dialogue Catholics must faithfully adhere to the principle that Judaism finds its fulfillment in Christianity and that the aim of dialogue is to arrive at truth rather than to exchange opinions.

The newswriter adds that "...the dialogue... has proceeded on the basis that both faiths were valid and that there would be no attempt at conversion." He quotes Rabbi Marc Tanenbaum as criticizing the Cardinal for failing to acknowledge "the vitality and autonomy of Judaism." He further identifies "Vatican policy" as acknowledging "a continuing independent covenant between God and the Jews" and quotes an Italian Jewish leader who views the Cardinal's statement as "an invitation to conversion."

These reflections on a complex issue may be helpful:

1. No inter-religious dialogue, whether between or among Christians or between Christians and Jews, Jews and Muslims or Muslims and Hindus seeks "conversion." Dialogue seeks greater mutual understanding based on

the authentic self-understanding that each religious faith has of itself. Dialogue seeks to identify and enlarge, if possible, areas of agreement and areas of cooperation and to generate loving relationships between individuals and communities. Dialogue of its nature is open to new insights and the possibility of needed self-correction. It is, indeed, more than an exchange of opinions. It must always seek truth.

2. Participants in authentic religious dialogue come together as equals, with total respect for the personal dignity, integrity and faith convictions of those with whom they dialogue. Such personal equality does not mean, however, that they consider the religion of the other, taken in its totality, as "equal" to their own or "equally valid" with their own. Dialogue does not imply the abandonment of one's faith convictions. A respectful, harmonious and productive dialogue is possible even when the faith convictions of the participants are, in important ways, opposed. Inter-Christian dialogue provides a signal proof of this.

3. When Catholics (and most other Christians) dialogue with believing Jews, they cannot abandon their conviction that Christianity is the fulfillment of Judaism. This principle does not, of course, describe adequately or fully the relationship between Judaism and Christianity. But it emphatically does not imply a failure to appreciate the Jewish faith or entail any questioning of the integrity, piety and profession competence of Jewish participants. Neither do the Jewish participants in the dialogue abandon their convictions and serious reservations about Christianity. We meet fully as equals though we do not evaluate our religious faiths as fully equal. This is a question of truth, not of integrity, virtue or competence or, we must add, of "who can be saved." Analogous "unequal" relations of faith content,

34

posited by the convictions of one or both sets of participants, characterize all the inter-religious dialogues.

When the Catholic Church dialogues with believing Jews, it is with the recognition, affirmed repeatedly by the highest authorities of the Church, that the Church itself, in the community of the first disciples, emerged out of believing Israel, convinced, as that community of disciples was, that God's saving promises to Israel had reached a definitive, initial fulfillment in Jesus of Nazareth, Emmanuel of God-With-Us.

Though the overwhelming majority of Jews then and since then did not receive, have not received and do not receive Jesus as the appointed Messiah and Savior – least of all as the Incarnate Word of the Father – both the New Testament Scriptures and the Church that wrote and continually transmits this Scripture teach that God steadfastly maintains his promises, his love and his covenant given of old to believing Israel. Romans 9-11 seeks to explore this mystery of acceptance/rejection, as does the continuing Church, without ceasing to proclaim that Jesus is Lord, the one Savior of Jew and Gentile, and that the Mosaic Covenant is now forever ordered to the Covenant of Calvary.

Catholics, like most other Christians, cannot abandon these convictions of faith they dialogue with Jews. Nor can they expect Jews to accept these convictions. The purpose of dialogue is not summary acceptance of one another's faith conviction – it is not "conversion" – but greater mutual understanding; the seeking of enlarged areas of agreement, if not total agreement; the promotion of mutual cooperation, based on convictions which are shared, for the common good; and the generation of reciprocal love. Some (for example, inter-Christian) dialogue may result in a mutual grasp of a deeper, fuller truth that ultimately unites the participants. But truth must impose itself; it cannot be imposed.

Jan 31, 1988   One name (way) only, not parallel ways

Editor: Your news columns, letters column and op-ed page have recently (11/18, 19, 20 and 26; 12/22; 1/28) reported or published serious and repeated criticisms of Cardinal Joseph Ratzinger for allegedly denying what has been variously designated by some Jewish religious leaders as the 'vitality and autonomy of Judaism," the "independent validity of Judaism," or the ongoing validity of Judaism." The Cardinal has also been censured for allegedly maintaining that the purpose of Catholic/Jewish dialogue is the conversion of Jews to Christianity. Following these repeated criticisms, no substantive clarification or response from Catholic side has been admitted to your columns.

In the original German text of his interview with the Italian magazine *Il Sabato*, the Cardinal had stated that in dialogue with the Jews Catholic proceed from the conviction "of both our duty with the faith of Abraham and the reality of Jesus Christ in whom, for us, Abraham's faith finds its fulfillment." This doctrinally unexplainable (for Catholics) statement finds equivalent expression in major authoritative Church documents dealing with Catholic/Jewish dialogue. Examples are Vatican II's (1965) Declaration on Non-Christian Religious (No. 4), the (1974) Guidelines and suggestions for implementing the conciliar Declaration 'Nostra Aetate' (No. 1, 2 and 3) and the (1985) Notes on the Correct Way to present the Jews and Judaism in preaching and Catechesis in the Catholic Church (I, 7).

Both Pope John Paul II and Cardinal John Willebrands, President of the Commission for Religious Relations with the Jews, have made the same point in a variety of addresses in recent years. Indeed, the Catholic

Church (cf. Vatican II's Declaration on Non-Christian Religions, Nostra Aetate) teaches that the Church of Christ is the community of salvation in which adherents of all other religions (for example, Buddhism, Shintoism, Islam) find or will find the fullness of the religious life intended for them by God's saving plan. This saving plan, first announced in the Hebrew Scriptures and partially fulfilled in Jesus' death and resurrection, has yet to reach its total fulfillment, which Christians associate with Jesus' Glorious Coming at the end of history, His Parousia.

Do these convictions entail the consequence that Judaism. With whom the Church has a special relationship (that it does not have with other world religions) has no ongoing validity? Certainly not. In the documents already mentioned, the Catholic Church teaches emphatically that Judaism has ongoing validity. This validity, however, cannot be seen (by Catholics) as separated from or independent of God's universal saving plan in Christ: "There is no salvation in anyone else, for there is no other name in the whole world given to man by which divine message teach that God steadfastly maintains his promises, his love and his covenant given of old to believing Israel. The New Testament Letter to the Romans, Chapters 9-11, seek to explore this mystery of acceptance/rejection of Jesus, as does the continuing Church today, without ceasing to proclaim that Jesus is Lord, the one Savior of Jew and Gentile, and that the Mosaic covenant is now forever ordered to the Covenant of Calvary.

In the words of the document "Notes…," mentioned above: "The Church and Judaism cannot then be seen as two parallel ways of salvation and the Church must witness to Christ as the Redeemer for all, 'while maintaining the strictest respect for religious liberty in line with the teaching of the Second Vatican Council" (No. 7).

Catholics, like most other Christians, cannot abandon these convictions of faith when they dialogue with

Jews; nor, on the other hand, can they ask or expect Jews to accept them. Jews cannot ask or expect Catholic to hold that Judaism is, in Rabbi Hertzberg's words (Op-ed essay, 12/23), "the principal heir and guardian of biblical truth." The purpose of Catholic/Jewish dialogue, as the documents listed above emphatically teach, is not acceptance of one another's diverse faith convictions – it is not "conversion," either way – but greater mutual understanding; reflection on those beliefs we hold in common; the seeking of enlarged areas of agreement; the promotion of mutual cooperation for the common good based on convictions that are shared; and the generation of reciprocal love.

Those distressed by the brief comments of Cardinal Ratzinger published, though not in their integrity, in *Il Sabato*, should consult once again the authoritative teaching documents given above. Cardinal Ratzinger's comments do not conflict with the authoritative teaching of the Catholic Church contained therein.

September 1, 1989
Some Jewish-Christian convictions can mutually pain one another

Editor: Professors Alice and Roy Eckardt (letter printed Aug. 31) appear to be using their own theological opinions as a standard by which to criticize Pope John Paul for speaking, during his early August general audience talks, of (ancient) Israel's infidelity to God, of the "new covenant" and of the new "People of God" constituted by Christ. They cite no authentic teaching statements of the Catholic Church to support their assertions that the Pope has somehow undermined or cancelled positions with respect to Judaism affirmed by the Church over the last few decades.

In his talks the pontiff recalled the covenants with Noah, Abraham and Moses and the announcement by the prophets of the coming new covenant (cf. Jeremiah 31:31ff.) that would effect a spiritual regeneration of God's people. This very same passage and many others (e.g., Isiah 8:5ff; Ezekiel 16) in the Hebrew Scriptures strongly lament the failure of God's people to keep his covenant.

The Christian Scriptures explicitly teach that the obedient sacrificial death of Jesus (and his subsequent bodily resurrection) established this new covenant, which embraces and perfects the Old according to the promise of God made anciently to Abraham and in fulfillment of the prophecy made through Jeremiah. These Scriptures also teach that the new People of God encompasses potentially both Jew and Gentile; in other words, all nations without distinction. In this new covenant there is no opposition between an "old" people and a "new" people, but rather a definitive new stage in the unfolding of God's saving plan which has forged one people of God from all nations.

To speak of the new covenant or to the new people of God implies no disparagement of the Mosaic Covenant or of the holiness of those who devoutly adhere to it. These terms express Christian faith convictions about the way God is now actually saving all people: "There is no salvation in anyone else, for there is no other name [other than that of Jesus] in the whole world given to men by which we are to be saved" (Acts of the Apostles 4:12).

Pope John Paul II faithfully teaches both that God's saving love for believing Israel is irrevocable (Romans 9-11) and that the Crucified and Risen Jesus is now the unique source of God's saving grace for all. The II Vatican Council's Constitution on the Church (Chapter 2) authoritatively explains the Church's teaching about the People of God in the Old and New Covenants. Pope John Paul II has not deflected from this teaching in any way.

Certain Christian and/or Catholic faith convictions are understandably received as painful by Jews, just as certain Jewish faith convictions are received as painful by

Christians. Jews are not "anti-Christian" nor are Christians "anti-Judaic" when they affirm these convictions.

November 26, 1989
Respecting the truth, respecting persons

Editor: In chiding San Diego Bishop Leo Maher (editorial, 11/26) for denying Holy Communion to "pro-choice" legislator Lucy Killea, you affirm, on the one hand that "a church's a right to discipline its flock is part of American liberty; but, on the other hand, you warn – with some high-sounding rhetoric – that such an action "threatens the truce of tolerance by which Americans maintain civility and enlarge religious liberty."

If bishops in Nazi Germany had been sufficiently aware of the progressive condemnation to the gas chambers of Jews, gypsies, homosexuals and mentally handicapped persons and had denied Holy Communion to Catholic government leaders who publicly advocated the permissibility of such actions, you would not be criticizing them today for an action evaluated as "forced obedience to a religious political agenda." You would be granting no plausibility to the defense of pro-choice legislators who maintained that, although personally opposed to the relegation of such persons to the gas chambers, they were unwilling to "impose their views on others."

Moreover, your appeal to Gov. Cuomo's defensive remarks sheds no light on the issue. The Governor confuses his church's position on abortion and capital punishment. The Catholic Church acknowledges the right of the state to inflict capital punishment but urges, for very cogent reasons, that in the conditions of our society this penalty be discontinued or not re-introduced. Church authority respects the views of those Catholics and others who disagree. Acceptance or non-acceptance of the current

Catholic teaching on capital punishment is by no means a test of one's adherence to the basic moral teaching of the Church.

The Church, on the other hand, has always and everywhere rejected abortion as a horrendous crime and is joined in this judgment by many citizens of other religions or of none. Furthermore, the Catholic holds, again with many other citizens, that bio-medical science unequivocally supports the judgment that the act of abortion violently terminates the life of an innocent preborn human being.

Though the step taken by Bishop Maher can be, and will be, debated both within and outside the Church as to its prudence and practical effectiveness, the bishop has only emphasized in a dramatic way that public advocacy of a permissive attitude to the slaying of innocent preborn children is incompatible with moral teaching of the Catholic Church and, indeed, with our civilization's dominant and long-held understand of what constitutes "civilizes.

December 1, 1989   More barking at the papal heels

Editor: Astonishing, indeed, was the appearance on your 12/1 Op-Ed page of an essay by former priest James Carroll seeking to discredit, even vilify, Pope John Paul II. On a day of particular triumph for the Pope – the day of his meeting with an ideologically transformed Mikhail Gorbachev, now amenable to protesting basic human rights, including that of religious freedom, in the Soviet Union – we are treated to some impromptu ferocious barking at the papal heels.

The charges James Carroll makes against the Pope have been made for more than a decade by a relatively small group of Catholic intellectuals based mainly in the Atlantic countries. Soon after John Paul's election in 1978 they realized that this extraordinarily gifted and accomplished Pope was not about to remodel the faith of the New testament and of the ancient Father's according to revisionist, evolutionist hypotheses proposed by some contemporary Catholic thinkers. Thus the highly intellectual Pope John Paul II has become the *beté noire* of this group of intellectuals who, either unable or unwilling to meet him on the level of patient and cogent theological discourse, resort to belittling him or damning him.

It is not only the Catholic Church, James Carroll should know, but also the Orthodox Churches, who profess that fidelity to the will of Christ manifested in the living tradition of the spirit-guided Church limits sacramental ordination as bishops and priests to men. It is not only the Catholic Church, but also the Orthodox Churches (the latter seeking reunion among themselves) who decline a quick reunion at the price of truth as they understand it. The Archbishop of Canterbury, whom Carroll wrongly thinks Pope John Paul has "shunned," admits the very serious problem of unacceptable diversity – in the sense of contradictory teaching – within his own communion. James Carroll's view of ecumenism is curiously shallow and myopic. His other charges against the Pope are equally partisan and baseless.

Those who are convinced, as this writer is, that Pope John Paul II is an authentic exponent, defender and exemplar of "Catholicism with a human face" sincerely hope and pray that our brother James Carroll may have a change of heart. Meanwhile we are grateful that he is a "former" priest and not an actually functioning one. The Catholic Church he presents is a Church of dissention, contradiction, doctrinal reductionism, relativism and discontent. "His" Church is not the Catholic Church we know and love and serve and represent.

Bishop repeated Church teaching to Governor; Act on principle then

Editor: Gov. Mario M. Cuomo takes the criticism of Bishop Austin Vaughan (news story, Jan. 24) and twists it to make the bishop look ridiculous.

First, Bishop Vaughan didn't "curse" the Governor. He simply stated Roman Catholic teaching about those who knowingly and deliberately reject the law of God in a grave matter and die impenitent. That penalty is eternal separation from God's presence.

Secondly, neither Bishop Vaughan nor any other pro-life advocate is asking Governor Cuomo to impose his private religious beliefs on others. Every public official has ethical standards he follows or should follow in personal life and in public life.

Is a public official who on principle opposes capital punishment seeking to impose his religious beliefs on others? Of course not. Is a public official who on principle opposes abortion - the deliberate slaying of an innocent preborn child - seeking to impose his religious beliefs on others? Of course not. One need have no particular religious convictions to recognize the biomedical evidence that a new human being begins at fertilization and develops continually through pregnancy, birth, infancy, childhood, adulthood and old age.

What the Governor's critics, including Bishop Vaughan, expect him to do is act in accord with his declared ethical convictions on abortion and seek by every legitimate democratic means to end public financing of abortion and legal approbation for this human slaughter. The Governor constantly takes refuge in depicting opposition to abortion as an expression of sectarian religious belief. It is impossible to believe that he could be so misinformed or so ignorant.

On capital punishment Governor Cuomo puts his mouth and his body where his ethical convictions are. Why will he not do so on abortion?

February 2, 1990   **Dissenting theologians**

Editor: It is ironic that Daniel C. Maguire of Marquette University (Op-ed "The Governor and the Bishop, 1/30) seeks to paint Bishop Austin Vaughan, a well-known theologian and past president of the Catholic Theological Society of America, as a theological illiterate. Upon close scrutiny, however, Prof. Maguire's assertions collapse.

No legislators or public officials can impose their "private moral views" (as Prof. Maguire alleges the bishop to be urging Gov. Cuomo to do) unless they happen to be US Supreme Court justices in a majority decision. Public officials and legislators can work only through the democratic process to achieve legislation that reflects their deeply held moral convictions on race, welfare reform, foreign aid, restraints on nuclear armaments, housing for the poor, the death penalty, criminal justice or abortion. The public debate associated with existing activity or with executive actions in accord with existing law can reflect, establish or change a public consensus on any particular issue.

Would Prof. Maguire have scolded legislators and public officials of former times when they opposed the Dred Scott decision or Plessy vs. Ferguson? Were such leaders creating chaos and undermining respect for law as Prof. Maguire alleges pro-life leaders are doing today? Are those who oppose apartheid in South Africa undermining respect for the law?

To be sure, some Catholic theologians in centuries past did defend therapeutic abortion in strictly limited cases. But Church authority rejected and continues firmly to reject (in Vatican II, for example) this position. The opinions of individual theologians, past or present, must not be confused with the binding doctrinal and moral teaching of the Catholic Church. Bishops, if any, of our own time or in the past who have made ambiguous statements about abortion are so exceptional that Prof. Maguire can rustle up only two alleged instances, which, in any case, do not support the abortion-on-demand policy now authorized by law in the United States.

The Catholic Church has never taught definitively when the new human being, present from fertilization, becomes a person. (And Bishop Vaughan made no statement on this point nor did he urge that Gov. Cuomo be denied the sacraments in his interview published in the New York Post.) But the Church as always rejected at any stage of the new human being's existence in utero. On moral and ethical grounds it has rejected the position that legislators may rightly support the introduction of permissive abortion laws (Holy See's Declaration on Procured Abortion, 1974). The US bishops only recently (Nov. 7, 1989) rejected once again and unanimously, on moral and ethical grounds, the contention of some Catholic politicians that they can oppose abortion (read, also, racism, apartheid, euthanasia) privately and support it publically.

If Prof. Maguire is convinced, as he alleges, that the majority of Catholic theologians support abortion in some cases, let him prove it. He is manifestly wrong in alleging that the miscarried or aborted fetuses cannot be baptized. Church law (Canon 871) reads: "If aborted fetuses are alive, they are to be baptized if this is possible."

The basic issue, however, is not the teaching of the Catholic Church (shared by the Eastern Orthodox Churches and some other churches) on abortion. The basic issue in a pluralistic society is the bio-medical evidence about the beginning of human life and the nature of abortion. This evidence is available to all and should be accepted by all. No less an expert than the agnostic physician and former premier New York abortionist Bernard Nathanson testifies to the bio-medical truth that abortion deliberately kills a human being. This is not a "privately held moral view."

Prof. Maguire has failed to place the shoe of theological literacy on Bishop Austin Vaughan. And there's no doubt on whose foot that shoe belongs.

February 2, 1990
Majority opinion does not make truth

Editor: Prof. Arthur Schlesinger, Jr. appears to hold that a majority vote should determine what is right or wrong, when he asserts (Op-ed, "O'Connor, Vaughan, Cuomo, Al Smith, J.F.K.,"2/1) that majority opinion in the United States does not evaluate "the freedom of choice" to kill a preborn human being as a "gravely evil course of action." He appears to regard any criticism of the existing law or public policy on abortion by citizens, whether bishops or public officials, as an attempt "to overrule the American democratic process."

When, in the past, religious leaders or public servants urged reversal of the Dred Scott decision or of Plessy vs. Ferguson, would this judgment have rightly been applied? Would this condemnation be visited upon religious leaders in South Africa who for decades have been urging political leaders to end apartheid? Is morality really a question of what a majority at any particular time judges to be right or wrong?

The only logical explanation for the criticism of Prof. Schlesinger is that he opposes racism in all forms but supports the right to abort preborn human beings. Do not both issues involve moral and ethical principles of the most fundamental kind? Are not both human rights' issues?

Religious leaders act consistently and in accord with conviction when they designate both racism and abortion as violations of fundamental human rights and call upon all citizens, including public officials, to oppose continues legislation of a grave evil – in the case of abortion, the slaying of a preborn human being.

To public servants like Gov. Cuomo, who publically acknowledge agreement with the ethical judgment that abortion is human slaughter, is it somehow out of order to urge that they therefore act publically in accord with this expressed conviction? Is it really in the public interest for a public official to act otherwise?

Prof. Schlesinger's usually helpful comments on public issues are regretfully spoiled I this instance by his inability to surmount that old stumbling block: "It depends on whose ox is being gored."

June 18, 1990
Always begging the question; never facing the issue

Editor: It's unfortunate that "The Cardinal Gets Tougher" (editorial 6/17) and A.M. Rosenthal's "The Cardinal's Crusade" (Op-Ed, 6/17) never zero in on the main issue. The main issue is whether or not the aborting of the fetus or young one from the womb is the deliberate slaying of an innocent human being.

Biomedical science answers unequivocally that a new human being begins at fertilization and develops continually through pregnancy, birth, infancy, childhood, adulthood and old age. No sectarian religious opinion or belief need to be invoked to establish this fact. Abortion terminates that new human life before birth.

If Cardinal O'Connor had stated that those "personally opposed" Catholic public officials who nonetheless supported or advocated and voted to fund "slavery rights," "racism rights," "anti-Semitism right's," or "genocide rights" ought to be made aware that they were placing themselves in danger of being excluded from sacramental communion with the Church, would anyone be criticizing him? Did you criticize the late Archbishop Joseph F. Rummel of New Orleans when, some thirty years ago and after several warnings, he excommunicated the racist Catholic politician Leander Perez?

Because abortion is the slaying of an innocent human being, as yet unborn, it is an evil equal to greater than all the others mentioned. No "truce of tolerance" should admit the one or the others. A re-write of your editorial or of the Op-Ed essay substituting any one of these other evils for abortion would make the point with ghastly clarity; and the Cardinal would then be effusively praised, not criticized, for his courageous leadership in opposing a major evil of our time.

Whereas civil officials are obligated to uphold and enforce the law, they are not required to acknowledge the rightness of a particular law or to refrain from using every democratic means to change the law. Many public officials of different religious faiths or of none disagree with the law permitting abortion on demand, as some of their predecessors did regarding laws on slavery and segregation, on the basis of moral conviction or religious teaching. They work legitimately by means of the democratic process to enact laws and public policies that protect the pre-born child from slaughter of abortion. In so doing they are faithful to the Constitution and to their oath of office.

Are only those civil officials who seek change on the abortion laws to be accused of being disloyal to the Constitution and their oath of office?

The scientific evidence shows that "aborting a fetus" is deliberately slaying an innocent human being. This, not the actions of some Catholic politicians, is the main - and in A. M. Rosenthal's phrase – the "deeply offensive" issue.

August 18, 1990   A splendid menu, not a cafeteria

Editor: Baptist Theologian Harvey Cox ("The Vatican Needs a Dose of Glasnost," Op-Ed, 8/17) complains of a chill generated by the recent (5/24/90) Instruction of the Holy See on the Ecclesial Role of the Theologian. Among other points, this document calls attention to the "serious harm done to the community of the Church by attitudes of general opposition to church teaching which even come to expression in organized groups." The reference is to some theologians organizing themselves and others against the Church's binding teaching. Prof. Cox fears that the new "ban" on public dissent will inhibit Catholic theologians from being objective and honest in theological research. He needn't worry. It won't.

A close reading of the Instruction shows that its concern is with those (relatively few) Catholic theologians who engage in public and contentious opposition to the Church's teaching and, who, in the words of the Instruction, present their "own opinions or divergent hypotheses as though they were non-arguable conclusions." Arguably, such theologians wouldn't be welcome even at Prof. Cox's Harvard Divinity School.   Freedom of theological (and every other kind of) research and publication is a value deserving careful protection. Attempting to have one's own theological opinions or that of a group nullify, or coercively be accepted as a substitute for, the binding teaching of the Church, however, violates the very nature of catholic theology.

The Catholic theologian is bound to Scripture, the Church's Spirit-guided Tradition (its lived experience of all the centuries) and its living Teaching Office, the college of bishops with the Bishop of Rome.   The Catholic theologian, precisely as <u>Catholic</u>, must work within these indispensable guideposts. The Teaching Office or magisterium, as it is called, functions not as an external policeman for theology but as an intrinsic and dynamic principle in the process by which theology better understands and expresses the Church's faith.

Catholic theologians who present hypotheses that differ with binding but not irreformable Church teaching in a manner that respects the Teaching Office's ultimate authority to decide disputed issues need have no concern about the so-called ban on dissent. Does the "Vatican need a dose of Glasnost"? No. But some Catholic theologians agree some of their colleagues in other Church communities need to understand better <u>the nature of Catholic theology.</u>

September 17, 1990   The always wrong is always wrong

Editor: Anna Quindlen's "The Nuns' Story" (Op-ed, 9/16) reeks with distain for the Catholic Church and its clergy. The columnist first offers an apologia for former nuns Barbara Ferraro and Patricia Hussey who because they publicly rejected over a long period of time a binding Catholic teaching, were required by Church authority to quit their Religious Life under vows. She then personally smears Catholic bishops and, by implication, Catholic priests, in a paragraph that may be the most venomous and offensive example of this genre that has appeared in the pages of The Times within recent memory.

"Tell me about it": bishops and priests allegedly lack the ability to listen with patience, sympathy and sensitivity to women who have had or who are contemplating an abortion. Ms. Quindlen clearly has no personal experience of the pastoral ministry of priests who daily counsel (tell me about it) both men and women with serious problems, including that of abortion, and who daily proclaim the Gospel of forgiveness to those who have sinned and a message of encouragement, hope and alternative solutions (alternative to the slaying of an innocent unborn child) to those who may be contemplating abortion or other wrongful act.

Priests cannot be effective pastoral ministers without endorsing and following the principle: "Tell me about it." But they can't advise a couple whose resident mother-in-law by intrusion or domineering is wrecking their marriage that killing mother-in-law is the right solution. And they can't counsel any couple or unmarried woman that a right solution to a problem pregnancy is slaying the unborn child. Not one of the "harsh laws of church and of state," this law is the law of God: Thou shalt not slay the innocent.

Ms. Quindlen quotes approvingly the Ferraro/Hussey dictum: "The Vatican's version of Catholicism is a culture of oppression... a church that is only about itself." These are "harsh words," she tells us. Indeed, they are, and false words. Only a species of ignorance could separate them from calumny.

October 8, 1990   **And the veil was taken away**

Editor: You praise Gov. William Weld of Massachusetts (editorial, 10/5) for seeking to make abortions easier to get in his state. "To a generation raised in the world of Roe v. Wade," you assert, "the idea that a woman can be forced to incubate a fetus may seem incredible."

This rhetoric depicts pregnancy as if it were an invasion and infestation by a lethal parasite. In the overwhelming majority of cases, pregnancy is the beautiful and often deeply longed-for natural result of the willing sexual union of a man and a woman. "Fetus" means the young one of the human species still in his or her mother's womb.

At just about the time your editorial appeared, Los Angeles Obstetrician Dr. George Flesh, writing in <u>Newsday</u> (10/7) and identifying himself as a religious Jew, recounted his own transition from willing abortionist – an "angel of death," his words – to one who now performs no abortions and holds that second-trimester abortions should be illegal.

By reflecting on what he was doing – "extracting a fetus, piece by piece," – and by later playing with a child he had not aborted because the parents changed their minds, r. Flesh tells us, "the connection between a 6-week-old human embryo and a laughing child stopped being an abstraction for me... While hugging my sons each morning, I started to think of a vacuum aspirator I would use two hours later.

Yes, "fetus" is the young one of the human species living in his or her mother's womb. Abortion, Dr. Flesh acknowledges, if belatedly, is the act which slays this very young and innocent human being. Weld for making easy what Dr. Flesh calls "an act of depravity that society should not permit?"

SECTION II: 1991- 2000

June 30, 1992   No more, sayeth the court, no more

Editor: A year ago, June 22, 1991, it was my turn as the Catholic pastor in Lindenhurst to give the invocation and benediction at the graduation ceremony for 440 graduates of Lindenhurst Senior High School. Although this was not the first time I so functioned, the U.S. Supreme Court's Lee v. Weisman decision, given June 24, has made it the last.

Gathered on a large athletic field that sunny Saturday morning were the graduates, their families, the faculty, the school district board and administration and other guests from the community. After the processional came the invocation. A moving reverential silence encompassed the assembly as I praised and thanked God for His blessings upon our country, our graduates and our community. I prayed that we might all continue to be worthy of and grateful for God's loving providence in our lives.

Your 6/25 editorial "Religion Remains Free, 5-4," derivative, to be sure, of the Court's decision, labels this invocation a "state-sponsored prayer... imposed on pupils... that invade the consciences of all the children... and violated the First Amendment's ban on the establishment of religion."

Such an analysis, I submit, is Kafkaesque. It does not meet your criterion of "what happens to real people in real situations." What I did, in that large Assembly of graduates, their families, their teachers and other community members, was to express religious sentiments and values that virtually all of us in this community share.

Decisions like Lee v. Weisman and your editorial strengthen the hand of a very small minority of Americans who, disliking all religion – period – seek to remove from the public forum every worshipful expression of that truth expressed succinctly by the late Justice William O. Douglas (Zorach v. Clauson, 1952):"We are a religious people whose institutions presuppose a Supreme Being..."

Nov. 21, 1992 Pub. NYT Dec. 5, 1992
The true meaning of being a Catholic

Editor: Pamela J. Maraldo, the newly elected president of the Planned Parenthood Federation of America, stated (Chronicle, Nov. 21) that, as a Catholic, she supports contraception and abortion and: "I go to church on Sunday but do not subscribe to many of the basic tenets of the church. That does not mean I am any less a Catholic."

Ms. Maraldo gravely errs in her final assertion. It is not any individual person, but Holy Scripture, the church's living spirit-guided tradition and its teaching office (of Pope and bishops) that authoritatively specify the Catholic faith as it is to be believed or lived.

By knowingly and deliberately committing certain sins, a Catholic, until repentant, excludes himself or herself from Eucharistic communion in the church; and, by rejecting certain binding teachings of the church, he or she becomes a dissenter, a heretic or even an apostate.

The Second Vatican Council in its Constitution on the Church, No. 25, clearly teaches the obligation of

Catholics to accept and live by all those teachings presented in a binding manner by church authority. Pope John Paul II spoke very explicitly on this point during his visit to the United States in 1987 when he addressed the United States bishops as follows:

"It is sometimes reported that a large number of Catholics today do not adhere to the teaching of the Church on a number of questions, notably sexual and conjugal morality, divorce and remarriage. Some are reported as not accepting the Church's clear position on abortion. It has also been noted that there is a tendency on the part of some Catholics to be selective in their adherence to the Church's moral teachings.

"It is sometimes claimed that dissent from the magisterium [teaching office] is totally compatible with being a 'good Catholic' and poses no obstacle to the reception of the sacraments.

"This is a grave error that challenges the teaching office of the bishops of the United States and elsewhere." (cf. "Origins," Vol. 17, No. 16, Oct. 1, 1987, p. 261.)

February 19, 1993
One vote only, one church only, one newspaper only?

Editor: Anna Quindlen (Op-Ed, Church and State, Feb. 17) lowers the boom on Cardinal O'Connor and, by implication, other Catholic leaders and citizens whose exercise of free speech and supervision of their own premises do not reflect her view of "what America expects of its citizens."

Cardinal O'Connor's support for the ousting of Schools' Chancellor Fernandez, the dispute over St. Patrick's Day Parade and Ms. Quindlen's own "disinvitation" to speak on a Catholic college campus are the basis for her charges that the Cardinal once again has "blurred the lines between politics and religion, church and state" and that he and other Catholic leaders are engaged in "politicking" and "lobbying" disguised as moral guidance. Very serious charges, these; and false ones.

Ms. Quindlen first inaccurately defines the disputed issues. She benignly describes the purpose and effect of Chancellor Fernandez's policies with "it's never too early to teach kids tolerance" and never "too late to offer sexually active kids condoms," thereby ignoring the judgment of many community leaders that these policies actually promote the acceptance of and practice of fornication and of homosexuality activity by the overwhelming majority of families who send their children to public schools.

Our columnist fails to mention that homosexual activists have marched before in St. Patrick's Day Parades, the issue now being, whether they should be permitted to march as an organized group under their own banner. Is this compatible with the religious convictions inherent in a privately sponsored observance of St. Patrick's Day? One's answer, to be sure, depends on one's moral judgment of homosexual activity. The Catholic Church, the Orthodox Churches, Orthodox Judaism and Islam judge such actions as always gravely wrong.

Ms. Quindlen further implies that churches, synagogues and religiously affiliated campuses, to qualify as "American," must admit to their premises speakers known to attack these one or more of the very principles upon which these religious communities are based. She confuses the public forum of a secular democratic state and the private for which that state exists to protect. Must one who may freely deny the Holocaust in a public forum be invited to a synagogue to do the same? Decidedly not the American way!

We read her contrasting "what America expects of its citizens and what Catholic Church expects of the faithful"; about the "ker-Klunk between democracy and theology," meaning Catholic moral doctrine; and about opposition between "authoritarian church and democratic state." It all sounds too much like the "You-can't-be-a-good-Catholic-and-a-good-American" charge that the Know-Nothings, Ku Kluxers and Paul Blanshards of days gone by have hurled at the Church and its leaders.

Acclaimed as moral prophets when they declare church teachings on, and actively campaign against, racism, anti-Semitism and social and economic injustice, Catholic clergy are severely criticized (by some) as "politickers" and "lobbyists" when they declare church teaching on, and actively resist, policies that promote abortion, fornication, and homosexual activity. It is no less a bashing of the Catholic Church, pace Ms. Quindlen, when its hierarchy is scored for specific doctrines such as those on Jesus, the Virgin Mary, and the Eucharist are attacked or lampooned. Our columnist seeks to isolate the hierarchy and its prophetic office from the reality of the Church as a whole. It can't be done.

Anna Quindlen has a right to voice her criticism of the Catholic Church and to tell us how she defines politicking and moral guidance. She cannot speak, however, as the "voice of America," but only, like the rest of us, as one voice in America. All religious leaders, like other citizens, have the right to share their views and urge their wider acceptance in accord with the democratic process. The Cardinal has done nothing other. Ms Quindlen clearly rejects, as she may, certain teachings of the Catholic Church. Her subtly implied "Back to the sacristy, priest, and attend to your spiritual duties," however, is just one more example of the authoritarianism she claims to deplore.

Editor: Jennifer Mattingly (letter, March 6) errs in asserting that the Catholic Church teaches that "ensoulment," a "theological" concept, "occurs at conception." Building on this mistaken premise, she concludes with reference to abortion that the Church "seeks to impose its theology on the law and therefore on the citizenry…"

The Catholic Church has no definitive teaching on ensoulment. Many theologians do hold that it is coincident with conception; others hold theories of "delayed hominization." Be that as it may, philosophical or theological concepts held by only some persons in a secular democratic society cannot be invoked as criteria to determine whether abortion does or does not slay a living human being. In this matter the only evidentiary criterion available to all is the bio-medical one.

Bio-medical science holds with certainty that a new member of the human species comes into being at conception and develops continually in the womb and outside the womb until death. This is not a "belief," but a fact.

Before birth the "little one" (fetus) produces heartbeats or brain waves at about three to four weeks, responds to sensory stimuli at about six weeks, grows hair on his or her head at about sixteen weeks, is able to live outside the womb at about 28 weeks (a period constantly decreasing), can walk at about a year after birth and talk at about two years and socialize more adequately only long after that.

Clearly, bio-medical science provides no basis for terminating the new human life at any stage within the womb or outside it. At all these stages, a living, developing human being is destroyed. Debatable biological, philosophical, psychological and sociological options do, however, lead some to conclude that the pre-born human being is of no value, not a "person," and therefore not entitled to any protection from the law. The consequence of one or more such debatable opinions is now imposed on the law and the citizenry.

April 2, 1993   **Right to choose? Choose what?**

Editor: Your editorial "So Poor Women Can Choose" (April 1) praises as "equal fairness, equal humaneness" the Clinton Administration's proposal to fund both the choice to give birth and the choice to abort.

The meaning of "to give birth" is clear enough; but the meaning of "to abort" is regularly obscured by a shroud of euphemisms and evasions such as pregnancy termination, the procedure, medical option, reproductive freedom and the right to choose. It is disingenuous, at the least, to keep using the slogan "freedom to choose" while sedulously avoiding discussion of what one does when one aborts: one wastes, destroys a human life, and violently so, before birth.

A New York physician specializing in abortion recently botched a late-term abortion in which he cut off the arm of the unborn child who was born the very next day. Had the doctor killed the unborn child, he arguably could have escaped, despite the late-term factor, criminal charges. But he failed to kill and now suffers a penalty only because the unborn child survived. In his defense the doctor maintains that the day he cut off the fetus's arm, she was not a person; only the next day, when she was born did it become a person. He did no harm to any person.

Please, where is the equal fairness, the equal humaneness in all this? Persons of whatever religious affiliation or none who identify abortion as the direct and illegitimate taking of an innocent life urge no "theology" on the law or on the citizenry. They urge the indisputable evidence of bio-medical science. Religious beliefs constitute no part of this evidence.

May 6, 1993   **Against priestly celibacy**

Editor: Rev. Paul E. Dinter (Celibacy and its Discontents, Op-ed, May 6) aggressively states his opinion that the Catholic Church's ordinary practice of ordaining as priests only men who profess themselves to have the charism of celibacy is mistaken, wrongful and harmful.

Unfortunately, the facts – recent sexual scandals involving some, we must forthrightly say, very few, Catholic clergy – Father Dinter alleges as support for his opinion do not in any way prove his case, even less so his vague, generalized attack on "Catholic sexual ethics."

Sexual scandals, regrettable and condemnable as they are, whether deriving from ordinary or pathological lust, affect persons in all walks of life, in all religious affiliations (or lack thereof), regardless of their single, married, divorced or celibate status. Indeed, the sin is all the more scandalous and condemnable in those who have professed themselves to live in chaste celibacy according to the model of Jesus their Lord, for the spread of His Kingdom and as a testimony to the truth that all human life achieves its true destiny and fulfillment only in the resurrected life of the world to come.

Fr. Dinter surely clutches at straws and gratuitously defames the "clerical establishment" when he uses these recent scandals as his battering ram against the rule of the Latin Catholic Church on priestly celibacy. Were this rule not in place, is any one so naïve as to think that all instances of lust, ordinary or pathological, would disappear from the Catholic clergy? Evidence from parallel cases involving married clergy of other Christian communions should lay this wishful thinking to rest.

Father Dinter could have offered us a reasoned discussion of celibacy, however brief; but, instead, as the editorial head on his essay aptly puts it, we are delivered only of his irate "discontents."

July 16, 1993
Marital love: two indivisible meanings; marriage and celibacy: two distinct charisms

Editor: In his bundle of gloomy assertions about the "collapse" of the "clerical order" in the Catholic Church and its "sexual absolutism" deriving from a "distaste for sex and its idealization of virginity," Thomas C. Fox ("Wrong About Sex, Absolutely," 7/16) finally identifies the object of his distain: the constant Catholic teaching, reaffirmed in Humanae Vitae (1968) and in many other authoritative Church teaching statements since that time that sexual relations belong exclusively to the marital covenant and in that context must always respect and never deliberately void either their love-giving or their life-giving meaning.

What Mr. Fox calls an "ingrained distortion" of human sexuality, the Church teaches as the divinely intended plan of conjugal love. It is curious that Mr. Fox attributes every clerical sin of a sexual nature ultimately to this teaching. If that is accepted, to what cause do we attribute the same sins and failures, amply documented but not profess this teaching?

The Catholic Church does not teach "distaste for sex" nor does it idealize virginity. In accord with God's Word, it teaches chastity within marriage and apart from marriage. In accord with the example and teaching of our Lord and St. Paul and of the whole of Christian Tradition, it teaches that an unmarried life for the Kingdom of God (not for any other purpose) is a charism greater than that of Christian marriage. These teachings are not peculiar to the Catholic Church, but are shared at least by the Byzantine Orthodox and other ancient Eastern Churches. More important, however, is not which charism is objectively greater, but which charism each individual person has received and how he or she lives it out for the glory of God.

November 18, 1993   **No official connection**

Editor: Anna Quindlen rebukes the U.S. Catholic Bishops for a "gratuitous attack" on Catholics for a Free Choice ("Authentic Catholics," Op-Ed, 11/18). On the contrary, given the purpose of CFFC – to promote acceptance of the choice to slay preborn human beings in their mother's womb – and the numerous media appearances of Frances Kissling, "who runs CFFC," to this end, the bishops' administrative committee wisely reminded rank-and –file Catholics and all other citizens that CFFC has no official or unofficial connection with the Church.

Ms. Quindlen seems unaware that long before Pope John Paul's encyclical "Spendor Veritatis" (1993), Vatican Council II (1962-65) had ruled (Decree on the Apostolate of the Laity, No. 24) that: "No project, however, may claim the name 'Catholic' unless it has obtained the consent of the lawful Church authority." To be Catholic, an organization must pursue its objectives in harmony with binding Church teaching. Catholics for a Free Choice, mainly a lobbying office and not, by its own admission, a membership organization, bases its program on the rejection of an essential and unchangeable teaching of the Catholic Church about the inviolability of innocent human life.

The Bishop of Rome and the other bishops of the Catholic Church indeed cannot speak for every person who identifies himself or herself as a Catholic – in every century and country some Catholics have embraced a variety of false and heretical teachings. But it's absolutely certain that the Pope and the bishops can and do speak in the assembly of God's faithful people as moral teachers endowed with the authority of the Risen Lord Jesus Christ (Luke 10:16). Even so, when they tell us that CFFC is not an authentic Catholic organization, they remind us only of what should be recognized as a self-evident truth.

May 28, 1994   **Total or limited autonomy**

Editor: "Mercy for the Dying" (Editorial, 5/28) means acknowledging the right of the individual to kill himself or herself when irreversibly dying and the right of other persons to assist the dying person in a self-inflicted death. Derived logically from your concept of the totally autonomous human person, this reasoning now leads to a "new frontier of freedom of choice," self-inflicted death.

A Washington federal judge recently held that the claimed and legally supported freedom of choice to bear or to slay the infant-in-the-womb constituted a milestone on the road to this new frontier of freedom of choice. But just as in this latter category of choice it has been exceedingly difficult, once the "right" has been legally enacted, to limit its exercise to specific circumstances, so, also, will it be exceedingly difficult to limit a legal "right to kill oneself and to assist another in doing so."

A different ethical framework, until recently firmly embedded in our civilized tradition and held no less firmly today by many millions of our citizenry, includes the indefeasible principle that deliberately taking innocent human life, one's own or another's, lies beyond the autonomy of the individual person or any collectivity of persons.

In the case of the irreversibly dying, it is indeed legitimate for the dying person – he or she has the right – to decline medical assistance that will only prolong the dying process and to seek (and therefore for others to give) every assistance that will minimize physical or emotional suffering in the dying process. But the dying person – and, a fortiori, any person who is not dying – has no right to take his or her own life nor is there a right for any other person as surrogate to execute this act or to assist its execution.

Yes, this latter logic derives in its full cogency from a framework of God the Creator and man (in both genders) his most noble creation, destined to live forever, just as the "total-autonomy" framework derives from the abandonment therefore. In this framework of Creator-creature, no direct taking of innocent human life, even dying human life, constitutes mercy. It remains forever a wrongful act to which there can be no right.

June 4, 1994   **Priestly ordination of women**

Editor: Anna Quindlen ("To the Altar, "Op-Ed, 6/4) states peremptorily that "those of us who believe women have a divine right to ordination believe the denial of that right is a moral wrong. Because of that it will not stand." She quotes two theologians known for their persistent rejection of a variety of binding Church teachings and cites a 1976 Biblical Commission study which concluded that the Bible alone cannot decide the issue of whether women can receive priestly ordination.

In fact, no one, man or woman, has a "divine right" to priestly ordination. The Catholic Church teaches that the conferral of this special requires a call from God, the genuineness of which the episcopal leadership of the

Church must first discern. Only then, a positive judgment having been made, is the gift actually bestowed by sacramental ordination. In particular instances diocesan bishops with the advice of their ordination committees decline to ordain men who claim to have a call "no matter how truly," to use Ms. Quindlen's terminology, [they believe] "it may resonate in their hearts." The felt call is not sufficient to gain ordination.

Respecting the person to be ordained priest, the Catholic Church and the Eastern Orthodox Churches have constantly taught and do teach that by the will of Jesus Christ the ministerial priesthood can be conferred only to men. This will of the Lord, constant from his public ministry through his men now exalted state in heaven and perduring until the day of his Great Coming, is discerned not exclusively from the texts of the New testament, but also from the living Spirit-guided Tradition of the Church – as this is articulated finally through the Pastors of the Church - the bishop - generally and that particular bishop who holds the Petrine primatial office, the bishop of Rome.

Developments in many Reformation Churches over the last thirty years have made the issue of women's ordination to the ministry a vigorously debated one. In this same period the Catholic Church and the Orthodox Churches have repeatedly affirmed their binding faith – conviction that only men can receive priestly or episcopal ordination. The Pope's May 30 declaration to this effect is only the most recent and, by its phraseology, the most decisive, definitive and unequivocally binding of these statements.

Anna Quindlen may believe that this teaching is a "moral wrong" and that "it will not stand." Theologians who follow the theological methods enjoined by the Second Vatican Council, however, know the criteria by which the will of Christ is discerned. They know that Christ's will can generate no moral wrong and that his unchangeable will stands forever.

August 10, 1994   **Abortion health care?**

Editor: Anna Quindlen (Op-Ed, The Conscience Clause, 8/10) favors health-care reform that compels religiously sponsored medical facilities to provide what she calls "commonplace medical procedures" (read <u>abortion</u>) and to provide such coverage for their insured employees.

Ms. Quindlen passes over rather quickly the several national polls that show an overwhelming majority of Americans opposed to such coverage. The Times Mirror Center poll, the results of which were released July 12, for example, found that 68 percent of Americans opposed including abortion in the basic benefits package for national health reform.

Her critique of "conscience clauses" and her indictment of "one religious group" – the Catholic Church – overlooks the special protection for religious freedom guaranteed by the first Amendment and the recently enacted Religious Freedom Restoration Act, passed to protect religious institutions and individuals from government-set mandates that run contrary to their consciences.

Beyond these important considerations, however, is the always sidestepped basic issue that abortion is not health care; it is the killing of an innocent human being. This is not mere opinion or somebody's "religious dogma." Bio-medical science confirms the human character of the embryo. From the moment of conception it is an original and biologically autonomous being, provided with an external design that develops uninterruptedly through pregnancy, birth, childhood and adulthood. What's debated is the <u>value</u> of this tiny human being.

Based on the data of science, philosophy and, for some, also, of religious belief, a very large number of Americans are convinced that this tiny human being should not be slain by abortion. The polls show conclusively that taxpayer-financed abortion should find no place in national health-care reform.

September 19, 1994   Fundamental right to abortion?

Editor: Alan Cowell (news report, "How Vatican Views Cairo," 9/18) concludes that the Pope's delegates to the Cairo Conference on Population and Development lost on the broad stage and prevailed only in details of the script.

To the contrary, when one considers the Clinton Administration's original objective, expressed in a March State Department cable instructing U.S. embassies to tell their host government: "The United States believes that access to safe, legal and voluntary abortion is a fundamental right of all women…," one can only marvel at the success of the Holy See in knocking this idea, disguised by euphemism in the working document, right out of the text, which now reads; "In no case should abortion be promoted as a method of family planning." That's a broad-stage victory.

In addition to those important textual changes by the papal delegates and cited by Mr. Cowell, others should be mentioned: 1) "pregnancy termination" was removed from the section dealing with health services for adolescents; 2) "including contraceptive services," was stricken from the section on family-planning for adolescents; and 3) these latter sections now stress the role of parents in guiding the sexual behavior of their children; 4) the vague, unprecedented phrase "sexual rights" was excised, as was 5) the reference to "other unions" (in addition to marriage) as deserving state support.

If the Holy See agreed (as it did) with major sections of the working document, especially those on economic development, education of both women and men and basic health care, why the hullabaloo over these areas dealing with the inviolability of innocent human life, the sanctity of marriage, parental rights, sterilization for the weak and artificial contraception for all? It is because the Church's ethical principles here – including the principle 'one may never do evil that good may come of it' – shared by many persons of other faiths or of none, are uncompromised.

Yes, we are ready to look like fools (Cowell's "villain of Cairo) to the worldly wise for the sake of the Gospel and the dignity of every human being from conception to natural death.

October 14, 1994   Abortion is homicide

Editor: Your 10/13 editorial "Abortion: Where are the doctors?" berates medical schools for not training abortion providers and berates doctors for failing to perform abortions because they are "cowed by harassment, taunts, threats, bombings and now murder…"

Did it not occur to you that, on the other hand, some medical schools and many thousands of doctors evaluate abortion as the deliberate slaying of an innocent human being in his or her mother's womb and that they are horrified by the suggestion that they should teach or perform what they evaluate as a distortion of the doctor's mission to heal?

Yes, some doctors no doubt refrain from abortion because they fear the more aggressive expressions of opposed public opinion; others make a lucrative trade of it; but still others evaluate abortion as the greatest deformation of their personal and professional mission.

November 15, 1994
The Bishop of Rome succeeds to Peter's teaching authority

Editor: "Rome's Lengthening Shadow" (Op-Ed, 11/14) by Thomas C. Fox seems calculated to generate hostility toward Pope John Paul II and the Holy See, particularly the Congregation for the Doctrine of the Faith (CDF). The "papal power plays" Fox deplores, are, contrary to his assertion and in the main, proper and needed acts of the Pope's teaching office, exercised either personally or through the CDF.

In teaching definitively that the Catholic Church has no authority to ordain women as bishops and priests, the Pope confirmed, despite some opposition, the constant doctrine of the Catholic Church and the Orthodox Churches. He did not order "no more discussion" on the subject, since, just as with the existence of God, discussion will go on forever. He declared, however, that the authentic and binding doctrine of the Church cannot be changed. Mr. Fox wants it changed.

And, so, also, with the teaching on the reception of Communion by civilly divorced and invalidly remarried Catholics: Mr. Fox wants it changed. Yet in deploring the CDF's letter to bishops reaffirming the Church's pastoral practice, he fails to mention a similar letter with the very same conclusion issued by all 17 Catholic bishops of the State of Pennsylvania on June 29, 1994, a full three months before the CDF letter. Are these bishops also guilty of a "narrow notion of marriage" or of insisting on an "unjust law." The real issue is the teaching of Jesus on the indissolubility of marriage and its consequences.

Questions about inclusive language in biblical translations are highly technical ones involving judgments about the exact intent of the biblical authors, as well as what language truly engages and enlightens people of today. Since U.S. bishops and biblical scholars will shortly be discussing this issue with the Holy See, it is reasonable to expect that the matter will be settled in a scientific and amicable way.

Thomas C. Fox wants various teachings of the Catholic Church changed. His tactic of arousing hostility to the Pope and the Holy See, however, is a poor substitute for informed and scientific discussion of the issues.

Jan. 9, 1995   Putting to death: two, but one is OK

Editor: Your 1/9 editorial on capital punishment "The Danger of Executing the Innocent" rightly stresses that this danger should argue powerfully against the re-introduction of capital punishment.

You label capital punishment "barbaric" and "vengeful" and judge it no effective deterrent. You state that a society which calls itself civilized and employs capital punishment without the utmost safeguards to protect the innocent "cannot for long live with themselves." Amen.

Why do you not also draw the conclusion that abortion, which always, definitely and certainly executes innocent human beings in the womb, ordinarily in a barbaric fashion, does nothing to prevent this daily, multitudinous execution of these innocents?

Nov. 25, 1995   Pub. NYT Dec. 2, 1995
The Catholic Church must remain true to itself;women
and priesthood

Editor: Thomas C. Fox (Op-Ed, Nov. 25) sounds like Hitler in his soon-to-be overrun Berlin bunker musing that his own army can still win the war.

The issue of women and the priesthood cannot intelligently be discussed by battering an authority one does not like, the Holy See, or by engaging in fanciful speculation about the future or by pretending that this issue is a struggle between so-called progressive, liberal and reform-minded Catholics against those nasty, closed-minded old "conservatives."

The issue is one of truth, of Christ's will for His church and how the church discerns that will.

The teaching that only men can receive priestly ordination is inerrant, the Holy See has declared, because it has been constantly taught and applied as of Christ's will by the universal teaching office of the church; namely, by the body of bishops with the Bishop of Rome at all times and places when this issue has been raised.

Pope John Paul II's 1994 apostolic letter on women and priestly ordination, it is maintained, only declared that to be a fact.

In the Roman Catholic and Orthodox church perspective, because the church is guided by the Holy Spirit, a teaching put forward uniformly throughout the centuries as deriving from the will of Christ must be inerrant. Men and women are indeed equal as children of God.

But just as a man is no less equal for being unable, in the order of nature, to bear a child, so a woman is no less equal for being unable, in the economy of salvation, to receive sacramental priestly ordination.

October 12, 1997   **Who killed Jesus?**

Editor: In "France's Bishops Apologize" (editorial, 10/12), we read that "the Second Vatican Council condemned anti-

Semitism and announced that the Jews had not killed Christ." On the second point the Council text (on non-Christians, No. 4) clearly acknowledges that some Jewish contemporaries of their fellow-Jew, Jesus of Nazareth, avidly sought his death but that "what happened in his passion cannot be blamed upon all the Jews then living, without distinction, nor upon the Jews of today.

In further asserting that Pope Pius XII "after the war, helped Nazi war criminals to escape justice," you accept the allegation made by some as undoubted fact. Surely Pope Pius XII deserves more nuanced treatment than your one-sentence condemnation of his (uninterpreted) silence and his alleged help to Nazi war criminals.

June 12, 1998
Other Western democracies have found a way. Why can't we?

Editor: The key principle stake in the school-vouchers debate (Breaching the Church-State Wall, editorial, 6/12) is that stated in the Universal Declaration of Human Rights (Article 26, par. 3): "Parents have a prior right to choose the kind of education that shall be given to their children." This is a natural and, fortunately, since 1925 in this country (Pierce v. Society of Sisters), a constitutionally guaranteed right.

Education, not be equated with transportation and garbage collection systems or recreational facilities, also paid for by public funds, is a unique service in that schools are surrogates for parents and inculcate values. Virtually all citizens, directly or indirectly, pay school taxes; and they are all compelled to send their children to school. Why is it that they can derive virtually no benefit from these compulsory taxes if they choose for their children non-public, often religiously sponsored schools?

You tell us that the First Amendment prohibits it. But the Founding Fathers and authors of the amendment, it can be demonstrated, had no such purpose in mind. Some state constitutions and US Supreme Court decisions, to be sure, have sought to limit or eliminate any tax assistance to religiously sponsored schools. Such provisions and decisions, however, can be reconsidered, refined and even reversed. Can we forget the sequence of Dred Scott, Plessy v. Ferguson and Brown v. Board of Education?

You tell us that vouchers threaten "the common schools that are essential institutions for a democratic society." Lurking ominously behind this statement is the secularist ideological bias (rejected by Pierce v. Society of Sisters) that all children must attend only one kind of school. In this country both "public" and "non-public" schools are common schools each serving large constituencies. Other Western democracies support both. Why can't we?

August 16, 1998
Political loyalties not religiously clear cut

Editor: Your columns (Aug. 16, pp. 1&4) continue the indiscriminate use of "Catholic" and "Protestant" to describe the terrorist groups wreaking havoc in Northern Ireland.

Whereas these religious designations may fairly identify the current minority and majority affiliations of Northern Ireland's people, they do not adequately describe their political affiliations; and, least of all, do they rightly describe those savages who murder and maim innocent men, women and children.

The political affiliations are "Nationalist" or "Republican," meaning a preference for union with the Republic of Ireland, or "Unionist," indicating a preference for continued union with Great Britain. Not all Catholics are Nationalists and not all Protestants are Unionists.

But one thing is sure: these terrorists – in the Omagh bombing, alleged to be a "Catholic splinter group" (is this a Church society?) – wherever they may have been baptized, act in a way diametrically opposed to their religion (if they have any), whether Catholic or Protestant. It is an insult to the various Church communities to identify these outlaws, brigands and desperados as Catholic or Protestant. Whether of Nationalist or Unionist sympathy, they are just dastardly criminals.

October 11, 1998
A political candidate in St. Patrick's Cathedral pulpit?

Editor: Baptist Minister Rev. Calvin O. Butts is reported in your Oct. 11 edition as endorsing Gov. George Pataki for re-election and, more importantly, inviting him to speak to his Harlem congregation on Sun., Oct. 11.

Currently or in the past, other Afro-American clergy and rabbinical leaders, individually or in concert, have endorsed political candidates and invited them to speak to their congregations. We do not hear any protest from Church-State separationist zealots, nor should we.

But suppose Cardinal O'Connor were to endorse a political candidate and invite him or her to speak to the congregation in St. Patrick's Cathedral. And if other Catholic clergy were to do the same. Would we hear a protest? Would The Times have a (critical) editorial?

Just a thought. And why the difference, if any?

November 11, 1998
Vouchers protect civil right and equality

Editor: "Vouchers for Parochial Schools" (editorial, 11/11)

74

reflects The Times's consistent distaste for schools, particularly religiously affiliated schools, that educate children apart from what is perceived as the normative common and now very secular public school.

The key principle at stake in this debate is: "Parents have a prior right to choose the kind of education that shall be given to their children" (UN Universal Declaration of Human Rights, Article 26, par. 3) a natural and, fortunately, since 1925 in this country (Pierce V. Society of Sisters), a constitutionally guaranteed right. Parents who exercise this right in the direction of a religiously affiliated school are uniquely and unfairly burdened.

All citizens, directly or indirectly, pay school taxes, including those citizens who at the same time pay (or have paid) tuition for their children in religiously affiliated schools or would do so if they had children to send there. The idea that vouchers for children in such schools forces all taxpayers to support religiously affiliated schools is pure nonsense.

Nov. 15, 1998   Pub. NYT Nov. 17, 1998
Ethical cell research

Editor: Re your Nov. 15 news article "Clinton Asks Study of Bid to Form Part-Human, Part-Cow Cells":

The production of human embryonic stem cells from the born human patient's own blood or skin grown in a denucleated cow cell -- if replicated by more research and if the method involves no mixing of the species and no production of an embryo rather than mere cells -- gives great promise of a universally acceptable ethical method of making available replacement human organs.

Earlier research producing such cells from discarded human embryos manufactured by in vitro fertilization or from the cells of aborted fetuses raised grave ethical questions, namely, the destruction of the human being at his or her beginning and the method by which these human beings as embryos were manufactured.

March 5, 1999   **Fairness and Civil Rights**

Editor: It is ironic that The Times (Rudy vs. Rudy) and Newsday (City Schools Need Both Crew and Voucher Plan) issued mutually opposed editorials on the same day (3/5) relative to Mayor Giuliani's school voucher experiment proposal.

In keeping with its long-standing ideology, The Times sees any such move as a threat to public schools and a violation of an absolute principle, no public money for private schools. Newsday, on the other hand, sees the proposal as benefitting poor children tied to filing schools that need competition to move them to reform.

In both approaches, however, one fundamental human-rights principle is consistently overlooked: The Universal Declaration of Human Rights (1948) Article 26, par.3 specified it best: "Parents have a prior right to choose the kind of education that shall be given to their children." This is a natural and, fortunately, since 1925 in this country (Pierce v. Society of Sisters), a constitutionally guaranteed right.

But in the USA, unlike most other Western democracies, this is a burdened right for parents who choose religiously affiliated schools for their children. Virtually no portion of their tax money can follow their children to a religiously affiliated school.

The tiresome "no public money for private schools" slogan fails to address the complexity of this basic human-rights issue.

May 2, 1999   Pub. NYT: May 6, 1999
Parents have a right to choose schools.

Editor: Your May 1 editorial "Florida School Voucher Scheme" does not mention a basic principle in the debate over school vouchers: both the United Nations, in its Universal Declaration of Human Rights, and the Supreme Court have declared that parents have the prior right to choose the kind of education their children receive.

Taxpaying parents who exercise this right by sending their children to religious, state-accredited schools derive virtually no benefit from the taxes they pay for public schools. Why must the exercise of their parental right to choose be so heavily burdened? What kind of guaranteed right is one you have to pay twice to exercise? Almost every other Western democracy has found a solution to this grave inequity. Why can't we?

May 25, 1999   Pub. NYT May 31, 1999
Ends and embryos

Editor: You report that the National Bioethics Advisory Commission will recommend that the Government begin to finance research on human embryos, saying that the moral evil in destroying human embryos is outweighed by the social good expected from this research (news article, May 24).

A key principle for all moral behavior is that one may never do evil that good may come of it. The end does not justify the means. It is a scientific fact that the human embryo is a new and unique member of the human species, containing everything necessary for development through all stages of human life. If it is morally acceptable to destroy the human being in the first stage of his or her existence, then why not also the born infant? The difference, after all, is not in kind but only in degree.

June 6, 1999   **Burger saw clearly**

Editor: Re the Clinton Administration's effort to get Supreme Court approval for giving computers and other instructional equipment to students in church-related school (news story, June 6), let the present Court heed Chief Justice Burger, Justices Rehnquist and White, who in their dissent in Meek v. Pittenger (1975) held that such children are denied specific benefits "only because they attend a Lutheran, Catholic or other church-sponsored school," a principle of discrimination which, they continued "does not simply tilt the Constitution against religion; it literally turns the religion clause on its head."

Calling Meek v. Pittenger "a gross violation of Fourteenth Amendment Rights" they expressed the "hope that at some future date the Court will come to a more enlightened and tolerant view of the First Amendment's guarantee of equal protection to children in church-sponsored schools and take a more realistic view that carefully limited aid to children is not a step toward establishing a state religion…"   Amen.

July 4, 1999   **A disservice to journalism**

Editor: Your news stories (6/30, 7/1, 7/2 and 7/3) on the UN Population Conference in New York last week frequently repeat the statement that "a comparatively small group of conservative (emphasis added) Roman Catholic and Muslim developing countries, with strong support from the Vatican, was blocking final agreement on several key aspects of the plan."

Again and again we read "conservative," "the conservative groups," "the small conservative faction."

Your reporter does not ideologically characterize the apparent majority group, some of whose opinions the smaller group opposes. Thus the reader is left with the impression that the majority, the "good guys," are being stymied by a small faction, the "bad guys."

If we are to have ideological labels, let's use them fairly across the board and not have news stories where the writer is, in effect, supporting one party to a dispute. Better, just explain the opposing positions; don't put labels on them.

Aug. 5, 1999   Important distinction

Editor: Your Aug. 5 news story and editorial on the homosexual scoutmaster fudges the key distinction between a virtually exclusive same-sex attraction – called the homosexual orientation – and homosexual genital activity.

Is homosexual genital activity wrongful (immoral) activity as is, for example, heterosexual fornication or adultery, or is it morally acceptable behavior? A great body of the citizenry is convinced of the former.

That a person has a homosexual orientation is nobody's business but his or her own and, like skin color, ethnic background or religious affiliation, provides no basis for discriminatory action. But if the homosexual person clearly states or implies that he or she is engaging in or seeking to engage in homosexual activity, doesn't that make a difference and one of the utmost importance to those who hold homosexual activity to be immoral?

To be concerned about the influence and effects of immoral behavior on others, particularly the young, is hardly bigotry. It is moral responsibility.

Aug. 30, 1999   Pub. NYT Sept. 3, 1999
Giving parents a choice will help students

Editor: "Parochial School Vouchers" (editorial, Aug. 29), which urges the Supreme Court to "declare voucher plans supporting religious education unconstitutional," conflates religious education and education under religious auspices.

Religiously affiliated schools provide the same basic education provided by public schools and other independent schools.

In addition, parochial schools offer character formation and religious instruction that parents seek and are guaranteed by their rights under the Constitution and international human rights covenants. All parents paying taxes and exercising their parental right of school choice should benefit in some way from those taxes.

The Supreme Court indicated the way not in 1973 but in 1997 when, reversing a 1985 decision, it held that public school teachers doing remedial teaching in religiously affiliated schools are not establishing a religion.

Sept 19, 1999   **The time to reconsider**

Editor: Will the Supreme Court ("Cases Give Court Chances to Define Church and State," Sept. 19) modify strictures that unduly burden taxpayers who choose religiously affiliated schools for their children?

In Meek v. Pittenger (1975) the then Chief Justice Burger, Justices Rehnquist and White held that such children are denied specific benefits "only because they attend a Lutheran, Catholic or other church-sponsored school," a principle of discrimination which, they maintained "does not simply tilt the Constitution against religion; it literally turns the religion clause on its head."

Calling Meek v. Pittenger "a gross violation of Fourteenth Amendment rights," they expressed the "hope that at some future date the Court will come to a more enlightened and tolerant view of the First Amendment's guarantee of the free exercise of religion, thus eliminating the denial of equal protection to children in church-sponsored schools and take a more realistic view that carefully limited aid to children is not a step toward establishing a state religion." Amen.

Sept 25, 1999   **Grotesque, savage**

Editor: In "Striking Down Abortion Bans" (editorial, 9/25), you cite the astonishing fact that 30 states have passed statutes prohibiting partial-birth abortion, though courts have blocked most of them.

What a groundswell of option throughout the nation against a "procedure" you describe elsewhere (9/25/99, B-5) as "a fetus is extracted from the uterus, all except the head, and a doctor then punctures the skull to remove the brain, before pulling the head out!"

Continued discussion and debate on partial-birth abortion will surely vindicate Op-Ed Columnist (and abortion-rights' advocate) Frank Rich's judgment (3/10/97): "By the second trimester, all abortion procedures are grotesque." We don't need euphemistic speaking or writing about a "procedure" but rather an exact description of what takes place.

Nov. 3, 1999   Pub. NYT Nov. 6, 1999
                    Pope Pius's silence in war: Why?

Editor: Re "Book revives Issue of Pius XII and Holocaust" (news article, Nov. 3): Archives of the Vatican for the

World War II years show Pope Pius XII concluding that a vigorous and public condemnation of Nazism or Bolshevism or both during the war years would have provoked an even greater destruction of innocent life and the dissolution of church structures in the areas controlled by these totalitarian regimes.

Pius XII's personal revulsion at Fascism and Communism is clear, and the papacy, before World War II, had already condemned both in famous encyclical letters.

If Pius XII refrained from what he judged as provocative acts, why are we Monday-morning quarterbacking him more than 50 years later? Can we prove him mistaken?

Nov. 20, 1999   **Adherence to truth**

Editor: Your 11/20 editorial "The Bishops and the Universities" rightly stresses that only some Catholic College and university officials or faculty fear lessened academic freedom as a result of new norms by which bishops will exercise authority already theirs by canon law respecting these institutions.

The neuralgic point has been the need for those (and only those) teaching theological disciplines to seek a "mandatum" or certification to teach. Why has this been thought necessary? Because some Catholic theology professors in some Catholic institutions worldwide have considered themselves justified in rejecting some definitive Church teachings and in encouraging their students to do the same. If they want to do that, the Church says, they must go elsewhere.

Academic freedom in theology, the Church maintains, is not based on the radically pluralistic view that there is no truth but only different positions. Rather the Church maintains that it has been given the office to declare the truth of God's Word and has the obligation to protect that truth in all its institutions.

December 14, 1999   Orientation vs. activity

Editor: The British Government (story, 12/14, p. 25) intends to establish a new policy on homosexuals in the military that emphasizes behavior rather than orientation. Sexual orientation is a private matter; illicit sexual contact with others is not. Such conduct, whether heterosexual or homosexual, involving on-duty personnel, would, presumably, in the new policy, like all other seriously wrongful acts, be a punishable offense.

The British appear to have identified a key principle toward achieving your goal (editorial, 12/14, "Investigating the Abuse of Gay Troops") of allowing both heterosexuals and homosexuals to serve in the military "on an equal, open basis." But it remains to be scientifically determined whether homosexual activity by its very nature, even if strictly off-duty, has a deleterious effect upon military discipline.

December 22, 1999
Free to change the nature of man

Editor: "Vermont's Momentous Ruling" (editorial, 12/22) favoring legal recognition of same-sex marriage casts aside the evidence of human nature and the ethical conviction of our Western civilization that marriage is exclusively the intended life-long union of man and woman in a covenant of love and mutual support open to the procreation of children.

If a handful of jurists, legislators, journalists or whoever can re-define the concept and reality of marriage to include persons of the same-sex, why can't they equally change the number of partners, same-sex or opposite sex, that will constitute "marriage"? The opponents of re-definition have entered an Alice-in-Wonderland world of intellectual and moral chaos.

January 8, 2000   Basic ethical questions avoided

Editor: Your characterizing ("The Debate on Gay Troops," 1/8) opposition to active homosexuals serving openly in the military as "bigotry" avoids addressing two basic questions: Is homosexual activity seriously wrongful, as our Western ethical tradition almost unanimously holds? And, why do our top military officers, past and present, (page 1, 1/7) judge the presence of active homosexuals as disruptive to military discipline?

Is it possible to draw sound conclusions on the issue of homosexuals in the military without thoroughly and cogently addressing these questions?

January 30, 2000   Basic question avoided

Editor: Embryonic stem cell research ("The Recycled Generation," 1/30) provides a feast of information but no cogent reflection on the main point: "in order to obtain human embryonic stem cells by currently available technology, you must destroy a human embryo."

Because the human embryo is a new member of the human species (no scientist denies this), those who declare immoral the destruction of this new human life are not irrational but radically rational about a basic ethical principle: Innocent human life must be free from deliberate attack. You may not do evil that good may come of it.

Arguing, in effect, that getting the embryonic stem cells by destroying the human embryo will do a lot of good for a lot of people is rank utilitarianism, practiced in another context by the Nazi doctor Joseph Mengeles. It's time in The Times for a lengthy debate by ethicists on both sides of the question. Let reason prevail!

January 30, 2000   **The truth is easy to find**

Editor: Al Gore (page 1 story, 1/30) now repudiates his 1987 written statement that abortion was "arguably the taking of a human life." He doesn't tell us why he held that position then or why he rejects it now.

One has only to consult a standard bio-medical textbook to learn the scientific truth that at the joining of the sperm and the ovum, fertilization, a new member of the human species comes into existence with everything needed, given a nurturing environment, to be called at a later stage of development, Al Gore.

It's strange that when it comes to abortion, scientific certainty yields to unscientific opinions. But is this tiny blastocyst-zygote-embryo-fetus a person? And what's a person? The answer involves philosophical opinions or, God forbid, religious convictions. Let's stick with the scientific fact: Abortion does take a human life.

Feb. 22, 2000   Pub. NYT Feb. 22, 2000
The French Solution?

Editor: Diane Johnson (Abortion: The French Solution, Op-ed, 2/22) builds on a false premise when she thinks that we can reduce abortions by adopting the "French Solution": providing teenagers with a pill that "prevents an already fertilized egg from implanting in the uterus."

By all bio-medical standards, the new human being with everything necessary, given a nurturing environment, to develop into a future Beethoven, Jesse Jackson or John Paul II comes into existence at fertilization. The progesterone pill thus actually causes an abortion, very early on and by chemical expulsion rather than surgical dismemberment, but an abortion nonetheless. The pill is manifestly not "late contraception"; once sperm and ovum have joined, it's too late for contraception.

March 14, 2000
Definitive Church teachings, not papal opinions

Editor: You state that the Pope's apology (editorial, 3/14) for, among other things, discrimination against women is "difficult to square with his continued opposition to abortion and birth control and to women in the priesthood." But these are not papal opinions.

Since it is both a scientific fact and a definitive Church teaching that abortion destroys the life of an innocent pre-born human being, no charge of "discrimination" for rejecting abortion can boast a moral foundation.

The Catholic Church rejects only those birth-control methods that denature the conjugal relationship or intentionally sterilize and, also, result in other moral evils. Though some may consider this teaching discriminatory, the Church judges it to be based on the nature of the human person and of his or her acts.

Finally, when the Church teaches that the ordained priesthood can be conferred only on men, it presents definitive teaching as the will of Jesus Christ. Holding to a divinely willed order cannot be discriminatory.

March 14, 2000   **Natural right, civil right**

Editor: The continuing debate over school vouchers, tuition tax credits and deductions (3/14, page 1) fails even to mention the fundamental principle at stake: the natural and constitutionally protected right of parents to choose their children's school. And, of course, having made a choice, tax-paying parents should suffer no undue financial penalty. Most industrialized democracies respect this principle and its logical consequence.

Whether students receiving vouchers fare better in independent schools or students in tax-supported schools do poorly are secondary, if important, points. This is a civil-rights' issue, the controlling principles of which were laid down by the US Supreme Court (Pierce v. Society of Sisters, 1925) and the United Nations (Universal Declaration on Human Rights, 1948) decades ago.

March 20, 2000   **Now, say a mule is a horse**

Editor: In holding (Legal Unions for Gays in Vermont," 3/18) that same-sex unions are "not a threat to traditional marriage and deserve the name of marriage as well as the law's full protection," you cast aside the evidence of human nature and the ethical conviction of our Western civilization that marriage is exclusively the intended life-long union of one man and one woman in a covenant of love and mutual support open to the procreation of children.

If a handful of jurists, legislators and journalists can re-define that concept and reality of a marriage to include persons of the same-ex, why can't they equally change the number of partners, same-sex or opposite sex, that will constitute "marriage"? The proponents of re-definition have surely entered an Alice-in-Wonderland world of intellectual and moral chaos.

May 13, 2000

Church teaching, not clergy opinion

Editor: By stating (editorial, 5/13) that New York's new Archbishop Edward M. Egan will "reinforce the pope's - and Cardinal O'Connor's – stern views on abortion, contraception and homosexuality," you suggest that the content and presentation of Catholic teaching on faith and morals are somehow linked to the positions and opinions of individual clergy.

On the contrary, what the Bishop of Rome and all other bishops and priests of the Church must teach on these issues and on all other doctrinal and moral issues is the same and can be found in the universal Catechism of the Catholic Church, 2nd. ed., 1997. In presenting such teaching, the clergy are not fairly described as "stern" or "theologically conservative," but just Catholic. Yes, they are, indeed, "reliable," "dependable" and faithful. And thank God for it.

[N.B. Bridgeport is a diocese, not an archdiocese.]

June 6, 2000   **To choose means to choose abortion**

Editor: A letter writer (June 5), seeking to clarify the object of the "right to choose," insists that it is a two-fold right: "to choose whether or not to have an abortion."

But who in the USA challenges the right of a mother to bring her child to birth? The challenge is all to the other possibility; namely, to terminate the pregnancy or, more precisely, to kill the child before birth. Thus, the "right to choose," in current usage, virtually always has as its understood object the latter, not the former, choice.

June 12, 2000   **Access to abortion**

Editor: Your story (6/11) on the recent UN follow-up conference on women's rights stated that certain Islamic nations were "most reluctant to advance women's rights" and "got strong support from the Vatican."

In fact, the delegation of the Holy See firmly supported women's rights and the General Assembly ban on reopening issues debated at Beijing. Some participants apparently wanted to "advance" beyond Beijing, as your story reports, by including "more explicit homosexual rights, broad definitions of "family" and more clearly stated support for safe and ready available abortions..." These efforts, judged morally harmful by the Holy See and other participants, failed.

June 12, 2000   **Competence to review?**

Editor: If Prof. Richard Rorty's summary of Gary Will's Papal Sin: Structures of Deceit is accurate (and I have no doubt that it is), then Gary Will who is deceived but, hopefully, not the deceitful deceiver that he takes most popes of the last 150 years to have been or to be.

Will's charges of papal cover-ups and unscrupulous steps to holster papal authority are familiar ones, if marked in this instance by extreme anger and vehemence; but they have been refuted many times by intellectuals and academics as eminent, if not more eminent, than Gary Wills. Indeed, it is a marvel that his book could receive such an extended and basically uncritical review by a scholar who does not specialize in Catholic theology or history and whose philosophical positions are hardly sympathetic to the Church.

One small point: When Pius IX in 1864 rejected "progress, liberalism and modern civilization," he was in context rejecting what we would label in context today as agnosticism, the oppression and attempted destruction of the Church, the denial of any objective moral order and ethical thinking divorced from any notion of God and the natural moral law. Pius's words and phrases were as different in their contextual denotation then as the word <u>gay</u> is today in relation to its meaning hardly fifty years ago.

August 6, 2000
Are homosexual practices right or wrong?

Editor: Two Long Island school districts (story, Aug. 6) are considering banning Boy Scouts from using their facilities because the Scouts allegedly discriminate against homosexual persons.

This discussion is constantly befogged by failure to distinguish between 1) the homosexual attraction, inclination or orientation and 2) homosexual practices. The former is morally neutral, if disordered, and the person's own business, nobody else's. Homosexual practices, on the other hand, according to the Judaeo-Christian-Muslim ethical tradition, are always wrong.

Thus when persons, usually adults, announce that they are practicing homosexuals (avowed homosexuals' in Boy Scout language) or when they seek to approve, defend, promote or advocate such practices, they can expect widespread legitimate rejection of their views as morally wrong and harmful to public morality, just as promoters or practitioners of any other wrongful activity would face.

Those who are convinced that homosexual practices are morally wrong and must not be approved, promoted or advocated in any way should not be accused of being discriminatory, homophobic or biased. Their position is one of deep conviction about right and wrong.

Aug. 25, 2000   Pub. NYT August 31, 2000
Sensible rules for stem cell research

Editor: Re "Sensible Rules for Stem Cell Research" (editorial, Aug. 25):

Your editorial seems to make light of the "clump of embryonic cells" that we all were in the first weeks of life. You seem perplexed that anyone regards an embryo as "a form of life that must be protected." But what cogent reason excludes new human lives from the protection against deliberate killing that all innocent human beings should enjoy?

Under the new federal guidelines, stem cells will continue to be obtained by deliberately destroying human embryos, if only frozen ones destined to be discarded by fertility clinics. Yet a substantial ethical gulf separates direct killing from "allowing to die."

Progress made possible by these rules will be achieved only by jettisoning the bedrock ethical principle: the end does not justify the means.

September 2, 2000
Separation of religion from public life?

Editor: Your concern (editorial, 8/31) to keep Sen. Lieberman's enthusiasm for a greater influence of religion on public life harmonious with your understanding of the prohibition of an "establishment of religion" leads you to employ phraseology far beyond the First Amendment when you endorse "the constitutionally based separation of religion from public policy."

If you mean that public policy should not be governed by a particular religion or religions, including secular humanism, all well and good. But if you mean that public policy should not be governed by ethical norms accessible to reason because they be reiterated or reinforced by particular religious beliefs, this would be an unacceptable ideological bias.

All citizens and legislators bring their basic ethical norms, regardless of their intellectual source, to bear on the formulation of public policy. Objecting to ethical norms accessible to reason because they are also religiously supported would indeed be anti-religion.

September 3, 2000 Scouts and active homosexual adults

Editor: You state ("Discrimination by the Scouts," editorial, 9/3) that "children cannot learn honor from an organization that views homosexuality as amoral defect." On the contrary it must be said that whereas homosexual persons have the same basic rights as all other persons, including the rights to justice, respect and friendship, homosexual practices are always morally wrong. That homosexual practices contradict the meaning of human sexuality is a conclusion readily accessible to human reason; and it is, in fact, reinforced by the teaching of the world's great religions.

The Boy Scouts are not asking young boys their sexual orientation, a probing completely inappropriate and unacceptable, as a test for membership. Problems some boys may have with this issue are surely private, in-flux as far as their development goes and a matter for discussion only with parents or parent-approved counselors.

The Scouts are concerned about having <u>adult</u> leaders who are <u>avowed</u> homosexuals; that is, persons who publicly declare that they engage in homosexual practices or who defend, promote or advocate such practices, which the Scouts and the majority of the world judge morally wrong. When The Boy Scouts of America decline to engage or to retain such leaders, they act in accord with just reasonable principle of discrimination.

September 19, 2000   To give no deadly medicine …

Editor: Your 9/19 editorial ("A Ban on Assisted Suicide") embraces the principle that persons, at least the terminally ill, have the right to kill themselves and that doctors should be permitted to assist them in their suicide. Further, to curtail this practice is "to use the power of the states to address the profound question of the right to die."

Most citizens of our country reject the idea of total personal autonomy, which you espouse and which is used to justify both self-killing and the killing of the preborn child. The Hippocratic Oath, moreover, mandates the physician "to give no deadly medicine to anyone if asked." That the projected Pain Relief Promotion Act would discourage doctors from giving appropriate pain relief to the terminally ill is pure speculation. Why not ask the doctors? Where is the evidence?

October 11, 2000   Pregnancy = two bodies, two persons

Editor: "The Enduring Battle Over Choice" (editorial, 10/11), misses the chief point at issue, which is not "reproductive rights" or "reproductive freedom," but killing preborn human beings.

Of course, man and wife have the freedom to generate offspring; but they do not have the moral right to kill their offspring, born or unborn. The right mothers have to "make medical decisions about their own bodies" ends with their own bodies. A woman who chooses to abort her unborn child makes a decision about a body-person within her that is not her own.

November 1, 2000   Wrongful means to a good end

Editor: Michael J. Fox (Op-ed, "A Crucial Election for Medical Research," 11/1) understandably wants to be cured of his Parkinson's disease and laudably hopes that others with similar devastating diseases may be cured.

But he proposes an immoral means; stem-cell research that destroys human embryos – which each of us were at our beginning. He avers that these surplus embryos, produced by in-vitro fertilization, will eventually be thrown away and die anyway. So why not destroy them through research that may help others to live?

The answer is simple: you may not do evil that good may come of it. What is referred to as a "microscopic clump of cells" is the human being at his or her beginning. Directly to destroy the incipient (actual not potential) human being is wrong. Allowing surplus human embryos (that ought not have been manufactured in the first place) to die is one thing; directly killing them is a entirely another. Moreover, adult stem cell research is showing more and more promise of achieving the goal Fox seeks.

Dec 4, 2000   All discrimination not wrongful

Editor: Schools Chancellor Levy has punished the Boy Scouts (story, 12/2) for their policy, labeled discriminatory, of barring avowed homosexuals – those adults who announce that they engage in homosexual practices and likely, also, approve, defend, promote or advocate such practices – from acting as scout leaders.

A great body of the citizenry, however, sees no unjust discrimination in barring such persons as role models any more than they would see unjust discrimination in barring heterosexual persons who announce themselves as practitioners and defenders of, for example, fornication or adultery. Such practices and all homosexual practices are judged wrongful by the ethical tradition of our civilization, a judgment fully accessible to reason though it may, in certain instances, be reinforced by religious conviction.

A small body of social revisionists apparently think they can shame with the labels discriminatory and biased those who on the basis of well-founded conviction draw the line between right and wrong and act consistently in accord with these convictions. The revisionists are engaged in one big grand begging of the question.

Dec 16, 2000
Punishment for choosing a religiously affiliated school

Editor: The "sound" decision (Another Setback for Vouchers," 12/16) of the Ohio federal appeals court disallowing vouchers is rather another setback for the human and civil right of tax-paying parents to choose schools for their children will attend.

Clearly the aid was "neutral" in that the parents could use it at any state-accredited school of their choice. What the court overruled was the parents' actual choice; that of a religiously affiliated school. Had they chosen, in the main, secular schools, no objection would apparently have been raised.

The 1973 Nyquist decision dealt with significantly different facts: the partially reimbursed parents had already made one specific kind of choice – the money could then go only one way. Thus it could be argued, though weakly, that religion was directly aided. But in Ohio the money was delivered prior to the implementation of any choice. It should be no business of the court what choice parents make. Once the particular choice is disallowed, free choice has disappeared.

SECTION III: 2001– 2010

January 21, 2001   **Right or wrong?**

Editor: Two well-known married politicians recently had a child out of wedlock (stories, Jan. 19, 20). The first, the Rev. Jesse Jackson, repented of his deed: "This is no time for evasions, denials or alibis. I fully accept responsibility, and I am truly sorry for my actions."

The second, Mayor Willie L. Brown, Jr. of San Francisco denied any impropriety in having an out-of-wedlock child: "There is nothing unseemly about this at all. She's a great friend."

Do we side with Jesse Jackson that adultery is immoral or with Willie L. Brown Jr. that it's just great?

Jan. 21, 2001   **An equivalent marriage?**

Editor: In granting health benefits to "domestic partners"-non-marital sexual partners – of senators or senate employees (story, Jan. 20), Republican State Senate leader Joseph L. Bruno sends yet another signal from civil authority that such partnerships, heterosexual or homosexual, are to be considered virtually the same as marriage.

Such decisions clearly undermine marriage as the uniquely rightful context for sexual relations and the begetting and nurture of children. It is particularly regrettable that a title to benefits is tied specifically to an illicit sexual union. Why not let employees designate another household member, family or non-family, as the secondary recipient of benefits. Why honor and reward persons for their choice of lifestyle our civilization has constantly judged immoral?

January 21, 2001   Research that kills. Yes? No?

Editor: Embryonic stem cell research advocates can't understand why opponents reject such experimentation even though it might (stress might) result in cures for various debilitating diseases. The answer is twofold.

First, you may not do evil that good will come of it. In procuring human embryo stem cells, the embryo is destroyed. And what's so bad about that?

Bio-genetics testifies with certainty that the human embryo is a new member of the human species containing all that is necessary, given the proper nurturing environment, to grow through all stages of human development. What? You mean this little cluster of cells is a human being? Yes, a human being in the very first stages of his or her development. Who would wish to have been destroyed, killed, when he or she was an embryo?

Secondly, adult stem cell research, which involves no destruction of the human embryo, shows great promise. We should concentrate on methods of cure that cause no harm, that do not kill. A human being should never be used as a means to an end.

February 16, 2001   **High-class degradation**

Editor: Missing from your reflection (The Mayor and the Arts, Round 2, editorial, 2/16) was artist Renee Cox's own comments (Newsday, 2/1, p. 2) on the intended meaning of her "Yo Mama's Last Supper," depicting Jesus at the supper as a nude woman.

"It's a critique how the Catholic Church has treated African-Americans and women ... [It] was meant to highlight legitimate criticism of the church, including the refusal to ordain women and accusations that church hierarchy remained silent during the Holocaust... The Catholic Church has to be held accountable... the Catholic Church is about big business."

The artist's intention to insult and pillory the Church thus becomes part of the meaning and message of her photographs. Artistic freedom and the right not to be penalized for "disfavored viewpoints" are irrationally used in this case to justify a deliberate, public and tax-supported community with the artist simultaneously declaring his or her contempt for the same.

No such lofty philosophical principles would be brought forward if the nude woman represented heros of the African-American community of the same.

February 22, 2001
          Preventing/ending the disease of pregnancy

Editor: You oppose ("New York's New Cardinal," editorial, 2/22) a conscience clause in a New York State Senate Bill that would, as you put it, allow religious groups on religious grounds unfairly to deprive female workers of important health-care coverage, namely, prescription contraceptives.

But some contraceptives are abortifacients; neither instrument is health-care but direct pregnancy prevention or termination. Pregnancy is not a disease. And unfair? What title does a person have to paid-for contraceptives or abortifacients?

Religious grounds? The Catholic Church's position on artificial contraception in marriage has a fully rational basis and its rejection of abortion, in addition, rests on undeniable scientific facts. Though both positions are reinforces by religious conviction, they are not at base religious. Even if they should be so perceived, the US Constitution prohibits forcing people to act against their religious convictions.

February 23, 2001   Distort and then target

Editor: In pursuing his analogy between the Clinton pardons and (the history of) indulgences, John Tierney (column, 2/23) uses terminology that can easily distort Church teachings or expose it to ridicule. Indeed, the indulgences "it's not a magic guarantee of absolution for all sins, in fact, it must be emphasized, it is not an absolution for any sins whatsoever.

To gain the indulgence, the person must first have repented, confessed his sins, promised to make restitution if required and have been absolved in the sacrament of penance. The Church, then, to whose ministers is committed the stewardship of grace (I Cor. 4:1; John 20: 21-23) , dispenses Christ's merciful grace to supply for the already forgiven sinner's indulgence does not forgive, pardon, or erase guilt; it only makes up for, in whole or in part, the reparatory efforts the forgiven sinner would need subsequently to make.

March 19, 2001   **Take my view or else**

Editor: The Rev. Carlton W. Veazey (letter 3/19) asserts that when religiously affiliated hospitals, insurers or managed care plans decline to provide their employees or the public with particular services judged (by them to be) immoral, they "impose their beliefs" on such persons.

Not at all. The public is under no obligation to patronize or seek employment with religious institutions whose ethical standards they do not share. Generally other providers are available. But even were they not, it is precisely in coercing persons forming the corporate boards of such institutions to act against their deeply held ethical standards or religious convictions that the imposition of a particular ethical or religious belief occurs.

Mr. Veazey seems to think that having a "secular" purpose, such as health care, exempts actions from moral evaluation or negates the religious character of the institution providing such care, and that if something is legally permissible, then institutions, if not individuals, should be coerced to provide the same. This latter view does not accord with our constitutional freedoms.

May 27, 2000   **"Right" to abort?**

Editor: The "fuzziness" in the abortion debate (editorial, 5/27) resided not in the degree of support or non-support for various abortional procedures or facilitating laws, but in the failure to designate candidly what an abortion is and what constitutes the object of the "right to choose."

Since bio-medical science identifies the new human being as beginning at fertilization and developing through various stages in the womb and then outside the womb, the abortional act clearly slays this new human being at some stage before birth and often in the most violent way. The "right to choose," in context, means the right to slay this preborn human being.

Because the life of an innocent human person is involved, many citizens and voters cannot accept this "choice" as an ethically defensible one or the description of efforts to limit it as an "intrusion into private medical decisions." Deliberately killing an innocent human being is never just a private medical decision.

September 16, 2002
A study paper, not official teaching

Editor: "Catholics, Jews and Their Work of Reconciliation," (The Week in Review, 9/15, p. 3,) refers repeatedly to the document "Reflections on Covenant and Mission," formulated by a Catholic-Jewish dialogue committee sponsored by the U.S. Catholic Bishops' Committee on Ecumenical and Interreligious Affairs, as a "bishops' " statement or an "episcopal" statement.

In fact, this scholars' document is a study paper carrying only the authority established by the evidence and reasoning offered by its signatories. It contains much that is positive, acceptable and laudable about the improvement in Catholic-Jewish relations since Vatican II.

But it also implies a very debatable understanding of God's enduring covenant with believing Israel as a saving relationship with no reference to Christ and His Church. This hypothesis requires broad and deep theological reflection on the Catholic side and a decisive judgment by the Church's teaching authority.

October 2, 2002
Accepting or rejecting the scientific certainty

Editor: "Slow Going on Stem Cells" (editorial, 10/2) again

sidesteps the basic issue, sloughed off as the opinion of "religious conservatives"; namely, what is the human embryo? Is it a human being at his or her beginning or just a clump of cells that we can dispose of at will?

The scientific evidence – no religious opinion – shows that the human embryo, given the proper environment, will develop through all growth stages of the human being before birth and after birth. Why don't we acknowledge the scientific evidence and admit that, in extracting stem cells from a human embryo, we are destroying a human being at his or her beginning? The end does not justify the means.

October 23, 2002
Sexual orientation means homosexual activity

Editor: Adding "sexual orientation" to the categories of persons protected by the State's Civil Rights and Human Rights Laws (story, 10/23) is intended to benefit homosexually active persons. If passed, the State for the first time will be giving special protection to persons not because of some innate morally neutral characteristic – race, ethnic origin, age, sex, etc. – but on the basis of a particular kind of sexual behavior.

The ethical tradition of our civilization, as of others, has judged all homosexual activity, just as non-marital heterosexual activity, as wrong. How can we confer a right precisely on the basis of a person's wrongful behavior?

Could fornicators, adulterers, bigamists and polygamists seek to become protected classes? Every person has the same natural moral rights and should enjoy the same civil rights. And all persons deserve respect and compassion. But no persons should have rights conferred on them because of their wrongful behavior.

December 10, 2002   **A moral revolution**

Editor: "Equal Rights for Gays." (editorial, 12/8) is certainly right in holding that all private wrongful acts need not be criminalized, especially if they do not violate the rights of others. But your staunch defense of homosexual activities omits any moral evaluation thereof. The moral tradition of our civilization judges homosexual activity to be wrong.

All persons must have the same rights, true; but there is no right to wrongful behavior and no special title to protection for any persons on the basis of their wrongful behavior. Do we punish polygamists "as a class by criminalizing an act that is central to who they are"? It seems that we do. The moral evaluation remains at the heart of it all.

December 17, 2002   Words obscure actual denotation

Editor: If "sexual orientation" ("Pass the New York Gay Rights Bill," editorial, 12/17) meant only what those two words denote – a more or less exclusive attractiveness to persons of the same sex or of the opposite sex – basic fairness would indeed require that all persons be treated equally regardless of sexual orientation.

But "sexual orientation" in context means homosexual activity – judged wrongful by the ethical tradition of our civilization – and the proposed bill would give special protection to persons precisely on the basis of their homosexual behavior pattern, a basis radically different from special protections granted to persons because of morally neutral factors such as race, ethnic origin, gender, disabled condition or religious persuasion.

You imply, moreover, that passage of such a bill is only a belated first step toward legalizing same-sex unions or registered partnerships of same-sex or opposite-sex couples in lieu of marriage.

And so the problem. The two words sexual orientation seem so uncomplicated; the moral, legal and social revolution they portend is so great.

January 2, 2003   Looking for changed teaching

Editor: Former priest Paul E. Dinter (Op-Ed, "A Catholic crisis, Bestowed From Above," 1/1) again sharply criticizes the episcopate under whom he once worked. Some of his criticisms, to be sure, have merit.

But with some of his "former colleagues" I wonder if his reforming proposals, whatever they may be, will produce something better or, rather, the chaos we see in non-Catholic Christian communities.

Moreover, as one who is convinced that the teaching of Humanae Vitae is irrefragably true, I do not see any contradiction between the teaching of that encyclical and the equally incontestable truth that "church teaching grows and develops," but not in demonstrable contradiction to the past.

Paul Dinter's hopes for the future underscore the truth that a big part of the "Catholic crisis" lies in dissent from definitive Church teaching.

January 22, 2003   Different basic principle

Editor: Your sainting of the late Assemblyman George Michaels ("A Forgotten Hero," editorial, 1/22) only emphasizes the huge gap between your philosophical position and that of those who reject abortion.

For you, killing an unborn child is part of "women's basic right to make her own childbearing decisions" and of "women's reproductive freedom."

For those who regard this position as tragically mistaken, a right is always a claim a person has on that which will achieve, enhance or protect human life and dignity. There can be no moral right to anything evil – lying, bribery, adultery, theft or abortion.

Man and woman indeed have a reproductive power, the moral freedom to exercise which being rightly confined to marriage. But once a child has been conceived, even apart from the marital union, no one has a moral right to kill that unborn child.

January 29, 2003   A "wall" for Catholics only

Editor: Mayor Bloomberg's politicking in five Protestant churches last weekend (news story, B4, 1-27) raises the more neuralgic issue of politicians campaigning during election years from church and synagogue pulpits and being cheerfully endorsed by clergy not in a private capacity as they are legally entitled to do but publicly in the midst of the congregation. This has happened regularly in recent years.

If a candidate were to promise himself and his platform in say, five Catholic churches, including St. Patrick's Cathedral, during an election campaign and be endorsed by the respective pastors of those churches, would this be acceptable? Why or why not? Does one rule apply to all?

March 2, 2003
Making humans to destroy them

Editor: You lament ("Cloning Countdown," editorial, 3/1) the House of Representatives' vote to ban so-called therapeutic cloning, as well as reproductive cloning. The latter creates a blastocyst with the aim of its continuing development through all other human stages. The former creates the blastocyst to be promptly destroyed for the harvesting of stem cells that <u>may</u> help cure certain human degenerative diseases.

Poor tiny blastocyst! Who are you? And does the purpose for which you are created make you a different kind of being? Science says absolutely not. You are in both cases a new member of the human species. But in the first case those who created you want to kill you, so that possibly your human parts may benefit bigger members of the human species; in the second, they want you to grow up as they did. Are you ready for the chopper?

How would we have answered?

March 12, 2003
Reproductive powers, not rights

Editor: By "reproductive rights" ("Reproductive Rights in Peril," editorial, 3/12), the editors apparently mean that human beings may exercise their sexual power in any way they please, even to the point of destroying the new member of the human species effected by fertilization.

Another ethical framework, more deeply based in the tradition of our civilization, recognizes that although all may have reproductive power only spouses have the right to exercise this power.

Moreover, even spouses have no "right" to a child (or to destroy the child once conceived), only a right to the spousal acts that may result in a child. Non-spousal conception may result from fornication, adultery, incest or the new manufacturing methods, such as in vitro and cloning.

The dire peril today is not to specious "reproductive rights" but to the ethical tradition of our civilization about the meaning and parameters of sexual love and the inviolability of innocent human life.

May 16, 2003

"400,000 Embryos and Counting"

Editor: Your reflection on what to do with the growing "stockpile" of "surplus" human embryos ("400,000 Embryos and Counting," editorial, 5/15) predictably recommends destroying at least some of them to harvest stem cells for research and "potential treatments for a wide range of illnesses."

You do not address the basic issue of whether in harvesting such stem cells the researcher is directly killing a human subject. The indubitable scientific fact is that in destroying a human embryo we are destroying a human being at his or her beginning. Your own reference to in vitro fertilization proves it. There is no way around this truth. But it can be ignored. And you have ignored it.

May 21, 2003   Call to approve homosexual practices

Editor: You are right in rejecting degrading language used to describe any group of human beings (Judicial Nominees and Gay Rights, editorial, 5/19). But in reproving Senator Rich Santorum, Alabama Attorney General Bill Pryor, Health and Human Services official Claude Allen – and implicitly millions of other Americans – for such alleged offenses, you overlook basic distinctions.

Linking polygamy, bigamy, pedophilia, pederasty, ephebophilia, homosexual activity, concubinage, bestiality and necrophilia does not entail the conclusion that these activities are the same or equally wrong. They are the same only in the sense that they are all morally wrongful actions (if not in the same degree) as judged by the ethical tradition of our civilization.

Your continuing editorial effort and that of the homosexual activists to promote the moral, social and legal acceptability of homosexual activity is the basic issue. Your position must be repudiated.

Respect for human dignity and commitment to basic human rights for all does not entail moral approval for specific activities in which particular persons may engage.

June 4, 2003   Ignoring the main point

Editor: In " 'Partial Birth' Mendacity, Again" (editorial, 6/4), you assert that this current House Bill, if it becomes law, would criminalize "the most common procedures used after the first trimester, but well before fetal viability." Drafters and supporters of the bill obviously don't think so and have denied the claim. Why not let the courts decide?

The omission of a women's health provision was prompted by the already common interpretation of the courts to include in this positive sounding phrase all kinds of social and financial considerations – nothing to do with health at all.

But the real mendacity, trickery and deception within this whole discussion, however, is the denial that when a "childbearing decision" is abortion, it is the decision to kill an innocent human being.

June 19, 2003   Overthrowing nature

Editor: Recent editorials (6/19), op-ed essays (6/18) and news stories (6/18) celebrate a supposed advance in social thinking, law and public policy represented by the approval in some countries of same-sex marriages. It is alleged that approving opposite-sex marriages but prohibiting same-sex marriages constitutes "discrimination" or "inequality" based on sexual orientation and activity.

The premise for this thinking is that marriage has no set definition in the nature of the human person as created male and female, as, inherently necessitating a sexual complementarity for the specific identity of conjugal love and for the procreation of children. To evacuate this understanding of marriage by personal or legal fiat and call the sexual intimacy of same-sex persons "marriage" is to overthrow not only the history of our civilization's thinking regarding marriage but to overthrow reason itself. The overthrow of reason is the enthronement of arbitrariness, another name for madness.

August 1, 2003   **Two basic differences**

Editor: "Playing It Safe on Gays" (editorial, 7/31) overlooks the basic philosophical or anthropological difference between the position represented by President Bush and that represented by those who favor homosexual unions:

The one, based on an analysis of human nature, which may or may not be buttressed by religious convictions, judges all homosexual activity as morally wrongful and holds that all heterosexual activity belongs exclusively within the marital union.

The other accepts both heterosexual activity in all contexts and homosexual activity as without ontological or moral distinction and holds that sexual activity is something human beings may enjoy at will.

From this distinction all the other differences arise. Why not identify and argue the main point?

November 30, 2003   **Every abortion is lethal**

Editor: The starting point for "Frank Talk About Abortion" (editorial, 11/30) is the mistaken principle "the fetus … is potential life."

"Life" here is synonymous with "human being." Biomedicine shows that a distinct, living if dependent human being exists from fertilization through the continuous and various stages of development before and after birth. What we have from the beginning is not a "potential" life but a human life with potential that will be exhibited in various ways at various stages of this human being's continuous development.

Thus there is no such thing as a "safe abortion." Every abortion destroys a human life. "Abortion mortality" attaches to every abortion since every abortion kills a developing unborn human being. That's frank talk about abortion.

What, then, is the answer to the abortion conundrum? Sex education, contraception; as you say? No. But that's another letter.

December 2, 2003   **A continuing injustice**

Editor: Though dealing only with state scholarships for theological studies on the college level, "Church, State and Education" (editorial, 12/2) asserts an over-riding principle – public funds to secular schools only – that effectively dissolves the natural, parental and civil rights of millions of Americans, those parents who choose religiously affiliated schools for their elementary and secondary school children.

Such education is compulsory and the taxation for it is compulsory; but only those who choose the "secular" school can benefit significantly from this mandatory taxation.

The late Chief Justice Burger, the then Justice Rehnquist and the late Justice White in Meek v. Pittenger (1975) stated that such a principle "does not simply tilt the Constitution against religion; it literally turns the religion clause on its head."

December 3, 2003 To benefit, only one practical choice

Editor: In U.S. Supreme Court argumentation on the Washington State college scholarship case, Locke v. Davey (news story, 12/3, p. 1), Justice Souter is reported to have observed that were vouchers denied to religiously affiliated schools, the argument could be made "that the religious student must somehow surrender a conscientious belief and enroll in a secular school to use the voucher." Exactly so.

This valid and compelling argument has been presented insistently for decades by parents who pay compulsory school taxes but who, unless they choose a secular school for their children, must surrender their constitutionally protected right to choose a state-approved but religiously affiliated school because they cannot afford to pay twice.

What greater burden could be leveled on the exercise of a constitutional right linked to religious conviction?

April 28, 2004 To retire is not to be removed

Editor: In a uniformly critical news story ("Archbishop of Dublin, Under Fire, Replaced, 4/27), Brian Lavery states that Cardinal Desmond Connell was "removed from his post." The context of the news story gives the verb replace, used in the heading and in one sentence, a very pejorative, even punitive meaning.

Over the past few years Cardinals Bevilaqua of Philadelphia, Hickey of Washington, D.C. and Connell of Dublin submitted their retirements at age 75, in accord with Canon Law; and these retirements were not accepted until several years later. We do not speak of them as having been "removed," or, in the pejorative sense, "replaced." They retired.

Editor's Note: Your 4/28 news story "Roman Catholic Priests Group Calls for Allowing Married Clergy Members," B5, states that the Rev. Andrew P. Connolly is the pastor of St. Francis de Sales parish in Patchogue, N.Y. In fact, he is a priest assigned to the Hispanic Apostolate who resides in the rectory of St. Francis parish, Patchogue.

May 10, 2004   Blind to the killing abortion is

Editor: In your "Church, State and Dinner" (editorial, 5/10), you lament the possibility of Senator Kerry's being excluded from the Al Smith dinner because of his avid and adamant support of "abortion rights."

To understand the position of the exclusionists, just change one word in your editorial. Write "slavery" rights for "abortion" rights. Then evaluate the "pluralism and tolerance" you would extend to this view and judge whether without a "slavery rights" advocate, the Al Smith dinner could measure up to its "grand heritage."

Opposition to abortion and "abortion rights" is not fundamentally a religious view – nor is opposition to abuse of prisoners, deportation of religious, racial or ethnic groups, segregation or racial discrimination. It is a human rights issue based on the science of human embryogenesis and intrauterine human development. Religion may support opposition to abortion and to these other ethical enormities, but it does not constitute the unifying basis for opposition: that basis is the dignity of the human person, human rights and natural justice.

Yes, one word proves the point.

May 11, 2004   Destroying the human embryo is wrong

Editor: "Republicans for Stem Cell Research" (editorial, 5/11) cites the hope of many that human embryonic stem cell research may help provide new treatments for various debilitating diseases. It is important to stress that so far such research has resulted in no successful treatments for these diseases. On the other hand, adult stem cell research has successfully generated such treatments.

More importantly, the basic question is the relationship of means to end. Does the end justify the means? It is a scientific certainty – in vitro fertilization proves it – that the "microscopic" embryo is the human being at his or her beginning. Is it right to destroy the human being at his or her beginning to obtain cells for treating other human beings in other stages of their development?

The answer must be a resounding "NO." It is wrong to do evil that good may come of it. The license to destroy hundreds of thousands of "excess embryos" produced wrongly in the first place only compounds the evil already committed. Allowing to die those who cannot be saved is radically different from deliberately destroying these tiniest of human beings. The end does not justify the means.

May 21, 2004 Diverse issues, diverse moral evaluations

Editor: Catholic legislators supporting "abortion rights" (story, 5/20) who protest criticism from bishops and possible denial of Communion on the basis of "we do not believe that it is our role to legislate the teachings of the Catholic Church" or who complain that legislators supporting the death penalty, the "unjust" Iraqi war or particular social programs are not equally censured misunderstand the essential differences between and among these various issues.

Church teaching does not unequivocally reject the death penalty; it has not declared the Iraqi war unjust or that particular social programs are the only way to achieve a needed social purpose. On these issues Catholics may legitimately differ and not be in conflict with definitive Church teaching. But on the direct killing of the pre-born human being no such difference is possible.

More importantly, abortion – like child abuse, slavery, active euthanasia, sterilization of the mentally defective, a child-soldier army, racial discrimination, segregation, anti-Semitism – radically assaults basic human goods and values: the inviolability of innocent human life, the dignity of the human person and natural justice. Religion may support these values but does not constitute their foundation.

By opposing the evils mentioned, including abortion, representatives of the people are asked not so much to legislate Catholic teachings as to uphold basic ethical values of a humane civilization. On such issues it would be unconscionable to separate public actions from personal beliefs.

May 24, 2004   Need to distinguish the difference

Editor: "Hustings and Pulpits," editorial, 5/24/ accents a misunderstanding generated by congresspersons who recently complained that some bishops were criticizing lawmakers who promoted "abortion rights" but not those who supported capital punishment and the Iraqi war. This is a case of apples and oranges.

Although the Church generally opposes capital punishment it does not unequivocally reject it; and, through the centuries, has consistently recognized the right of the state to inflict it. To be sure, some Church leaders, including the Pope, have opposed the Iraqi war; but the Church's teaching office has not declared this war unjust. Everything is different, however, with the killing of the pre-born human being in the womb. Church teaching definitively rejects such killing.

More importantly and to the point: Church leaders are not asking lawmakers to legislate "religious tenets" or to "toe a doctrinal line." They were not doing this in the civil rights marches of the 60s, in protecting apartheid, in opposing the sterilization of the mentally defective or now in opposing active euthanasia, abortion, assisted suicide or the tearing apart of the human zygote for research. These issues are human rights issues supported by religious beliefs, indeed, but firmly founded on the ethical goods and values that undergird a humane civilization.

June 9, 2004   **Mrs. Reagan doesn't get the point**

Editor: "A Fitting Tribute to Mr. Reagan," editorial, 6/8 suggests this tribute would be Mrs. Reagan's hoped-for vigorous promotion of embryonic stem cell research. Principled ethical opposition to such research is mentioned in a kind of by-the-way – "because stem cells are extracted from microscopic embryos, which are destroyed in the process."

Yes, stem cell research does destroy – kill – the human embryo which we all were at our beginning. It is asserted that we should not "turn our back" on this research that "might" alleviate so much suffering.

Military personnel in the Abu Ghraib prison didn't turn their backs on the debasing and degrading of prisoners to make them talk. But they used a wrongful means the world has judged abhorrent. We should find even more abhorrent the destruction of an innocent human being at his or her beginning.

It is difficult to think that Mr. Reagan would regard the destruction of any innocent human being as fitting tribute to him.

June 17, 2004   Pub. NYT June 22, 2000
Risking censure from the Bishops

Editor: "Politics, Religion and Silence," by Joyce Purnick (Metro Matters, June 17), suggests that opposition to abortion is a religious position. To the contrary, it is based on the irrefutable facts of genetics, embryogenesis and human development testifying to the origin of the new human being at fertilization joined to the moral principle that directly and deliberately destroying an innocent human being is wrong.

The same moral reasoning, with no needed reference, leads us to reject slavery; child abuse; ethnic, racial or religious cleansing; racism and anti-Semitism.

If a politician maintained that "I'm personally opposed to slavery, but I wouldn't impose that (supposedly religious) view on others," we would simply laugh. For a large portion of the citizenry, the same is true for abortion.

June 17, 2004 Science proves abortion slays living being

Editor: Joyce Purnick ("Politics, Religion and Silence," 6/17) bolsters confusion over abortion, religion and politics by labeling opposition to abortion as a "religious" position. Mario Cuomo and Geraldine Ferraro are described as politicians who personally oppose abortion but who "would not impose that view on others."

To the contrary, opposition to abortion is based on the irrefutable facts of genetics, embryogenesis and human development testifying to the origin of the new human being at fertilization joined to the moral principle that directly and deliberately destroying an innocent human being is wrong.

The same kind of moral reasoning, analogously, with no needed reference to religion, leads us to rejection of slavery, child abuse, ethnic, racial or religious cleansing, sterilization of the mentally deficient, racism and anti-Semitism. Many religions support these conclusions and reinforce the reasoning from natural moral law but they do not constitute the basis for the positions.

If a politician maintained, "I'm personally opposed to slavery, but I wouldn't impose that [supposedly religious] view on others," we would simply laugh. For a large portion of the citizenry, the same is true for abortion.

June 30, 2004
Bio-medical science tells us when human life begins

Editor: Gary Wills ("The Bishops vs. the Bible," Op-Ed, 6/27) makes a valid point in holding that the issue of abortion can and should be argued without reference to religion. But he does not reflect the Church's self-understanding in stating that it can teach only what is found explicitly in the Scriptures. The Church teaches the biblical message as this is understood and interpreted by the Spirit-guided life of the Church – what we call Tradition. From the beginning this Tradition – this Church – has always definitively rejected abortion.

The Church also affirms, however, its office to interpret the divine natural moral law, a form of reasoning,

Wills rightly notes, open to all. Under this heading, however, as under that of divine revelation, the Church holds abortion to be gravely wrong.

Religious communities have the same right as all other citizens to declare and urge acceptance of ethical positions they hold. In the case of abortion, philosophical theories about personhood do not provide commonly accepted criteria of judgment. Biomedical science, however, does: at fertilization the new human life begins.

July 24, 2004   If we don't like it, it's radical

Editor: "A Radical Assault on the Constitution," editorial, 7/24, so characterizes a procedure – regulating the jurisdiction of the Supreme Court and implicitly that of the lesser courts – granted to the Congress by Article III, Section II, No. 2 of the US Constitution itself.

Be that as it may, your vehement opposition to limiting the jurisdiction of the federal courts in redefining marriage accents the need for a Federal Marriage Amendment, which no courts can overthrow, to protect he concept and legal wisdom of our civilization from time immemorial.

This proposed amendment unfortunately failed on a procedural basis in its first test in the Senate. Now it is up to the House and the Senate (once again) and a tidal wave of the citizenry to demand its passage.

August 2, 2004   Maneuvering for partisan objective

Editor: The public be damned! better describes the action ("Equal Coverage in Suffolk," editorial 8/1, The Long Island Section) the action County Executive Levy and his special labor-management committee took in by-passing the Legislature with his labor-management committee and extending health benefits to domestic partners (read non-marital sexual partners) of county employees.

Already defeated in principle twice in the Legislature, this action conferring benefits on the homosexual partners and on the non-marital heterosexual partners of county employees creates a substitute for marriage and at the same time discriminates and excludes by favoring only partnerships based on a criterion of illicit sexual relationships.

Your plea for "tolerance" and "equality" summarily rejects the convictions of the majority of the citizens that (1) homosexual activity is wrongful and, if tolerated, is not to be rewarded by becoming a title for benefits; and (2) that no question of equality is involved since an apple is not a gooseberry; a sardine is not an elephant. The ethical tradition of our civilization testifies to the truth that a homosexual relationship cannot be termed marriage.

Moreover, if domestic partnerships are to be recognized by law and become a title for benefits, they should include persons committed to live together for mutual support and security on other bases; for example, two sisters; or an adult child caring for an aged parent or a parent caring for a disabled child; two non-related adults living together on a permanent basis to meet an economic crunch.

By acting against the unique social status of marriage and by favoring domestic partnerships based solely on illicit sexual relationships, Mr. Levy and his committee have callously decided: the public be damned!

August 8, 2004 Pub. NYT August 8, 2004
                                        Domestic partnerships

Editor: The public be damned! Better describes the action

that the Suffolk County executive, Steve Levy, and his special labor-management committee took in bypassing the Legislature and extending health benefits to domestic partners (read nonmarital sexual partners) of county employees ("Equal Coverage in Suffolk, editorial, Aug. 1).

Already defeated in principle twice in the Legislature, this action conferring benefits on the homosexual partners and on the nonmarital heterosexual partners of county employees creates a substitute for marriage and at the same time discriminates and excludes by favoring only partnerships based on a criterion of illicit sexual relationships.

If domestic partnerships are to recognized by law and become a title for benefits, they should include persons committed to live together for mutual support and security on other bases; for example, two sisters; or an adult child caring for as aged parent or a parent caring for a disabled child; or any two nonrelated adults living together on a permanent basis to meet an economic crunch.

Sept. 1, 2004   **Their moral sense cries out**

Editor: In declaring the partial-birth abortion law unconstitutional (story, Aug. 27), Federal District Judge Richard C. Casey cited a US Supreme Court decision of four years ago that necessitated his overruling a law passed overwhelmingly by Congress last year and signed by President Bush.

With fierce repugnance, however, he characterized the partial-birth abortion procedure as "gruesome, brutal, barbaric and uncivilized." Yet he struck down the law. Why? The bottom line: The US Supreme Court made me do it.

When will a courageous judge stand up, sweep away this legal formalism and. braving, of course, the certain overthrow of his own decision, point to the scientific evidence, the relevant ethical principles and declare: The US Supreme Court has erred; we are wantonly killing innocent human beings; the Court must stop this now!

September 7, 2004   Meddlesome cleric? An old charge

Editor: Vacation prevented me from reading on time "Saying No to Turkey" (editorial, 8/15) which labels Cardinal Joseph Ratzinger a "meddlesome cleric" for stating his view in a French newspaper that Turkey should not become a member of the European Union.

In the article the Cardinal expressed his own opinion, a prudential judgment, not a Catholic teaching or even a declared official policy of the Holy See.

Deeply troubling about this editorial, however, is the: "meddlesome cleric" label foisted on the cardinal. Eight centuries and more ago Henry II of England reportedly so characterized Thomas Becket, Archbishop of Canterbury, for differing with the King's policies and thus incited Becket's murder in his own cathedral.

From the old Testament prophets to Archbishop Oscar Romero of San Salvador and beyond "meddlesome clerics" have raised their voices in behalf of human dignity, justice, mercy and the common good. We will thank you for retiring the thinly disguised anticlericalism and secularism of "meddlesome clerics" for clergy whose only "offense" is to differ with your views.

September 13, 2004
You ca choose it only if you can afford it

Editor: The basic problem for religiously affiliated

elementary and secondary school parents ("Employment by Dogma? (Whatever that means) Lay Teachers Challenge Catholic Church," story, 9/12) is that they cannot benefit significantly from the compulsory educational taxes they pay unless they choose one kind of school, the public secular school.

Critics say, "Send your children to the public schools. What do you expect, a special police force, fire department or sewage system because you pay taxes like the rest of us?" The fallacy here is that the right to choose the school one's children attend is a natural, parental and civil right guaranteed by the U S Constitution as interpreted by the US Supreme Court and specifically upheld by the UN Universal Declaration of Human Rights. Other Western democracies fully respect this right and give equitable aid to such parents or such schools.

Thus we are being squeezed out of existence. I am the rector of a 475 pupil elementary (N-8) school, I know.

September 23, 2004
It's certain: embryonic stem cell research kills

Editor: "California's Stem Cell Challenge," editorial, 9/23, admits that no one knows whether embryonic stem cell research will bring cures of various diseases and that, in any case, clinical cures would be years away. (On the other hand, no mention is made of significant advances in cures brought about by research on various forms of adult stem cells.)

The editorial cites but does not endorse the ethical objection to destroying human embryos while extracting their stem cells. But surely this is the basic issue: whatever the ultimate purpose, are we killing (which all admit) a human being (which some dispute) at his or her beginning when we extract stem cells from a human embryo?

Responses should stick to the scientific evidence and accepted ethical reasoning.

September 30, 2004   Disparaging another view

Editor: Your "Feeding-Tube Posturing Struck Down" (editorial, 9/29) chastises the Florida Legislature "prodded by religious conservatives" for requiring that feeding and hydration tubes be restored to Theresa Schiavo who breathes on her own in a persistent vegetative state but has required such assisted feeding to live.

Why label disparagingly those whose reasoned ethical convictions tell them that withdrawing this nutritional support will cause Terri to starve to death? Should those who would deny Terri this nutritional support then be called "liberal secularists"? The conflicting ethical positions should be argued out, not dismissed with ideological labeling.

October 16, 2004
                    Clerics should keep quiet – one kept quiet

Editor: You support Harvard's bid ("A Promising Cloning Proposal," editorial, 10/15) to pursue so-called therapeutic cloning, but quickly pass over the basic issue: If, as you admit, cloning destroys an innocent human embryo by extracting its stem cells, are we not thereby deliberately killing a human being at his or her beginning? And what ethical principle justifies the deliberate killing of an innocent human being at any stage of his or her development?

Your same-day huffy jab ("Blessed Charles I") at John Paul II for beatifying the late (and last) Emperor Charles I of Austria-Hungary calls to mind your August 15

("Saying No to Turkey,") editorial labeling Cardinal Ratzinger a "meddlesome cleric" for expressing a personal negative opinion on Turkey's bid to join the European Union. Should the pontiff now reprove a "meddlesome journalist" for poking his nose into internal church affairs? Or is it possible that there is a Catholic mole on the editorial board?

October 25, 2004   **Yes, it is absurd**

Editor: Jennifer Lymneous (letter, 10/25) might see the weakness of her reasoning for choice in abortion if the issue of slavery were uniformly substituted for abortion in her text. Thus –

"Laws supporting the right to hold slaves acknowledge each citizen's right to decide whether slavery is moral or immoral. Laws restricting slavery make one decision for everyone.

"Life is unpredictable. I would never force another citizen to keep a slave against his or her will. Why should I be forced to free a slave against mine?"

October 25, 2004
It depends on whose campaigning in whose Church

Editor: Various news stories in recent weeks (ex., p.1, 10/25) have reported candidates for major public campaigning in tax-exempt houses of worship. Is this not a grievous breach of the so-called wall of separation between church and state? Community groups and media that usually rail against such violations are curiously silent. Has The Times changed its view?

Editor: Senator Kerry recently complained that bishops "have suggested that as a public official I must cast votes or take public positions – on issues like a woman's right to choose and stem cell research – that carry out the tenets of the Catholic Church." He is profoundly mistaken.

The choice to slay an innocent human being clashes with a moral principle recognized by the whole world, though not observed by all: to respect, never to violate, innocent human life. No political candidate or legislator is expected to write into law tenets that have their unique source in Catholic teaching but only those that have or should have their support from the consensus of rational and civilized people. Like slavery, euthanasia, sterilizing the innocent, unjust discrimination based on racial, ethnic, gender or religious criteria, civilized people, growing in moral insight, reject slaying the innocent. Religious convictions may reinforce these positions drawn from human reason and experience but they are not the basis for them.

And what about those who say, we consider ourselves rational, civilizes and humane but we do support the killing of pre-born children and the willful destruction of human embryos? We respond, consider the scientific evidence. It is irrefutable that a new human life begins at fertilization. Observe an abortion; watch the young one (fetus) scalded and dismembered in his or her mother's womb; or watch the child's head bludgeoned into pulp just before it emerges from the birth canal. Tell us what you see happening. Tell us how you evaluate these actions. What do you say?

January 2, 2005   **There is an explanation**

Editor: David Brooks ("A Time to Mourn," Op-ed. 1/1) laments the vicious human destruction caused by the tidal waves, for which, for him and for many others, philosophically speaking, there is "no explanation."

But classical Christianity has an explanation for such events, which, while viewing them as no less mournful and cruel, sets them in a context of meaning and hope. The material world and the human person are disordered. Whence this disorder? The primordial transgression of the head of the human race, whom the Bible calls Adam. Thus sin, a very particular sin, not God, is the cause of sickness, suffering, death, natural disasters and those effected by human decision.

Christmas, the Cross and the yet-to-come Glorious Advent of the Messiah are the antidote to it all. In the meantime the grace of salvation is offered to all.

Those who reject classical Christianity as "myth" have seldom confronted a scientific apologetic defending the truth of the biblical message. Those who have, mourn no less the vicious cruelty of the tsunamis, the Black Plague or Hitler's genocide of the Jews; but they all see these disasters in a framework of meaning and hope.

February 11, 2005   **Equal but not interchangeable**

Editor: State Senator Thomas K. Duane (letter, Feb. 10) apparently thinks that men and women are interchangeable in all respects when he asserts that persons of the same sex have the right to civil marriage. To hold otherwise, he tells us, is "discrimination."

On the basis of biology, reason, history, law and experience, other citizens reject this view as ill-founded and as contrary to nature and the common good. They hold, with due respect for those who propose same-sex marriage as a civil right, that the institution of marriage requires a man and a woman and that no discrimination emerges in law or in fact from respecting this objective reality.

May 19, 2005
The Rabbi judges the pope. He doesn't mind.

Editor: Writing on the Op-Ed page of The New York Times for May 14 (The Vatican's Sin of Omission), the distinguished rabbi and author, Arthur Hertzberg, declared his uncertainty that over the last forty years "a new age in Jewish-Catholic relationship had dawned." The stumbling block for the rabbi is that the pope, like his immediate predecessors, while acknowledging that some individual Catholics on all levels had failed to speak out loudly for the Jews during the Nazi period, maintains nonetheless that the pope himself of that time (Pius XII) and the Church itself as such cannot be faulted. He attributes this position to the Catholic doctrine of papal infallibility.

In fact, Pope Pius XII did speak out many times about Nazi and Stalinist atrocities, but not as loudly, as specifically and as frequently as Rabbi Hertzberg and some others, looking back 60 years after the events, would have liked. The pope's decisions, however, had nothing to do with the Catholic conviction about the guidance – yes, infallible – enjoyed by the whole Church, the episcopacy and the Bishop of Rome in very special circumstances. The pope's decisions on what to say, how strongly and specifically to speak and how frequently to speak were (and are) linked to his own assessment of events in the context of the time and of the good and bad effects that such statements would have. Historians, striving for the fullest objective and balanced evaluation, will give us the best reading of these events.

But the distinction between the Church and its individual members is one Rabbi Hertzberg understandably does not understand. The Church is a communion of grace, a sharing by persons in God's life, a fellowship that transcends this world and has its center in the Heavenly Jerusalem, with the Glorified Lord Jesus and the angels and the righteous of all ages, from the Covenant with Adam through the Covenants of Sinai and Calvary. When those of us still on our pilgrim way deliberately sin by commission or omission, we wound our fellow wayfarers.

Thus we do not say that the Church, so understood, is the perpetrator of any evil, but rather, understood as the Body of Christ and the communion of grace, she is the "mother" of every blessing. If, on the basis of historical facts as he sees them, the rabbi expects us to flail Pope Pius XII, he is chasing the wind. We do not see the facts of those decades as he sees them. God is the pope's judge and the rabbi's judge and the judge of us all.

May 23, 2005 Pub. NYT May 24, 2005
A critical juncture on stem cells

To the Editor: "A Surprising Leap on Cloning," (editorial, May 24) does not address the basic question in the debate over human embryonic stem cell research. When a human embryo is produced, what kind of entity is it, and what respect does it demand?

Biomedical science tells us that the human embryo, however produced, if maintained in the proper environment, will develop from the beginning through various stages before and after birth and becomes an adult person.

Tacking "therapeutic" onto cloning provides a euphemism to hide the truth that the embryo is being produced to be destroyed by harvesting its cells for research.

This discussion has nothing to do with religion. The facts, accessible to all, derive from biomedical science.

May 26, 2005   **The scientific facts**

Editor: "The President's Stem Cell Theology" (editorial, 5/26) ought to have been headed "The President's Stem Cell Ethics." Mr. Bush cited only scientific facts and (implicitly) the ethical norm that one may not do evil that good may come of it in his decision against embryonic stem cell research.

The biomedical facts about the embryo are undisputed: From the beginning it is a new member of the human species and, given the proper environment, will develop through various stages before and after birth into an adult person. That some embryos naturally die does not compromise this fact.

True, people do have different moral codes; and you accuse the President of seeking to impose a particular moral code on a pluralistic society. But all legislation derives from a particular moral vision and the norms that accompany it. Elected officials must certainly abide by their conscientious convictions.

The President's ethical reasoning based on indisputable scientific fact is particularly cogent. Your moral code permits the deliberate killing of an innocent new member of the human species; his does not. Let's have a referendum to determine whose code has the greater support.

June 17, 2005   **Exactly what happened**

Editor: The bottom line on Terry Schiavo ("Autopsy on the Schiavo Tragedy," 6/17): Terry was severely brain-injured, not recoverable, but certainly not dying. The pathologist's report designates the cause of her death as "marked dehydration," What caused this? The withdrawal of her gastric feeding tube. Why was it removed? Her husband said Terry said (years ago) she wouldn't want to live this way. You conclude she was "allowed to die." In reality, she was forced to die. The direct cause of death was the removal of her gastric feeding tube. What severely disabled but not dying person so nourished will be next?

June 20, 2005   **Natural science proves it**

Editor: The basic fallacy in Gov. Mario Cuomo's effort ("Not on Faith Alone," Op-Ed, 6/20) to keep religion out of the embryonic stem cell debate is his failure to recognize that natural science cannot at any point in human development – not only ar fertilization – declare the product of human conception to be "sacred," a human being, a person. Human reason makes that recognition.

Natural science – the indisputable facts of genetics, embryogenesis and human development – provide the evidence for the origin of the new human being at fertilization and the continuous development, given the proper environment, through all stages of human development, before and after birth.

Of course, not all participants in this agree on the respect due to the human embryo, but those who do are convinced that the scientific evidence for this rational conclusion is overwhelming and coercive. No need to keep religion out. It shouldn't be there in the first place.

July 11, 2005   Pub. NYT July 17, 2005
Religious education and school taxes

Editor: As the rector of a religiously affiliated (Catholic) elementary school, I can readily support positions set forth by Erin Harrington in "Keeping the Faith" (Op-Ed, July 10).

Basic to the survival of these schools is a practical recognition of the natural, human and civil right of parents to choose the school their children will attend. But a severe penalty attaches to exercising it; such parents must suffer the loss of virtually all benefits from the compulsory school taxes they and all others must pay. This policy is strangling our school and most other religiously affiliated schools.

Why should the exercise of a constitutional right to choose a service for which all pay compulsory taxes result in such a heavy burden for those who choose a religiously affiliated school?

Objectors say: "You want your own school -- or your own police force, fire department, sanitation service or library? Then pay for it." This reproach neglects the special nature of the school in the education and character formation of children.

The Constitution gives citizens no right to separate services of the kind mentioned, but it does guarantee parental rights in the choice of schools.

Other Western democracies don't strangle religiously affiliated schools by their tax policies. Why should we?

July 15, 2005   When you err, retract your error

Editor: "The Dark Side of Stem Cell Politics" (editorial, 7/15) chides Senate Majority Leader Frist for changing from support (2001) to opposition (current) respecting embryonic stem cell research and for backing a new third way to produce these cells without killing a human embryo in the process – craven acts, you opine, in deference to the Bush Administration.

But changing one's mind can result also from learning new facts. Nothing is clearer from bio-medical science than that the human embryo, that little dot, is a new member of the human species. That's not ideology or theology, but undisputed scientific fact. Harvesting stem cells from such "surplus" or cloned embryos destroys a new member of the human species. That's another indisputable scientific fact. That you may not do evil that good may come of it is a basic ethical principle. No dark side this, but the side of luminous light.

July 20, 2005   **Plan B clearly aborts**

Editor: "Governor Pataki and Women's Rights," (editorial, 7/19) urges the governor to sign a bill that would allow pharmacists and nurses to dispense emergency contraceptive drugs without a doctor's patient-specific prescription, allowing females of any age to obtain these high-hormone drugs without a physician's examination and without parents' knowledge or oversight.

You describe this drug – called Plan B – as a contraceptive not an abortifacient; but the manufacturer, Barr Pharmaceuticals of Pomona, NY, states that the drug can prevent implantation of the embryo in the uterus. Clearly, it can expel the new member of the human species.

It is false to identify Plan B as merely a contraceptive and thus deny women the right to have fully informed consent about the drug they are taking.

Moreover, because neither parental consent nor age restriction applies, young girls of any age will be able to access these drugs repeatedly, putting their health at risk and infringing on parents' rights to make healthcare decisions for their children. Governor Pataki should veto this bill.

July 30, 2005   Pub. NYT August 2, 2005
Stem cells and Senator Frist

Editor: Bill Frist, the Senate majority leader, offers a baffling logic in his turnaround on human embryonic stem cell research when he states that "it's a fact of science" that the human embryo is "nascent human life" but that the potential of this research - "a theory, a hope, a dream" - justifies this destruction.

He says, in effect: the end justifies the means. A human being at his or her beginning can rightfully be destroyed for a hoped-for benefit to other human beings. If such a human being can rightfully be destroyed for this purpose, why not a human being at any other stage of his or her existence?

Senator Frist offers us not the logic of reason and principle but of politics - of Machiavelli.

August 3, 2005   Deception or contraception

Editor: It is patently deceptive to make the unqualified claim as you do ("Governor Pataki's Veto," editorial, 8/2), that the so-called morning-after pill (Plan B) is "a form of contraception, not abortion." The manufacturer, Barr Pharmaceuticals, candidly states in its literature that the drug can prevent implantation of the embryo in the uterus.

Contraception prevents the union of sperm and ovum. Plan B can operate this way, but it can also cause the already conceived embryo to be expelled. Bio-medical science universally affirms that a new human life begins at fertilization. It's immaterial whether the drug dislodges the embryo from the uterine wall (which it does not) or prevents it from lodging therein. This distinction is without a difference regarding the effect deliberately intended and achieved; namely, the expulsion of the embryo from the womb.

Falsely identifying Plan B as only contraception also denies a woman – and yes, the teenager under 16 – her right to have fully informed consent when she chooses this drug.

October 14, 2005
Ephebophilia and pedophilia are distinct

Editor: Your criticism ("The Stonewalling Shepherd," editorial, 10/13) of Cardinal Mahoney refers to the "pedophile priests" and the "pedophile scandal," despite the unquestioned data of the John Jay College Report which shows that 78% of those clergy alleged to have sexually abused minors in the period of 1950-2002 were accused of the sexual abuse of post-pubescent males. Pedophilia refers to pre-pubescent children. The attraction of adult men to adolescent males is generally referred to as ephebophilia, a classic expression of homosexuality.

Both pedophilia and ephebophilia are dangerous tendencies and need to be effectively addressed. But they are distinct and should not be confused.

March 11, 2006   **The final solution!**

Editor: John Tierney was surely laughing all the way as he wrote his jeu d'esprit (Who's Afraid of Polygamy? Op-ed, 3/11). It must be comforting for professional women to learn that here's a way – be one of eight wives, like the

Utah lawyer and journalist Elizabeth Joseph – to insure round-the-clock day care for the kids.

But don't we need a companion essay – Who's Afraid of Polyandry? Think how all the men could chip in for the one wife and the limited number of kids and be off, in turn, having a good time.

Menu supreme! Affordable living! Maximum services! Why has it taken so long to laud the virtues of polygamy and polyandry? We need a college course with a textbook. The author? You guessed it. Polyanna.

December 23, 2005
Reason, not experimental science provides the answer

Editor: "Intelligent Design Derailed" (editorial, 12/22) signifies the legal disqualification of this thesis as a proper component of a natural science or biology curriculum but it leaves unanswered basic questions that have pressed the thinking mind for millennia.

Is experimental natural science the only path to truth or to the verification of truth tentatively attained? If I can confidently say that my wrist watch was not blown together by the wind or assembled by a monkey, cannot I reflect upon the order of nature and of the universe and conclude that they are not the explanation of themselves?

Philosophical science and biological science should not be confused. Neither should be expected to respond to questions it has no tools to answer or to intrude on the realm of the other.

June 10, 2006   Face the basic question

Editor: "A Start on Research Cloning" (editorial, 6/9) again sidesteps the basic and hugely important ethical issue of destroying human embryos, naturally conceived or cloned by extracting their stem cells for whatever purpose. The issue is one of ends and means.

Scientists agree that a new human life begins at fertilization or by the substitute act of cloning. The embryo is then deliberately destroyed for its stem cells possibly to benefit a living human being distinct from the one destroyed. If human life can be deliberately destroyed at its beginning for a therapeutic purpose, why not at any other stage?

Research on adult stem cells, notably those taken from umbilical cords, involving no ethical problem has yielded extensive therapeutic benefits. Why is not this research more broadly cited and generously funded in contrast to embryonic stem cell research which destroys innocent human life and to date has yielded no benefits?

July 14, 2006 Pub. NYT July 18, 2006
Debating the value of same-sex marriage

Editor: Controversy continues over the New York Court of Appeals rejection of arguments that the equal protection laws demand the legalization of same-sex marriage.

Neither the court nor its critics, however, have identified the basic reason marriage is limited to a man and a woman: it is the nature of the human person as male and female, a distinction that makes impossible any total interchangeability of man and woman.

No man can bear a child; no woman can by and of herself conceive. It is nature, not opinion or long custom, or the curious "reckless procreation" argument that dictates marriage as exclusively a man-woman relationship.

Persons have rights, and all persons have the same basic human rights. But a line of distinction drawn on the basis of (wrongful) activity is fundamentally different from that drawn on the basis of age, race, sex, disability or ethnic background.

Interracial marriage, for example, and same-sex marriage are not comparable, despite the opinion of the minority in the court ruling. It is an authentic philosophical anthropology that proves these points.

July 19, 2006   **Logic to madness**

Editor: In "Standing Up for Stem Cell research," editorial, 7/18, you state: "It is no more immoral to create and destroy embryos for therapeutic purposes than to create and destroy surplus embryos for fertility purposes." As stated, you're right.

Both are grossly immoral because they deliberately destroy nascent human life. And you admit, while denying that these human embryos have any [visible] human attributes, "sitting outside the womb," they have "no chance of developing into babies."

This is troublesome logic. To manufacture and destroy human embryos for whatever purpose is wrong. Yet this is precisely what we should and must do? Such logic can lead to madness.

August 7, 2006   Pub. NYT August 13, 2006
Consider alternatives to abortion

Editor: Lynn Harris (Op-Ed, Aug. 6) tells how she houses young girls and more mature women overnight so that they might obtain abortions, often late term, in New York and then return to their out-of-state homes.

She thinks she is engaged in a humanitarian task -- facilitating the dismemberment and killing of preborn human beings.

How is it possible to be so blind to the nature of abortion?

September 21, 2006   Intolerance masking as tolerance

Editor: I don't have the text of that "mischievous amendment empowering "evangelical" chaplains to speak in the name of Jesus at interreligious military gatherings" (editorial, 9/21, "Keep Christ out of the Christmas Tree). But I am bold to say that if any religious representative is invited to pray at an interreligious gathering, military or otherwise, that person should proclaim the prayer in accord with his or her religious beliefs.

To ask for a prayer and then require that it be sterilized according to somebody's least common denominator is the real intolerance. Listen respectfully – that's tolerance – or opt for no prayer. That's your right.

October 3, 2006   Espionage journalism

Editor: Your 10/3 news story ("A Coming Papal Visit Focuses Anger Among the Turks") reports a fear among some Turks that the Greek Orthodox Patriarchate in Istanbul is actively seeking Vatican City-like status for itself. The story does not directly cite any official or unofficial Turkish source asserting this fear or any other basis for the alleged fear and, importantly, no comment from the Ecumenical Patriarchate itself on the issue. This seems a critically inadequate journalistic way of publicizing such a potentially explosive political issue.

December 20, 2006

Yes, it still holds. One may not do evil that good may come of it

Editor: Nicholas Kristoff ("When Prudishness Costs Lived," Op-Ed. 12/19) plays the consummate pragmatist when he raps the Bush Administration and, of course, the Catholic Church for opposing the use of condoms to fight AIDS. The Church is the nongovernment agency with the largest world-wide program to fight AIDS.

Yes, the Church does oppose the use of condoms because of themselves and by themselves – intrinsically, apart from the agent's intention – their purpose is to impede the transmission of life and to divide a relationship (love and life) proper only to spouses.

Though individuals may be guiltless because they do not share or they feel compelled to transgress this norm, we cannot say: Do what is always objectively wrong and harmful because in this instance, some good may come of it – no more that we can say: Commit fornication, adultery, sodomy; kill the unborn child; abandon or kill this severely disabled neonate; assist in this suicide or perform this euthanasia; destroy this human embryo – because this may produce some good. One may not do evil that good may come of it.

Give the Catholic Church credit – and, I do not hesitate to say, respect – for its worldwide efforts to combat AIDS, and its deeply held moral values and norms. We cannot do evil that good may come of it.

July 10, 2007   **Begging the question**

Editor: You brand Dr. James Holsinger's view on male homosexual activity ("A Nominee's Abnormal Views,"

140

7/10) as "benighted" and "abnormal" because in a 1991 paper on male homosexual activity he did on anatomical and physiological grounds so qualify such intercourse and called it "unhealthy" in that it "can lead to rectal injuries and sexually transmitted diseases."

Does anyone doubt that male homosexual activity is statistically, anatomically and physiologically abnormal? Does anyone doubt that it can lead to the evils specified? Are we living, like The Times board, with Alice in Wonderland?

You berate Dr. Holsinger for not citing the evil effects of male-female anal relations or the fact of heterosexually transmitted diseases – not the subject of his essay. Completely omitted in his essay and in The Times critique is any mention of the ethical principles involved. One begs the question in assuming that any kind of homosexual activity is right.

Millions of Americans and countless other millions throughout the world are convinced on ethical and moral grounds that both male and female homosexual activity is against the nature of the human person and therefore wrong and abnormal, apart from any consideration of possible injurious medical effects. To be so convinced is not "benighted" or an "aversion," but an affirmation of a profoundly ethical conviction.

February 15, 2008
Christians are still Christians and Jews still Jews

Editor: You report ("Resolution on Prayer Is Approved", 2/9, 2/14) that Conservative rabbis and other Jewish organizational leaders strongly oppose the new papal formulation of a Good Friday prayer from the seldom-used 1962 Missal because it continues to pray that Jews will recognize Jesus of Nazareth as their Messiah and Savior.

The essence of the Gospel and the specific, explicit

teaching of the New Testament Scriptures is that the Great Obedience of Jesus, the God-Man, upon the Cross is the cause and source of salvation for all, the Jews <u>first</u> and then all other peoples.

In recent decades, some Jewish and some Christian dialogue partners have tended to obscure this teaching by positing two distinct and separate covenants, one for the Jews and the other for all other peoples.

It is understandable that believing Jews would want Jesus completely out of the picture. The Church must indeed clarify its own teaching on the relationship of the "two covenants". But just as Jews cannot recede from their conviction that the Trinity represents idolatry, so Christians cannot recede from their conviction that Jesus is the universal Savior.

No offense intended by either position to the other side and no setback to the dialogue for those who respectfully the conviction of their dialogue partner.

February 24, 2008   **No solution only more issues**

Editor: David Blankenhorn and Jonathan Rauch (Op-Ed,2/22) propose a "reasonable accommodation" on same-sex marriage: All should accept a federal law sanctioning same-sex marriages and civil unions granted by the States that have "robust" religious conscience exceptions with the federal bill guaranteeing the same. Such a bill would confer on civil unions most or all of the federal benefits of marriage. The law would be analogous, it is said, to abortion laws which allow for the conscience of those who cannot approve or take part in what William Saletan in a same-day op-ed piece calls the killing "of a developing human being."

To this ingenious compromise, this writer must say no. Why not? Such a "compromise" would immediately and legally entrench an intrinsic evil-homosexual relations - and legitimate such unions all over the country. Without necessarily using the word "marriage," it would overturn the sexual ethic of our civilization based on the natural moral law accessible to all persons by their reason and based on the nature of the human person and of his or her acts; that is, based on a philosophical anthropology, a philosophy of man.

It would lead further to the manufaction of children, erode the nature of the family as the fruit of heterosexual spousal love and never satisfy, as the 2/24 editorial. "Gay Marriage Needs a Vote" categorically maintains, those who hold that same-sex marriage is a "right."

Firm, respectful discussion that accuses no one of malice or bad faith must be embraced by both sides as they continue to uphold what they are convinced is the truth.

August 30, 2008   **Voting for Evil?**

Editor: Peter Steinfels (Beliefs, 8/30) gives Prof. Douglas G. Kmiec generous space to justify his position that, as a faithful Catholic opposed to killing the unborn, he may nevertheless vote for a candidate (Candidate A) strongly supportive of, and, indeed, a champion of, so called abortion rights for other weighty reasons; namely the opposing candidate's (Candidate B) perceived lesser general conformity (than Candidate A) to the body of Catholic moral and social values. And, he implies, other faithful Catholics may do the same.

Prof. Kmiec accuracy cites pertinent moral principles:1) you may not support Candidate A because he embraces an intrinsic evil, but 2) you may vote for him/her for other weighty reasons, suggesting the seriously defective position of Candidate B. But Dr. Kmiec is mistaken in applying the second principle to this case. And he also overlooks the issue of priority: a lie and a homicide are both evil; but the latter overwhelms the former in its degree of evil.

Space needs to be given to a competent moralist and political science scholar to prove these points. A letter won't do.

June 2, 2008   **A make-believe world**

Editor: Legalizing same-sex marriages will not serve justice as you maintain (editorial, 5/30), but only legal positivism: the theory that government can establish as a "right" whatever it chooses, provided the public does not respond with massive dissent.

So a legislature could not (today) enact laws that permitted slavery or the deportation of particular racial, ethnic or religious groups without meeting massive public rejection. So at the present time would laws purporting to establish polygyny, polyandry or incestuous unions as a "right" be similarly rebuked.

Until recent decades the same could be said for same-sex unions of any kind, much more so those that purport to be "marriages." Holding that persons with an exclusive same-sex attraction have a "right" to marry one another evacuates marriage of its basic meaning, which involves the mutual giving and receiving of the right to the sexual union that ordinarily produces children. Persons of the same sex are naturally incapable of doing that. Only man and woman can mutually bestow this gift and so can be said to have a right to marry.

The mutual sexual exchange between same-sex partners amounts only to a collection of masturbatory practices that no moral system has accepted as a good for the human person. Of course, all human beings have the same basic rights, which the legislature should recognize and enact in law and in public policy and the executive, implement. Same-sex marriage, however, is not one of these basic rights. Legalizing same-sex "marriage" is not a step closer to justice but to a world of make-believe.

One cannot have a right to something nature universally disqualifies a particular group of persons from having. Two men or two women cannot forge the sexual bond that permits the conception of a child. Thus nature universally says no to same-sex marriage.

August 4, 2008
Humanae Vitae, greater depth than first seen

Editor: Peter Steinfels's commentary ("After 40 Years, a Debate Reverberates, 8/2) on Humanae Vitae, the 1968 encyclical in which Pope Paul VI reaffirmed the Catholic Church's constant teaching on artificial contraception, lacks specific mention of two important themes of that letter.

First, the pope declares that both contraception and marital oppression in the conjugal act violate the two-fold inseparable meaning of love-giving and life-giving, essential to the conjugal embrace.

Second, he affirms that this understanding derives not merely from the natural moral law – the law inherent in the nature of the human person and of his or her acts – but from that law "enlightened and enriched by the Gospel." Throughout the encyclical the pope cites the numerous values and norms flowing from the divine revelation that bear upon this meaning. His teaching is essentialist not consequentialist (what happens if...).

The entire teaching of the encyclical and its central judgment about frustrating love or frustrating potential life rest upon this total view of human life implicit in the Church's constant teaching and, now (in 1968), in this latest authoritative reaffirmation of that teaching.

August 30, 2008   **Voting for evil?**

Editor: Peter Steinfels (Beliefs, 8/30) gives Prof. Douglas G. Kmiec generous space to justify his position that, as a faithful Catholic opposed to killing the unborn, he may nevertheless vote for a candidate (Candidate A) strongly supportive of, and, indeed, a champion of, so called abortion rights for other weighty reasons; namely the opposing candidate's (Candidate B) perceived lesser general conformity (than Candidate A) to the body of Catholic moral and social values. And, he implies, other faithful Catholics may do the same.

Prof. Kmiec accurately cites pertinent moral principles:1) you may not support Candidate A because he embraces an intrinsic evil, but 2) you may vote for him/her for other weighty reasons, suggesting the seriously defective position of Candidate B. But Dr. Kmiec is mistaken in applying the second principle to this case. And he also overlooks the issue of priority: a lie and a homicide are both evil; but the latter overwhelms the former in its degree of evil.

Space needs to be given to a competent moralist and political science scholar to prove these points. A letter won't do.

November 8, 2008   **Take a look, folks.**

Editor: Peter Steinfels "Catholics and Choice (in the Voting Booth)," (Beliefs, Nov.8) cautiously but nonetheless sharply criticizes U.S. Catholic Bishops as "big losers" in the Nov.4 presidential election for their "perceived" (that wiggly word) designation of abortion or "abortion rights" as the decisive criterion for casting one's vote. Readers should re-read his essay substituting each time for abortion and "abortion rights" slavery and "slavery rights." They'll get the point.

Those who have never viewed the atrocity of a child slain by dismemberment or scalding in the womb or half out of the womb, or left to die totally out of the womb may indeed comment "why all this fuss about abortion?" For those who have seen an accurate depiction, it must be termed a horror.

Adherents of the truth are never "big losers" although they may be "perceived" as such. Here the words of Scripture resonate: "The wisdom of this world is foolishness with God" (I Corinthians 3:19).

November 14, 2008   Op-Ed.
Reproductive rights – another view

Op-Ed Editor: Encouraged by the public editor's 11/9 essay "The Perilous Interaction of Art and Religion," by his endorsement of executive editor Keller's description of The Times as "tolerant and curious about a wide range of views and behaviors" and, finally, by his own conclusion that the "editors need to be sure that the wide range includes the views of the religious," I present this widely accepted (but not by The Times) alternative philosophical view, also endorsed in the main by the major world religions, of reproductive rights, also called reproductive freedom.

Coincidentally, on the same day that the public editor's essay appeared, another of the familiar and fairly frequent Times' editorials on reproductive freedom also appeared. Usually such editorials appear in the context of a perceived (by The Times) threat to "a woman's right to her own childbearing decisions." And the 11/9 editorial was no exception. The "right" in question is to make the decision to seek and direct the expulsion and destruction of the new human life – be it called zygote, embryo or fetus (according to its stage of development) - in her womb. This is what

The Times means by "reproductive freedom" and "reproductive rights."

But what is a "right?" and where does it come from? What is the basis for a right? A right is a claim human beings have as persons to that which is needed for the good of the person. Others have an obligation to respect our human rights and, perhaps, to supply or facilitate the "good", whatever it is, or at least not to inhibit the exercise of the right.

Where do these rights come from? Our Declaration of Independence tells us our most basic human rights are intrinsic to our nature as created by God. They are not gifts to us from the state or from the majority in a particular society. Human reason identifies these rights; legislatures may enact them into civil law and courts give them fuller exposition. But basically they are not legally fabricated; they are recognized as due to the human person. As civilization progresses, reason may see these rights more clearly whereas in other earlier contexts they had lain dormant or even denied. Also, what we once saw as a right can later be recognized as doing injury to another; for example, the right of a certain class of persons to own slaves.

The right of persons of diverse races, genders or ethnic origins to participate fully in society, to have food, clothing, shelter, employment, medical care, to vote, to send their children to the schools of their choice are examples of rights recognized and protected by law. But all these rights are seen first as intrinsic to the human person and for the good of the human person. Legislation that goes against the good of the human person is deprived of any basis in reason and can establish no moral obligation, even though the law may be a coercive one. The Nuremberg laws in Nazi Germany are one example of such laws.

Do men or women have reproductive rights? An

ethical heritage deeply embedded in the history of our civilization holds that neither men nor women have reproductive <u>rights</u> and certainly no reproductive freedom. Both men and women do have, however, a complementary reproductive <u>power</u>; but only spouses have the right to exercise this power. Moreover, even in the case of spouses, such a right is not a right "to a child" or, perish the thought, to destroy a human being already in the womb, but a right only to the marital embrace that may be productive of a child.

Conception may, indeed, result from acts that are not spousal. Fornicators, adulterers, incestuous persons and rapists may conceive a child or cause a child to be conceived; but they have no right to exercise their reproductive power in that context. I prescind here from any discussion of conception apart from the marital embrace, e.g., artificial insemination or in vitro fertilization where the husband is the donor.

I take as an indisputable datum of bio-medical science that a new human life begins at fertilization. (It is curious that some intelligent people, in the face of the unanimous scientific testimony may still deny this fact.) Equally indisputable is the fact that, given the proper environment (the womb), the fertilized egg develops progressively – zygote, embryo, fetus, neonate, toddler, schoolchild, teenager, young adult, middle-aged adult, senior. I write as one who was once a fertilized egg. My mother and father knew that their marital embrace could result in conception. They intended or at least allowed this to happen. I have gone through all the stages in the womb and out of the womb.

Did my mother have the "right to make her own child-bearing decisions?" which, in the rhetoric of The Times, means a right to destroy me before I was born? Was that her "reproductive right?" A manifestation of her reproductive freedom?

The natural moral law tradition, bolstered by but not based on religious convictions, says NO. I was a human being from my beginning as a fertilized egg, then zygote, and an embryo. Like every other child I was a gift to my parents. I have had from the beginning a right to life. Nothing justifies the direct and deliberate killing of this new human being whether parents wanted it or not or fornicators, adulterers or sexual oppressors want it or not! One may not do evil-that good may come of it.

It has been my purpose here to discuss related issues such as criminalization – who should be punished and how or what services society should provide to dissuade women with problem pregnancies from having recourse to abortion. These are other very important, related but separate issues.

The question addressed is a simple one: Does man or woman have a reproductive right? NO. Do they have a reproductive power? Yes. Can they exercise this power in any way or in any context they choose? NO. What is the rightful context for the exercise of their power? The marital union of one man and one woman. Does either husband or wife have the right to destroy the fruit of their marital embrace? NO. They have been given a gift to respect, to treasure and to bring to the same maturity they enjoy.

Reproductive rights and reproductive freedom understood as the right and freedom to destroy the new human being present in the womb have no basis in a sound philosophy of the human person and are gravely injurious to third parties, those who exercise this so-called right and to the general societal attitude of respect for the inviolability of innocent human life.

December 12, 2008   **Machiavelli lives!**

Editor: So the defense and promotion of human rights is a "certain utopianism" or "Angélism," French foreign minister Bernard Kouchner tells us ("French Foreign Minister Voices Doubts on Human Rights Push," 12/11). "And there is a permanent contradiction between human rights and the foreign policy of a state," he says.

All these decades (since the Universal Declaration of Human Rights (1948) I have been thinking that the defense and promotion of human rights was the pursuit of justice and respect for the inviolable dignity of every human being.

How mistaken I have been! Could the foreign minister be referring to the permanent contradiction between good and evil?

February 2, 2009   **Defer to the wise hand**

Editor: Peter Steinfels ("The Holocaust Furor and the U.S. Bishops," 1/31) is worried about Pope Benedict's decision to lift the excommunications from four schismatic bishops, including Richard Williamson, who (the latter) recently made, almost simultatouesly with the Pope's generous gesture, outrageous public comments about the Holocaust. Why aren't the U.S. bishops, Mr. Steinfels implies, raising Cain?

The Holy See repudiated Williamson's remarks, as did his own religious community, the Society of St. Pius X – which in addition asked forgiveness for his comments and barred him from repeating them; and the U.S. Conference of Bishops' representative also repudiated them. Too much attention is being paid to this one schismatic bishop on the margins of his Church and of his own Society.

The real problem for Mr. Steinfels and (on this point) his would-be fellow doom-sayers seems to be, however, the very fact of the Pope's outreach to reconcile these ultraconservative dissidents. Why aren't the U.S. bishops raising Cain about Benedict's gesture? Whoa!

Clearly the Pope, mindful of the perduring so-called "Old Catholic" Schism after Vatican I (1869-70), does not want any perduring schism after Vatican II. Give way to the judgment of the Bishop of Rome. Recall, schismatica and other obstinate dissidents are dealing with the former Cardinal Joseph Ratzinger.

March 3, 2009
The law treats all religion, including secular humanism, alike

Editor: In her dense Op-Ed essay "Keeping the Faith, Ignoring the History" (3/1), Susan Jacoby proclaims herself a "thoroughgoing secularist" and asserts that it is both dangerous and unconstitutional to allow "faith-based communities" to receive federal funding to implement social service programs for the general public.

Ms. Jacoby seems shocked that the Obama Administration should continue such programs initiated by the Clinton and the Bush Administrations because, she claims, such programs cannot be kept free of proselytism and selective hiring practices.

Indeed, proselytizing, which entices people to embrace a particular religion, should definitely not receive federal funding; but hiring practices needed to preserve the sponsor's value system in accord with the law is a different issue.

Our country's religion is not one of secularism or secular humanism (Torcaso vs. Watkins, 1961) any more than it is some form of Judaism, Christianity or Islam. Religious groups should not be discriminated against because they provide social, health or educational services both in accord with the civil law and with their value systems.

March 10, 2009
Good intentions do not sanctify bad actions

Editor: "Science and Stem Cell Research" (editorial, 3/10) blames "religious conservatives" for the now-lifted "Bush administration's restrictions on federal funding for embryonic stem cell research."

In fact, those who support all forms of stem cell research except the embryonic form do so because of bedrock ethical principles; innocent human life is inviolable; it may not be deliberately attacked; you may not do evil that good may come of it.

To extract stem cells from a human embryo is to kill that embryo; it is to destroy a human being at his or her beginning. Ironically, in the science section of your same 3/10 issue, Nicholas Wade points out the many successes of non-embryonic stem cell research, which may eclipse the need perceived by some to manufacture and destroy more human embryos for research.

The ethical principles that forbid the destruction of human embryos are an "ideology" only for those who embrace a different "ideology"; namely, if you have a good purpose, it's OK to destroy human embryos.

We should all refrain from blackening the opposition (either side) and seriously discuss the agreed scientific facts and ethical principles that govern human (including natural scientific) activity.

March 18, 2009   **Condoms always distort**

Editor: Re: Your editorial, "Pope on Condoms and AIDS", 3/18:

The ethical framework on sexual issues from which the Pope speaks is radically different from that of The Times. Sexual union (the conjugal union), for the Pope, is proper only to husband and wife (man and woman) in the permanent, faithful and monogamous bond called marriage.

To a host of other sexual practices The Times has expressed no objection and, indeed, at times given explicit or implicit approval. Condoms can give an often false sense of security to those who use them – security from the transmission of AIDS, as well as from conception, since the condom always distorts the nature of the conjugal act.

Whereas some statistics may show that certain condoms, when properly and consistently used, reduce the transmission of AIDS, such ideal circumstances are unusual and the inherent wrongfulness of the condom always distorts the nature of the conjugal act.

Thus, the logic of the Pope's remarks, given his ethical framework, even in the absence of universal supporting statistical evidence, upholds his judgment that condoms in the context of widespread illicit sexual practices, will only increase the transmission of AIDS.

March 23, 2009   **Concerned for discrimination**

Editor: The rhetoric of "A Window of Justice" (editorial 3/23) unabashedly reveals itself as explicitly aimed at the Catholic Church, as is the discriminatory proposed Child Victims Act which it supports.

You said: "The bill does not explicitly target any institution." But it makes no mention of public institutions and their personnel for which a different and more difficult process must be followed to file civil suits for alleged sexual abuse crimes.

Fairness to alleged victims and alleged victimizers demands that no obstacles be placed before those who would introduce civil court suits against public employees such as those of public schools, for which, statistics show, a far greater number of sexual abuse claims have been alleged in a shorter period of time than against any particular group of clergy.

Your intent to nail the Catholic Church by a discriminatory law couldn't be clearer.

March 24, 2009   **Defeat the enemy at all costs**

Editor: Following The Times's 3/18 editorial ("Pope on Condoms and AIDS") harshly scolding Pope Benedict XVI for an in-flight to Cameroon response to a reporter's question, the editorial page has admitted no letter in the pope's defense. It seems to me a particularly cavalier and biased judgment that would so pounce on the world's foremost spiritual leader and admit no letter in his defense. I perceive a trend of squeezing out the Catholic Church and an accurate presentation of its teaching, when that is called for, from the editorial and op-ed pages.

March 25, 2009   **The whole truth, please.**

Editor: Your 3/25 editorial "Broader Access to Morning-After Pills" praises a federal judge's decision to lower the age requirement for non-prescription purchase of the pill from age 18 to at least 17, but does not mention how the pill may work.

You speak of "block a pregnancy," "preventing unplanned pregnancies or abortions." But Barr

Laboratories, manufacturer of the pill, speaks clearly and specifically: in different cases the pill may inhibit ovulation, act as a contraceptive or as an abortifacient, preventing the fertilized ovum from lodging in the uterus.

What you refer to as removing an "ideological" obstacle to completely free access is, in reality, adherence to a fundamental ethical principle: respect for the inviolability of innocent human life that may have begun, as all bio-medical science freely admits it begins, at fertilization.

You take a neutral stand on the judge's recommendation that all age and other restrictions be removed in purchasing the drug, "potentially allowing children as young as 11 or 12 to take the drug without medical prescription" and presumably without mom's and dad's permission. Wow!

April 7, 2009   **Debasing nature**

Editor: "Iowa Decency" (editorial 4/5), praising that state's Supreme Court's legalizing of same-sex marriage, declares "shameful" the failure of most other states to do the same. Your view and that of the Iowa State Supreme Court proclaims the total interchangeability of men and women and effectively abolishes the natural moral law – the "law of nature and of nature's God" in the words of our Declaration of Independence – which underlies our civil law and in which our civil law and that of most other civilized nations.

Manifest physical impossibility – even in this new purely positivistic legal framework – prevents courts from declaring a man's right to bear a child without at the same time recognizing the impossibility of natural sexual and generative relationships between two persons of the same sex, thus preventing the possibility of designating such a union as marriage. So football is tennis and cricket is soccer and baseball is ping pong, as long as the court says so.

What is actually shameful is the rejection of the natural moral law and the declaring as legal and moral whatever relationships human beings choose to have.

April 13, 2009   Men and women not interchangeable

Editor: "A Mission for Gov. Paterson" (editorial, 4/10) describes same-sex marriage as a "basic civil right." You are mistaken. One cannot have a right to have or to do something for which nature universally or the civil law reasonably makes one ineligible

A man cannot bear a child. Therefore he cannot have such a right or a right to pregnancy leave. No person, man or woman, can have a right to practice medicine unless he or she is qualified by law.

Your position assumes that men and women are totally interchangeable. Nature says they are not. The conjugal union is by its nature potentially generative of children. A same-sex union is radically incapable or such generative power.

Indeed, persons of both sexes should have the same basic human and civil rights, except those for which nature itself universally disqualifies them. The harmful consequences of abolishing the natural moral law by legalizing same-sex marriage are innumerable. Governor Paterson's mission should be to protect the common good of society and to veto any such proposed law.

April 17, 2009   Determined to exclude any other view

Editor: Three times within two weeks you presented your

readers with editorials ("Iowa Decency," 4/5, "A Mission for Gov. Paterson,"4/10 and "New York's Missing Civil Right," 4/17) strongly advocating passage of a same-sex marriage law in New York State as a "basic civil right." No letter contesting this view has been admitted to date in your columns.

Your position assumes that men and women are totally interchangeable. Nature says they are not. Marriage, the conjugal union, is by nature potentially generative of children. A same-sex union is radically incapable of such generative power.

Moreover, for example, a man cannot bear a child. Therefore, he cannot have a basic civil right to bear a child or to enjoy the benefit of pregnancy leave. Comparisons with the right to women's suffrage or of equal rights for the disabled or people of color have no objective relevance. Such persons are not radically incapable, by nature, of enjoying the right sought.

Indeed, persons of both sexes should have the same basic human and civil rights, except those which nature itself universally disqualifies them. Recent legislation in Washington State has insured that members of all legal partnerships enjoy the same rights without calling any same-sex partnership "marriage."

The harmful consequences of abolishing the natural moral law by legislating same-sex marriage are innumerable. New York's (and the nation's) "missing civil right" is not same-sex marriage but the right of the pre-born child to life and not to be killed in, or while emerging from, his or her mother's womb.

April 20, 2009   Intrinsic evils—never justified

Editor: Correspondents (letters, 4/19) supporting Notre Dame's invitation to President Obama to give its commencement address and receive an honorary degree despite the President's vigorous advocacy of abortion "rights" in conflict with the university's public commitment to Catholic teaching about the intrinsic evil of abortion fail to recognize the radical difference between abortion and those other issues cited - such as preemptive war, capital punishment, help for the poor and support for basic workers' rights. Previous presidents, it is maintained, differed with Church teaching on such issues but nevertheless received like invitations without criticism.

The legitimacy of capital punishment in limited circumstances can be debated without objection in the Church and those other issues cited are freely debated as to their legitimacy (preemptive war) or the proper and most effective steps to help the poor or protect workers' basic rights.

To cite an impedient issue comparable to abortion one would need to conceive of an elected official who vigorously supports slavery "rights" or the state's "right" to deport members of a particular racial, religious or ethnic community. If the official held such views, the current critics of highlighting a single issue would certainly appreciate why a great body of the citizenry regards the unbearable horror and injustice of deliberately slaying the innocent preborn child in the womb or as emerging therefrom as such a gravely impedient issue.

May 6, 2009   **Hate crimes unequivocally rejected**

Editor: Your editorial "Matthew Shepard Act," 5/6, rightly states that hate crimes against any class of persons, including homosexually active persons, deserve unequivocal rejection and condemnation.

We must guard against, however, one possible and dangerous result of such an act; namely, that those ethicists and moralists representing the philosophical or religious position that all homosexuals acts are always wrong would be judged by the very fact of such teaching or preaching to be inciting or abetting hate crimes.

Free speech and freedom of religion must be guaranteed. Infractions of these rights must be rejected and condemned with equal force as the hate crime themselves.

May 8, 2009   **Not fairness but manifest facts**

Editor: Your editorial " 'This Is a Question of Fairness' ", (5/8), the fourth in a month's time advocating the legalization of same-sex marriage -with, to date, no substantive letter or op-ed essay admitted to your columns contesting your view - indeed makes to ring hollow the Public Editor's statement (11/9/08) quoting the executive editor that The Times is a liberal newspaper, "tolerant of and curious about the wide range of views and behaviors"; and he added: "the editors need to be sure that the wide range includes the view of the religious."

Your position on same-sex marriage assumes that men and women are totally interchangeable. Nature says they are not. Marriage, the conjugal union, is by nature potentially generative of children. A same-sex union is radically incapable of such generative power.

Moreover, for example, a man cannot bear a child. Therefore, he cannot have a basic civil right to bear a child or to enjoy the benefit of pregnancy leave. Comparisons with the right to women's suffrage or of equal rights for the disabled or people of color or seniors have no objective relevance. Such persons are not radically and universally incapable by nature of enjoying the right sought.

Indeed, persons of both sexes should have the same basic human and civil rights, except those for which nature itself universally disqualifies them. Recent legislation in

Washington State has insured that members of all legal partnerships enjoy the same rights without calling any same-sex partnership "marriage."

The harmful consequences of abolishing the natural moral law by legislating same-sex marriage are innumerable. This is not a question of fairness but of nature and nature says no. To find out what the voters of New York State think, let's have a referendum.

May 12, 2009   **Only one side is heard**

Editor: Your 11/9/08 essay endorsing Executive Editor Keller's description of The Times as "tolerant and curious about a wide range of views and behaviors" and your own conclusion that "the editors need to be sure that this wide range includes the views of the religious" persuades me to write once again (earlier letter 3/24/09 – attached) about the failure of The Times's letters column and its Op-Ed essay page to exemplify these characteristics in the case of same-sex marriage.

In the space of about one month (4/5-5/6) four substantial editorials appeared vigorously supporting the legalization of same-sex marriage in New York State: Iowa Decency, 4/5; A Mission for Gov. Paterson, 4/10; New York's Missing Civil Right, 4/17; and 'This Is a Question of Fairness', 5/8.

On a question of such a fundamental social change one would expect at least one substantive letter and one op-ed essay to appear contesting The Times editorial board's view. None have appeared but letters supporting same-sex marriage (related to other articles) have appeared. I know that at least one (my own) contesting essay and one substantive letter have been submitted.

Without a doubt, The Times has many important issues for which it needs to allow letters space and op-ed space. But a more radical social change than same-sex marriage can hardly be imagined. Why is it that only letters supporting same-sex marriage have been printed and no essay contesting The Times's view has appeared on the op-ed page?

Your essay of November 9, 2008 quoting Editor Keller's broad tent view and your concluding admonition to the editors seems to ring hollow.

May 21, 2009   **Opposition may not be heard**

Editor: "Gay Marriage Slow to Draw Opposition" (5/20, p.1) provokes the question: Can the opposition be heard?

Those in favor call this an issue of equal rights. If a man and a woman can get married, why can't two men or two women, or, we might add, some other combination of men or of women? Why can't any partnership be a marriage?

Here's why: Nature says no. Marriage is a union of a man and a woman for a bonded, permanent relationship that usually brings forth children and constitutes the family, the basis of society as we know it.

Two persons of the same-sex cannot do this. Giving same-sex partners the right to marry is like giving a man the right to bear a child. He can't do it. And so he can't have or be given the right to do it. Nature says no. And nature says no to same-sex marriage.

Equal rights? Indeed, all persons have the same basic rights and should enjoy them, except when nature itself universally disqualifies a certain class of persons for a particular right.

Applied to same-sex marriage, "equal rights" is a red herring used to distract people from the true purpose of the "pro" lobbyists: full societal acceptance and full legal approval of homosexual relations. Let's have a referendum.

May 28, 2009   Equality is not interchangeability

Editor: Your editorial "Setback for Equality" (5/27) features the red herring constantly invoked in the same-sex marriage debate.

If men demanded the right to bear a child – to be equal to women – or women demanded the right to father a child – to be equal to men – what answer would be given? Answer: It's impossible for a man to bear a child or for a woman to father a child. Nature itself universally disqualifies men and women from the right they would be seeking. What nature universally denies no law can give.

And so it is with same-sex marriage. Neither two men nor two women can marry because they cannot establish the lasting conjugal bond that ordinarily generates children and to create a family, the basic unit of society. The issues of equality and discrimination do not even arise. Nature has settled the matter for all. The real goal of same-sex marriage advocates is full societal acceptance and full legal approval for homosexual relations.

June 4, 2009   Heavy hand of censorship

Editor: I have counted at least six major editorials over the last two months in favor of same-sex marriages (the latest, "Vote on Gay Marriage," 6/4) but have seen no letters or op-ed essays opposed. Strange! On such a fundamental social change, no dissent?

Those in favor call this an issue of equality, of "basic civil rights." If a man and a woman can get married, why can't two men or two women, or, we might add, some other combination of men or of women? Why can't any partnership be a marriage?

Here's why: Nature says no. Marriage is a union of a man and a woman for a bonded, permanent sexual relationship that usually brings forth children and constitutes the family, the basis of society as we know it.

Two persons of the same-sex cannot do this. Giving same-sex partners the right to marry is like giving a man the right to bear a child or a woman the right to father a child. He/she can't do it. And so he/she can't have or be given the right to do it. Nature says no. And nature says no to same-sex marriage.

Equal rights? Indeed, all persons have the same basic rights and should enjoy them, except when nature itself universally disqualifies a certain class of persons for a particular right.

Applied to same-sex marriage, "equal rights" is a red herring used to distract people from the true purpose of the "pro" lobbyists: full societal acceptance and full legal approval of homosexual relations. Let's have a referendum.

July 27, 2009   **Censorship enforced**

Editor: In two month time (4/5-6/13/09) six substantial editorials and at least one op-ed essay appeared vigorously supporting the legalization of same-sex marriage in New York State: Iowa Decency, 4/5; A Mission for Gov. Paterson, 4/10; New York's Missing Civil Right, 4/17; and 'This Is a Question of Fairness', 5/8; Setback for Equality, 5/27, and Vote on Gay Marriage, 6/4. The Op-ed piece "Why I Now Support Gay Marriage" appeared on 6/13.

Such a proposed fundamental social change should warrant at least one substantive letter and one op-ed essay to appear contesting The Times editorial board's view.

None have appeared but letters supporting same-sex marriage (related to other articles) have appeared. I know that at least one contesting essay and one substantive contesting letter have been submitted.

Without a doubt, The Times has many important issues for which it needs to allow letters space and op-ed space. But social change more radical than same-sex marriage can hardly be imagined. <u>Why is it that only letters supporting same-sex marriage have been printed and no article contesting The Times's view has appeared on the op-ed page?</u>

Thus your essay published November 9, 2008 quoting Editor Keller's broad tent view and your concluding admonition to the editors about including a variety of views ring hollow.

July 29, 2009 - Op-Ed.
Reproductive rights—another view

The Times vigorously champions "a woman's right to her own childbearing decisions," phraseology taken from an 11/0/08 editorial but repeated equivalently in many other editorials on reproductive rights. In context this right denotes the right of a woman to direct the expulsion and destruction of a new human life – be it called zygote, embryo or fetus (according to its stage of development) - in her womb. This is what The Times means by "reproductive freedom" and "reproductive rights."

But what is a "right?" and where does it come from? What is the basis for a right? A right is a claim human beings have as persons to that which is needed for the good of the person. Others have an obligation to respect our human rights and, perhaps, to supply or facilitate the "good", whatever it is, or at least not to inhibit the exercise of the right.

Where do these rights come from? Our Declaration

of Independence tells us our most basic human rights are intrinsic to our nature as created by God. They are not gifts to us from the state or from the majority in a particular society. Human reason identifies these rights; legislatures may enact them into civil law and courts give them fuller exposition. But basically they are not legally fabricated; they are recognized as due to the human person. As civilization progresses, reason may see these rights more clearly whereas in other earlier contexts they had lain dormant or were even denied. Also, what we once saw as a right can later be recognized as doing injury to another; for example, the right of a certain class of persons to own slaves.

The right of persons of diverse races, genders or ethnic origins to participate fully in society, to have food, clothing, shelter, employment, medical care, to vote, to send their children to the schools of their choice are examples of rights recognized and protected by law. But all these rights are seen first as intrinsic to the human person and for the good of the human person. Legislation that goes against the good of the human person is deprived of any basis in reason and can establish no moral obligation, even though the law may be a coercive one. The Nuremberg laws in Nazi Germany are one example of such laws.

Do men or women have reproductive rights? An ethical heritage deeply embedded in the history of our civilization holds that neither men nor women have reproductive rights and certainly no absolute reproductive freedom. Both men and women do have, however, a complementary reproductive power; but only spouses have the right to exercise this power. Moreover, even in the case of spouses, such a right is not a right "to a child" or, perish the thought, to destroy a human being already in the womb, but a right only to the marital embrace that may be productive of a child.

Conception may, indeed, result from acts that are not spousal. Fornicators, adulterers, incestuous persons and rapists may conceive a child or cause a child to be conceived; but they have no right to exercise their reproductive power in that context. I prescind here from any discussion of conception apart from the marital embrace, e.g., artificial insemination or in vitro fertilization where the husband is the donor.

I take as an indisputable datum of bio-medical science that a new human life begins at fertilization. (It is curious that some intelligent people, in the face of unanimous scientific testimony, may still deny this fact or assert that it is a "belief," not a fact.) Equally indisputable is the fact that, given the proper environment (the womb), the fertilized egg develops progressively – zygote, embryo, fetus, neonate, toddler, schoolchild, teenager, young adult, middle-aged adult, senior. I write as one who was once a fertilized egg. My mother and father knew that their marital embrace could result in conception. They intended or at least allowed this to happen. I have gone through all the stages in the womb and out of the womb.

Did my mother have the "right to make her own child-bearing decisions?" which, in the rhetoric of The Times, means a right to destroy me before I was born? Was that her "reproductive right?" A manifestation of her reproductive freedom?

The natural moral law tradition, bolstered by, but not based on, religious convictions, says NO. I was a human being from my beginning as a fertilized egg, then zygote, and an embryo. Like every other child I was a gift to my parents. I have had from the beginning a right to life. Nothing justifies the direct and deliberate killing of this new human being whether parents wanted it or not or fornicators, adulterers or sexual oppressors want it or not! One may not do evil-that good may come of it.

It has not been my purpose here to discuss related

issues such as criminalization – who should be punished and how or what services society should provide to dissuade women with problem pregnancies from having recourse to abortion and support those who have given birth. These are other very important, related but separate issues.

The question addressed is a simple one: Does man or woman have a reproductive right? NO. Do they have a reproductive power? Yes. Can they exercise this power in any way or in any context they choose? NO. What is the rightful context for the exercise of their power? The marital union is of one man and one woman. Does either husband or wife have the right to destroy the fruit of their marital embrace? NO. They have been given a gift to respect, to treasure and to bring to the same maturity they enjoy.

Reproductive rights and reproductive freedom understood as the right and freedom to destroy the new human being present in the womb have no basis in a sound philosophy of the human person and are gravely injurious to third parties (the unborn child), those who exercise this so-called right and to the general societal attitude of respect for the inviolability of innocent human life.

August 10, 2009   **Hypocrisy at its height**

Editor: Paul Vitello's post-mortem (8/10, p. A-11) on the Markey Child Victims Act at least had the effect of exposing the hypocrisy of some (was it many?) NYS Assembly members who voted (over three years) for this bill as long as they knew that it had no chance in the Senate. They were ready to be crowd-pleasers but not to face reasoned, organized opposition in their districts.

The emotion-laden title of the bill belied its real purpose, described by Newsday (April 26 editorial) as an act of vengeance against the Catholic Church. An earlier Times editorial (March 23) had concluded that the Catholic Church should take its medicine. And a hand-out from the Markey office, while lauding the public-school authorities for their handling of abuse cases, identified the Catholic Church as deserving punishment while defending the bill's practical exemption of public schools and other municipal institutions from its effect.

The rank discriminatory character of the Markey Bill didn't seem to bother people until almost the very end of the debate. Opposed by Catholic and Orthodox Jewish authorities and by those against changing statutes of limitations, the bill finally met rejection also from a host of public-school and municipal-organization officials; when they realized how radically they could be affected by it. This proposed act of vengeance against the Catholic Church deserves eternal rest.

August 20, 2009   **Nature rules**

Editor: Your page-one feature (8/19) on lawyer Theodore B. Olson and his championing of same-sex marriage reports him as applying the "equal-rights" and "discrimination" principles to this issue. Like many others, he completely overlooks the testimony of nature.

Nature's construction of man and woman shows that they are destined to be united with one another and to bear and raise children. Two persons of the same sex cannot do this. Giving same-sex persons the right to marry is like giving a man the right to bear a child or a woman the right to impregnate herself of herself and by herself. He can't do it; she can't do it. And so neither can have the right to do it. Nature says no universally; and nature says no universally to same-sex marriage.

Questions of discrimination and equal treatment do not even arise. Supposed analogies for overcoming discrimination or achieving equal rights drawn from struggles over slavery, segregation, women's suffrage, inter-racial marriage, etc. have no relevancy. In no case has nature itself universally disqualified persons in those alleged parallels from exercising the rights they sought. Nature does, however, issue a universal disqualification in the case of same-sex marriage.

September 14, 2009
Wrongful activity deserves no protection

Editor: Your "The Rights of Gay Employees," (editorial 9/13) urges "all who believe in workplace fairness" to support the Employment Non-Discrimination Act," which will include persons experiencing same-sex attraction, bi-sexuals and the trans-gendered. All well and good.

Those you call the "religious right" definitely support workplace fairness but they disapprove of any law that legitimates homosexual <u>activity</u> or the promotion of such in the workplace, just as they would object to any law legitimizing non-marital heterosexual or bisexual activity or the promotion thereof in the workplace.

The law should and does protect persons of different racial, ethnic and religious groups, women, seniors and the disabled from discrimination in the workplace. No such person by reason of his or her condition is doing anything wrong. But if same-sex inclined persons act out their inclination or promote it in the workplace, they act wrongfully and cannot claim discrimination "when their actions are disapproved or disallowed." This distinction between <u>condition</u> and <u>activity</u> is key in formulating a law that truly insures workplace fairness.

October 1, 2009   **Masking the truth**

Editor: Your editorial "Abortion and Health Care Reform" (10/1) misses the point of the position you reject: Abortion is not health care; it is the butchering of an unborn child in his or her mother's womb. So horrifying is this action that most people recoil from having to view it taking place or even a photograph thereof.

Why then should all taxpayers be compelled to pay directly or indirectly for abortions on the irrational premise that abortion is health care? If you deny the scientific facts, look again.

October 7, 2009   A metaphorical wall prejudice built

Editor: As usual, your editorial (in this case, "The Constitution and the Cross," 10/7) identifies the establishment clause of the First Amendment with "the founders' direction that there must be a wall of separation between church and state."

Everyone knows or should know that the authors of the First Amendment gave no such direction in forbidding any federal law respecting an "establishment of religion" – in historical context meaning a state church such as existed in England – and in forbidding any law "prohibiting the free exercise thereof."

To the stonemasons and rhetoricians at The New York Times belongs the categorical insistence on this overblown image of the "wall." Like the Berlin Wall, it needs dismantling to permit a peaceful, just and respectful solution on a contended issue, in this case, the California VFW cross.

October 15, 2009   **Attack on religious freedom**

Editor: "Faith-Based Discrimination" (editorial, 10/14) demands that religiously affiliated organizations sponsoring social or other public-service programs and receiving federal grants be prohibited from employing only personnel in agreement with (or at least not opposed to) their ethical, moral and religious principles – as authorized by a 2002 presidential directive and a "constitutionally suspect" 2007 memo from the Justice Department.

To the contrary, religiously affiliated organizations need to preserve the institutional integrity of their units and services. They should not be forced to employ persons whose views and actions evidently will compromise, undermine or disrupt this integrity. Such religious freedom should be preserved. The quality and effectiveness of the programs such organizations deliver should be the criterion of their eligibility for federal grants, not a hiring policy that could be self-destructive.

October 21, 2009
        Pope accedes to earnest plea of some Anglicans

Editor: "Vatican Bidding to Get Anglicans to Join Its Fold: Luring Conservatives," (10/21, p. 1) misleadingly, even odiously suggests that the new overture of the Holy See to (some) Anglicans who already accept the Catholic faith is a kind of greedy proselytizing, whereas it is, in fact, a generous, long-awaited response to urgent, insistent requests from Anglicans in various parts of the world to recover their full communion with the Catholic Church without abandoning their entire liturgical and spiritual patrimony.

One such group of Anglicans, relatively small in

number but world-wide in extension and "Anglo-Catholic" in persuasion, calling itself the "Traditional" Anglican Communion, made a formal approach to the Holy See in 2007 and have waited two full years for a substantive response, which now has come.

An initial form of this new canonical framework announced Oct.20 was given to the United States in 1980 (see NYT, 8/21/80, p.1), called the Pastoral Provision, as a result of which about 100 Anglo-Catholic clergy have been received and ordained as Catholic priests and six small Anglican-Use congregations established.

This new improved canonical framework will permit all Anglicans (so-minded) throughout the world on an equal basis to restore full communion with the Catholic Church without abandoning their liturgical and spiritual patrimony.

October 26, 2009   **A humble petition granted**

Editor: The Gospel reading for Sunday (Oct.25) following Pope Benedict's overture to those Anglicans seeking full communion with the Catholic Church was Mark 10:45-52 – a blind beggar, told that Jesus was passing by, cried out to him for the gift of sight.

Jesus, then, in a "gambit" (Oct.25), "invites" (Oct. 24), "bids" (Oct.21), "lures" (Oct.21) or "woos" (Oct.24) him to join his flock. Yes? No! Jesus mercifully responded to the petitioner and gave him his sight. So Pope Benedict graciously responded to the Anglican petitioners by granting their petition.

Why do we look for evil or crassness in the good?

October 28, 2009   **Portraying killing as a good**

Editor: "Oklahoma vs. Women" (editorial, 10/25) trots out The Times's familiar hobby horses: reproductive rights and reproductive freedom, fictive rights that denote a (usually troubled) woman's recourse to having the child in her womb killed. This is not a right but a wrong. Man and woman, if married, certainly may exercise their mutual right to acts that ordinarily result in conception; but they have no right to kill the child conceived. Troubled pregnant women need our help but not in this way.

Pregnancy is not a disease. Abortion is not health-care, but the killing of an innocent human being. To such an act there can be no right.

October 29, 2009
The famous (fake) "wall of separation"

Editor: Your Finish Line 2009 (Oct. 29, p.23) feature on Mayor Bloomberg's effective courting financially and otherwise of key members of the city's black clergy "who together preach to tens of thousands of congregants each week" raises the question of political endorsements by clergy personally and in their tax-exempt pulpits. This church-state issue usually generates intense interest from The Times.

If this amazing story were one of the Mayor's courting of Catholic clergy for the same purpose, wouldn't the editors roll out on stage their handy prop stressing the absolute separation of church and state?

October 30, 2009   Why same-sex relations are harmful

Editor: Evan Wolfson (letter printed 10/29) finds it strange that California Lawyer C.J. Cooper was initially baffled by Judge Vaughn R. Walker's question as to why it would be harmful to permit homosexual men and lesbians to marry. It was strange. But one lawyer's bafflement should not be thought widespread.

Here's why legalizing same-sex marriage would be very harmful:
1) It will give legal and social approval to homosexual relations and put them on the same level as heterosexual conjugal relations; 2) It will promote those homosexual relations that are physically dangerous; 3) It will legitimize the view that there is no ethical difference between homosexual relations and the conjugal union; 4) It will reverse the immemorial judgment of our country and our civilization that homosexual relations are unnatural and immoral; 5) It will implicitly teach our youngsters that they have for marriage a range of sexual choices – heterosexual, homosexual, bi-sexual – and, when public opinion accepts it – polygamous, consensually incestuous and group marriage; 6) It will impair the psychological health and development of children (now perhaps manufactured), which, scientific studies show, need ideally the influence of a father (male) and a mother (female) and it will erode the understanding of the traditional family as the basic unit of our society.

Of course, sterile couples and elderly couples cannot conceive but they are not by nature itself disqualified for the conjugal union. No same-sex union can be a conjugal union.

FedEx to lawyer C. J. Cooper and the Federal Judge Vaughn R. Walker in San Francisco.

November 8, 2009   **The end in view**

Editor: I have counted at least seven major editorials over the last several months in favor of same-sex marriages (the latest, "Equality's Ragged March," 11/8) but have seen no letters or op-ed essays opposed. Strange! On such a fundamental social change, no dissent?

Those in favor call this an issue of equality, of "basic civil rights." If a man and a woman can get married, why can't two men or two women, or, we might add, some other combination of men or of women? Why can't any partnership be a marriage?

Here's why: Nature says no. Marriage is a union of a man and a woman for a bonded, permanent sexual relationship that usually brings forth children and gives rise to the family, the basis of society as we know it.

Two persons of the same-sex cannot do this. Giving same-sex partners the right to marry is like giving a man the right to bear a child or a woman the right to father a child. He/she can't do it. And so he/she can't have or be given the right to do it. Nature says no. And nature says no to same-sex marriage.

Equal rights? Indeed, all persons have the same basic rights and should enjoy them, except when nature itself universally disqualifies a certain class of persons for a particular right.

Applied to same-sex marriage, "equal rights" is a red herring used to distract people from the true purpose of the "pro" lobbyists: full societal acceptance and full legal approval of homosexual relations.

November 23, 2009   **Bending nature to our will**

Editor: For the eighth time (by my count) since March, The Times ("The Church and the Capital," editorial, 11/23) has endorsed same-sex marriage with no published rebuff. And this time, in a solemn, pontifical introductory one-sentence ipse dixit – "Gay people will eventually win full civil rights – including the right to marry – throughout the United States." Amen.

Of course, the rest of us, those who disagree on a

purported right, will now roll over and die <u>or</u> may we differ with the Mighty One? And say that the arrangement made by Catholic units in California and Georgetown, clever though they may be, are a big wink? And that civil and religious officials should not now prepare to engage in a nation-wide hoodwink?

Yes, man, get yourself pregnant to show that you are equal to woman. Never mind that nature says it's not possible. If you say you can do it, you can do it. Nature will bend to your will. And if you want to marry another man, just do it. Nature must obey your will.

November 27, 2009   What the editors have done!

Public Editor: Your 11/9/08 essay endorsing Executive Editor Keller's description of The Times as "tolerant and curious about a wide range of views and behaviors" and your own conclusion that "the editors need to be sure that this wide range includes the views of the religious" persuades me to write once again (earlier letters 3/24/09, 5/12/09) about the failure of The Times's letters column and its Op-Ed essay page to exemplify these characteristics in the case of same-sex marriage.

In the space of eight months (4/5 – 11/26/09) nine substantial editorials have appeared vigorously supporting the legalization of same-sex marriage in New York State (and New Jersey): Iowa Decency, 4/5; A Mission for Gov. Paterson, 4/10; New York's Missing Civil Right, 4/17; 'This Is a Question of Fairness', 5/8; "Setback for Equality," 5/27; "Vote for Gay Marriage," 6/4; "Equality's Ragged March," 11/8; "The Church and the Capital," 11/23 and "New Jersey's Marriage Moment,"11/26.

On a question of such a fundamental social change one would expect at least one substantive letter and one op-ed essay to appear contesting The Times editorial board's view. None have appeared but letters supporting same-sex marriage (related to other articles) have appeared. I know that at least one contesting essay and one substantive letter have been submitted.

Without a doubt, The Times has many important issues for which it needs to allow letters space and op-ed space. But a more radical social change than same-sex marriage can hardly be imagined. Why is it that only letters supporting same-sex marriage have been printed and no essay contesting The Times's view has appeared on the op-ed page?

Your essay of November 9, 2008 quoting Editor Keller's broad tent view and your concluding admonition to the editors rings hollow, indeed.

November 27, 2009   **Écrasez l'infame - Voltaire**

Editor: In nine major editorials over eight months (the latest, "New Jersey's Marriage Moment," 11/26), The Times has told its readers that same-sex marriage ("marriage equality") is a fundamental civil right demanding enactment into law. We have read no published dissent.

Forgive a pontifical dictum similar to your opener in "The Church and the Capital," (editorial, 11/23): There is no such thing as a fundamental right to same-sex marriage; Why not?

One cannot have a right to something nature universally disqualifies a particular group of persons from having. Two men or two women cannot forge the sexual bond that permits the conception of a child. Thus nature universally says no to same-sex marriage.

November 27, 2009 A force-feed of New York citizens

Editor: Governor Paterson and some Albany legislators evidently think they are going to force a same-sex marriage law on many millions of fellow New Yorkers very soon. They know what we want or should want and they are going to let us have it. They have everything ready and are just waiting for the proper moment – enough votes in the State Senate – to bestow their gift.

The Governor, it is said, once had cherished relatives, now deceased, who lived in a same-sex union that embarrassed at least some members of the family. Now he wants to clear the air and sweep the path so their counterparts today may say loudly and proudly "we're married."

The legislators in favor insist that this issue is one of "equal" rights. If a man and a woman can get married, why can't two men or two women? And, we might add, why not some other combination of men and of women? Why can't any kind of partnership be a marriage? Yes, a partnership of two or more persons who are committed to one another and promise to live with one another at least until they break up should be deemed a marriage.

Why not? Here's why not: Nature says no. Marriage is the union of one man and one woman for a bonded and permanent life together that usually brings forth children and constitutes the family, the basis of society as we know it. Marriage is not a new invention. Establishing the fundamental unit of society, man-woman marriage has been characteristic of virtually all societies from time immemorial. Nature's construction of man and woman shows that they are destined and fitted to be united with one another and to bear and raise children. Two persons of the same sex cannot do this. Giving to same-sex persons the right to marry is like giving a man the right to bear a child. He can't do it. And so he can't have the right to do it. Nature says no and nature says no to same-sex marriage.

Of course, sterile couples and elderly couples cannot conceive but they are not by nature itself disqualified for the conjugal union. No same-sex union can be a conjugal union.

But, again, what about equal rights? Indeed all persons have the same basic rights and they should enjoy them except when nature itself universally disqualifies a certain class of persons for a particular right. Because two men or two women can't establish the sexual bond that ordinarily generates children, produces a family and gives children the required material and psychological support they need to grow up successfully, they cannot marry. Scientific studies show the benefits of having a mother and a father and the disadvantages suffered by children not so fortunate. How, then, can two men or two women marry or be supposed to have a right to do so?

Oh, we know that today families can be manufactured by various scientific means. What science can do and should do are separate issues. We have yet to see over time the social effects of human manufacture compared with the nature's millennia of procreative marriage and the family. Same-sex marriages, duos or other combinations, like polygamy and polygyny, conflict with the natural moral law. What is the proof? It stares you in the face. Millennia of history re-enforce this truth.

Further, what about equal-rights parallels? Same-sex marriage promoters regularly cite the woman's suffrage movement, the struggle against slavery and segregation, the battle to allow interracial marriages and achieve rights for the disabled and seniors as parallels for the effort to obtain equal rights for partners of the same-sex to marry. These comparisons have no relevancy. In no case has nature itself universally disqualified persons in the alleged parallels from enjoying and exercising the right they sought. Nature does issue a universal disqualification in the case of same-sex marriage.

Finally, legalizing same-sex marriage would over time be very harmful:
1)It would give legal and social approval to homosexual relations and put them on the same level as heterosexual conjugal relations; 2) It will promote those homosexual relations that are physically dangerous; 3) It will legitimize the view that there is no ethical difference between homosexual relations and the conjugal union; 4) It will reverse the immemorial judgment of our country and our civilization that homosexual relations are unnatural and immoral; 5) It will implicitly teach our youngsters that they have for marriage a range of sexual choices – heterosexual, homosexual, bi-sexual – and, if and when public opinion accepts it – polygamous, consensually incestuous and group marriage; 6) It will impair the psychological health and development of children (now perhaps manufactured), which, scientific studies show, need ideally the influence of a father (male) and a mother (female); 7) It will erode the understanding of the traditional family as the basic unit of our society; and 8) It will cause social service agencies whose ethical principles disallow same-sex "marriage" to be accused and convicted of discrimination and forced to end their public service.

If the Governor and his friends in the Legislature insist on their goal, let's have a referendum first so that we know where all New Yorkers stand.

December 3, 2009   Nature determines who qualify

Editor: "Voting for Discrimination" (editorial, 12/3) labels the NYS Senate's failure to vote for same-sex marriage as "voting for discrimination." You continue your long series of editorials vigorously promoting the legalization of such marriages by recourse to rhetorical red herrings, such as equality, fairness, justice, courage, decency basic civil rights and discrimination.

If an intelligent, well-educated young person of 17 claims discrimination for being denied a "right" to vote in civil elections, we must reply, "you don't qualify." The well-founded judgment of society enacted in law requires you to be 18 to vote.

If a person well-educated in the science and art of medicine complains that he or she, not having a license, is being denied a "right" to practice medicine, we must reply "you don't qualify." The well-founded judgment of society enacted in law requires you to have a license to practice medicine.

Similarly, persons of the same sex seeking to "marry" one another don't qualify, not only by the well-founded judgment of society but also and principally because nature itself universally disqualifies two persons of the same-sex from marrying. They cannot forge the permanent sexual union that permits the conception and birth of children and the establishment of a family, the basic unit of society. This law inherent in nature obviously raises no questions of discrimination, denial of rights, injustice, unfairness, equality, lack of respect for others or basic civil rights.

December 7, 2009 Nailing the Church to an old response

Editor: "Bishop's Words" (editorial, 12/7) admits that your lawsuit forcing the Bridgeport diocese to release more than 12,000 pages of confidential documents on child-abuse allegations involving seven priests over several decades yielded little information.

Your unabashed, open effort, however, to nail the

then (1997, 1999) bishop of Bridgeport, Edward M. Egan, to the wall for responses in legal interrogations at the time considered indifferent to victims and zealously protective of priests falls somewhat flat when one recalls that lawyers in a legal deposition will seize upon any unguarded comment to build the case for their clients.

Contrasting Bishop Egan's 1997 response in that legal context and time with Dublin Archbishop Diarmuid Martin's open, free and realistic reflections (2009), when the legal wrangling was over and the government report issued seems a bit mean. The two bishops would hardly disagree on the outrageous evil of child sex abuse and on the need to heal victims.

We have long since entered a new highly protective environment for our youth. It is not a time to tarnish the Church anew for past failures.

December 11, 2009   Crush Nature's Law

Editor: "Uphill Toward Equality" (editorial, 12/10) alleges for the umpteenth time that nature's institution of marriage as the permanent sexual bond between a man and a woman denies "equality" to persons of the same sex who wish to marry and thus denies them a fundamental human and civil right.

But you can't have a right to something nature universally disqualifies you from having. A man can't bear a child or a woman conceive a child of and by herself. Thus neither can have a right to what nature disallows. And so it is with the "marriage" of two persons of the same sex. Nature says no. *C'est impossible!*

On the other hand, all persons, married or unmarried, should have equal status as persons and so be entitled to the same basic human rights.

January 19, 2010   **Blind to the obvious truth**

Editor: Maureen Dowd's reflection ("An Odd Couple…" Op-Ed, 1/17) on the legal twosome Olson and Boies seeking to overthrow Proposition 8 and sanction same-sex marriage in California includes the judgment that proponents of man-woman marriage as nature's exclusive intent are just biased old fogies who won't acknowledge homosexually active persons "as normal, or human beings."

Were a man seeking a legal right to bear a child and breast-feed him or her, how would we respond? He can't do it. Nature universally disqualifies men from this function. Such a legal claim would have no foundation. So it is with same-sex "marriage." Two (or more) persons of the same-sex are universally disqualified by nature to forge the conjugal bond, the essence of marriage. They cannot marry or be given the right to marry. Nothing odd about that.

January 19, 2010
                    Some similarities, but many differences

Editor: Nicholas D. Kristof (Religion and Women, Op-Ed, 1/16) rightly deplores offenses against women and denial of their rights which have been associated in the past or the present with various religions of the world. Religions, however, are radically analogous and often have little similarity other than the basic questions they address: the relationship of humankind and of the universe to a being, person or persons beyond one's experience and responsible in some way for our existence.

The laudable goal of The Elders (including President   Robinson- Ireland- Carter, Mandela, and Anglican Archbishop Tutu), cited by Mr. Kristof, of eliminating all oppression of women associated with religion will encounter disputes over some beliefs and practices of some religions.

For example, the Catholic Church and the Orthodox Communion of Churches hold that the Lord Jesus Christ has not authorized His Church to ordain women as priests and bishops. The divine will is not to oppression, they say. President Robinson and Archbishop Tutu, with many others, are likely to disagree on that point. It is a complex issue that cannot be dealt with in a letter.

January 29, 2010   **Military Discipline**

Editor: Your plea for "Ending Don't Ask, Don't Tell" (editorial, 1/28) must, indeed, include testing the verifiability of the so-called canard that "unit cohesion would be harmed" if homosexually active "service persons were allowed to be open about their sexuality." More importantly, however, such a change would need to be accompanied by a strong policy directive that homosexual activity or any invitation thereto are absolutely incompatible with military service, as are any forms of heterosexual harassment or invitations to illicit heterosexual conduct.

February 24, 2010   **Good God—merciless catastrophe**

Editor: James Wood ("Between God and A Hard Place, Op-Ed, 1/24), seeks to reconcile the concept of a loving Creator God with the merciless destruction of human life and property (Haiti is the example) caused by earthquakes, tidal waves and other natural disasters presumably permitted or willed by God.

Orthodox Christian doctrine offers a solution that, without fully plumbing (impossible) the mystery of God shows that God is no monster: these events are truly compatible with our conviction that God is love.

The Catholic Church teaches that the disorder in nature and in the human person leading to natural destruction or to personal sins is the result of a personal, originating and catastrophic sin of our first father Adam, assented to by his wife Eve – together, these parents, specially graced and honored by God, of our present human race. Adam's sin – the Scripture calls it a transgression – had enormous negative consequences. It affected himself, his wife and his progeny, the whole human race to follow, together with the earth that they and we inhabit. Disorder in the natural world. Personal sin in the human world.

Because God is the God of love, however, he has overcome this great disorder in principle with His mercy, culminating in the sending of His Beloved Son, the Word of God, into human nature to be the light of the world and, most importantly, to present the sacrifice (of the cross) to God the Father, which sufficed for all the disregard of God's will and law (sin) in the world. By its merits, the forgiveness of sins can be had by all, beginning with Adam and Eve who ever lived or will ever live in this world. All discord and imputable sin are rooted however, in human choice will not be removed until the Last Day when Christ, the Savior, comes in glory to judge the living and the dead. Then the understanding of God's love and mercy will be clear to all.

Even though we know that the loss of life in tragedies and catastrophies can be tragic and humanly inexplicable, God has given and does give sufficient graces to all to be saved by the reason of the Sacrifice of Christ, His Son. The final tragedy is not death, or physical destruction but the loss of one's eternal salvation. This –

loss of salvation – no one should fear who perseveres to know and serve the God of creation and salvation.

Some will say, Oh all this is Christian myth, a story told to calm people down. But for Christians it is, of course, the revealed word of God. Because it is a mystery, a truth beyond one's comprehension. It is not a fully satisfactory resolution for us, of the mystery. But it is coherent: God is not a monster, who arbitrarily destroys what he has made. But the world has been and is tainted by sin. The sins and finiteness of mankind have established the basis for human tragedy.

March 11, 2010   **We are not a law onto ourselves**

Editor: "Laws, Lies and the Abortion Debate"(editorial, 3/10) illustrates The Times's continuing fixation on "reproductive freedom" and "reproductive rights," which suggest the image of people copulating with multiple partners and producing scores of children like Osa the Taliban king and, less liberally, a sitting African president in the news these last few weeks.

Of course The Times means to suggest no such craziness but only the "right" to kill a preborn child in the womb, the most innocent and vulnerable of human beings.

In truth, there is no such thing as "reproductive freedom" or "reproductive rights". Human beings have a reproductive <u>power</u>, which they may use, the ethical tradition of our civilization teaches us, in the context of monogamous marriage to seek the conception and birth of a child, a gift, not a possession to manipulate or destroy. The so-called right or freedom to kill is the real demon in this controversy.

March 15, 2010   **A basic principle**

Editor: Your lengthy editorial ("More than Onerous," 3/15) chides those members of Congress who, in your view; are willing to scuttle the current health-care bill because they judge it ineffective in fully removing the possibility of taxpayer funding of elective abortions. You urge them, in effect, to "embrace evil for the greater good."

Of course you do not see the deliberate killing of an innocent child in the womb as a grave, an enormous evil. They do. Sorry, we may not do evil that good may come of it. This onus is too grave to bear.

April 26, 2010
   Are we too sensitive? Look at the evidence

Editor: Your Public Editors' column for 4/25 points to some excessive sensibilities on the part of some Catholic critics regarding The Times's recent coverage of sex-abuse of minors incidents by Catholic clergy. Not to take issues with your every point, but overall, I would say we (Catholics) feel that our Church is a convenient and always newsworthy punching bag (for The Times) for any scandal that may involve members of our Church. Perhaps it has to be that way. The Times is a completely secular newspaper that emphatically does not share most of the truths and values that constitute the very raison d'être for the Church's existence.

Let me illustrate by citing some related facts: sex-abuse of minors is a widespread and serious problem in the USA and throughout the world; and it is horrible. Only a very small percentage of perpetrators are clergy, even a smaller percentage, Catholic clergy; they deserve to be exposed. Go for it. Scores of abuse cases from police rolls have been reported by the Catholic League to the

Associated Press; but AP is not interested. If a case were to involve a Catholic priest - Wow! A brief report would be filed and a reporter (from The Times) would likely have raw meat for a major feature. Why? Because the Catholic Church is involved.

Over the last year there have been abuse cases involving a Pennsylvanian Episcopal bishop's shielding his brother, also an Episcopal priest, the bishop (then a priest) was a parish rector having his brother as his assistant at a church in California: a big case but no mention in The N Y Times. Why? Who's interested? A New York City rabbi got caught recently – but not a word. You alluded to the public schools sex-abuse – a substantial problem in the New York City public school system – is The Times interested? The public would be. But then there are the teachers' unions.

Certain groups in N.Y.S. are preventing passage in the legislature of a proposed law (supported by the Catholic bishops in NYS) that would require clergy to report the sex abuse of minors to the enforcement agencies. Who is preventing passage of this law and why? A good feature but we won't see it. Why? The Catholic Church is a better target. We don't want the teachers' unions, and Planned Parenthood or its affiliates down our backs.

Not all this is completely logical. But life is not completely logical. Catholics want to know how come we are the big news story when the same abuse is going on in spades elsewhere and in other contexts. And the latest story of the priest in Chile: The abuse started with the man when he was 17 and continued until he was 36. Whoa! Excuse me. That's a case of a homosexual relationship beginning, perhaps, as ephebophilia, (not pedophilia – attraction to pre-pubescent children) but clearly homosexual, then and in the subsequent adult years.

One final point which is unquestionably logical, I think. Over the past year you received at least two (email) letters from me concerning a case of bias in The Times which I monitored carefully. For about 10 months at least ten editorials appeared vigorously supporting same-sex marriage – a fundamental social change favored by The Times. No letter and no op-ed essay were admitted to publication that differed substantively from the position of The Times. Strange. Very strange. In fact, inexplicable. You ought to have a response to that.

April 27, 2010   Markey Bill—Rank discrimination

Editor: Prof. Lawrence Lessig ("A Better Chance at Justice for Abuse Victims," Op-Ed, 4/27) surely hasn't done his homework when he supports the original Markey Child Victims Act, which proposed a statute-of-limitations waiver in the case of sex abuse of minors allegedly committed by employees of <u>private</u> (read <u>Catholic</u>) institutions. The proposed Child Victims Act pro preserved the sovereign immunity of <u>public</u> school and other <u>public</u> institutional staffs from such suits and thus was rankly discriminatory.

In her promotional literature, Assemblywoman Markey acknowledged that her proposed legislation was aimed at the Catholic Church. A Times editorial of March 23, 2009 unabashedly supported this targeting. Shamed into revising her bill so that it would apply equally to all institutions, Ms. Markey still suffered defeat in the NYS Assembly.

Prof. Lessig seems to want the original bill which will "assure that potentially thousands of victims who have been abused by <u>priests</u> [my emphasis] will have the opportunity for compensation..." What about the potentially tens of thousands of victims abused over the last sixty years by employees of public institutions? No matter. It's <u>priests</u> we want to get.

May 17, 2010   **Hypocrisy at its highest level**

Editor: "Justice for Child Abuse Victims" (editorial, 5/16) signals your continuing effort to nail the Catholic Church in the matter of the Markey bill, earlier versions of which (2006, 2007 and 2008) you cite approvingly, despite their manifestly biased and discriminatory nature in targeting private institutions but leaving public institutions, like the city and state school systems – with thousands more potential litigants – shielded from the effects of the bill. Newsday on April 26, 2009 labeled Markey an act of vengeance against the Catholic Church.

　　Now, in its amended form, including all public as well as private institutions, Markey is poised to bankrupt both. Opponents of the new Markey include the New York State Council of School Superintendents, the State Association of Counties, the New York State Conference of Mayors, the New York State Boards Association, Agudath Israel, and the New York Association of Criminal Defense Attorneys.

　　The way forward on this issue is with the Lopez-Kruger bill, which extends the statute of limitations forward, with no backward open window. Let's hear from Mayor Bloomberg and his superintendent of schools.

May 27, 2010   Pub. NYT May 28, 2010
　　A Nun, a bishop and a decision about abortion

Editor: Nicholas D. Kristof is undoubtedly right in citing, with others, the praiseworthy compassionate qualities of Sister Margaret McBride, who authorized the abortion of an 11-week-old developing child in utero because of the "high probability," a medical judgment, that the mother, suffering from the pathological condition of pulmonary hypertension, would otherwise die.

The medical facts in every such hard case are crucial to a right solution. Taking them as given, we must still say that the solution authorized was wrong.

What, you say you would let the mother and the nonviable child die? Unintended physical death is not the greatest of evils, since we will all ultimately die. But directly killing an innocent person is a grave evil.

The compassionate Sister Margaret undoubtedly thought she was making the right decision. But she erred in her judgment. The mother and the child in utero deserved the finest continuing medical treatment available. The child did not deserve to be killed. Indeed, we may not do evil that good may come of it.

June 14, 2010   Nature says no

Editor: When the U.S. Supreme Court declared marriage "A Basic Civil Right" (editorial, 6/11), the justices referred, of course, to the marriage of a man and a woman. Your shift of that designation to same-sex marriage is cute, facile and mistaken.

We'd laugh if men claimed a basic civil right to bear or nurse a child. They can't do it. Nature disqualifies them universally. Discrimination? Really! In the same way two persons of the same sex cannot claim a civil right to marry, since marriage requires in principle the ability to generate a child. They can't do it. Nature universally disqualifies them.

Civil law can grant rights to many different kinds of partnerships and confer upon them appropriate benefits. But when nature universally says NO, defying nature is the path to chaos.

July 9, 2010   **Hiding the truth**

Editor: "The Pope's Duty" (editorial, 7/9) perpetuates the confusing and misleading equivalence between pedophilia and homosexual abuse of minors. Scientific psychological criteria designate pedophilia as the abuse of pre-pubescent children, a distinction clearly made in your 4/10/10 Beliefs column – A 20. The overwhelming majority of credibly identified clergy abusers, however, have been male abusers of post-pubescent <u>male</u> minors, an abuse called ephebophilia, a classic form of male homosexuality.

The Chilean case highlighted in your 6/21 - A12 issue and earlier, indirectly also in your editorial, concerned a 17-year old male who began to be abused at that age and for almost twenty years afterwards.

This and other cases of male abuse of male teenagers can hardly be classified as pedophilia.

August 5, 2010
Constitutional juggling does not yield "same-sex" marriage

Editor: "Marriage Is a Constitutional Right" (editorial 8/5) marks your thirteenth (list attached) editorial since April 2009 advocating same-sex marriage without admitting to publication any letter or op-ed essay disputing your view. Fortunately, your reasoning, like Judge Walker's in his 8/4 decision, falls to the ground.

Objections to same-sex marriage do not rest on a discriminating conviction, a "private bias", Judge Walker calls it, that opposite-sex couples are "morally" superior to same-sex couples, but rather on the rational certainly that the ability to perform the generative act is a basic constituent of marriage and always has been.

Nature universally disqualifies same-sex persons

from engaging in the generative act. No question of discrimination arises; nature has made men and women sexually different, not the same. Marriage is, indeed, a constitutional right – if one qualifies. Same-sex persons do not qualify; they cannot be the subject of a right to marry one another.

That's nature and the natural moral law, which the civil law flouts at society's peril.

August 9, 2010   The best of several possible choices

Editor: Ross Douthat ("The Marriage Ideal," Op-Ed, 8/8) begins by briefly citing "commonplace" arguments for heterosexual marriage and then abruptly states "they're wrong."

Grateful for his pontifical and apodictic judgment, we must next look to his reasons. Marriage customs vary in accord with diverse world cultures – some do it one way; others, another, he tells us. Polygamy in its male or female form has actually prevailed world-wide. Child-rearing also has been communal as well as two-parent.

The columnist does not seem to have any ethical or evaluative standard to apply to different marriage customs, just as if, in agriculture, he might observe that some prefer water buffalos to tractors for plowing. What about the dignity of the human person in the marriage union? And is the homosexual union just a new variety in this great toss-up? Does nature have nothing to say about human coupling?

In the end Ross Douthat comes down on the side of the heterosexual monogamous union. But it seems for him to be only a "better" marriage union in association with other "good" unions. A rather casual approach to an issue of tremendous social importance!

August 9, 2010   Nature is the heart of the matter

Editor: "Heart of the Matter" (editorial 8/8) like Federal Judge Walker in his 8/5 decision, succumbs to emotion rather than to reason.

Objections to same-sex marriage do not rest at base on a discriminating conviction, a "private bias", Judge Walker calls it, that opposite-sex couples are "morally" superior to same-sex couples, but rather on the rational certainly that the ability to perform the generative act is a basic constituent of marriage and always has been. Same-sex couples are constitutionally unable to do it.

Nature universally disqualifies same-sex persons from engaging in the generative act. No question of discrimination arises; in fact that charge is a red herring. Nature has made men and women sexually different, not the same. Marriage is, indeed, a fundamental right – if one qualifies. A father cannot marry his daughter or a mother her son. Brother and sister cannot marry. A seven year old male and female cannot marry. Same-sex persons even more radically do not qualify; they cannot in nature be the subject of a right to marry one another.

That's nature and the natural moral law, which the civil law flouts at society's peril. There lies the heart of the matter.

August 16, 2010   A claimed legal basis that is void

Editor: "In Defense of Marriage," editorial 8/14, ironically applying now in your view to both opposite- and same-sex marriage, continues to assume the validity and cogency of Judge Walker's applying the principles of equal protection of the laws and due process to justify legalizing same-sex marriages. But his reasoning is specious.

Same-sex couples by reason of their sexual

sameness cannot place the marital act (the act of sexual intercourse) with one another. Nature has made this universally impossible for them.

Thus there is no basis in fact for alleging a denial of equal protection of the laws because the law cannot supply for the maintained cause of grievance, a universal deficiency of nature. Nature itself makes it possible only for two persons of the opposite sex to have the martial act. In their natural and universal inability so to act, persons of the same sex cannot claim any undue burden from application of the laws.

Thus the claimed application of equal protection of the laws and due process has no relevance to the case of same-sex marriage.

August 16, 2010   **Manifestly prejudiced**

Editor: The New York Times has shown itself to be manifestly intolerant and biased on the issue of same-sex marriage by not admitting to publication in its opinion pages (4/1/09 – 8/15/10) any substantive letter or op-ed essay opposed to The Times's pro-homosexual marriage position expressed in at least fourteen editorials and several op-ed essays during the same period.

After twelve editorials since April 1, 2009 advocating the legalization of same-sex marriage, The Times published a thirteenth (based on Judge Walker's California ruling) on August 5, 2010 and, then, for the first time, printed one the very next day (Aug.6) four letters, one of which opposed The Times's and the Judge's view. The writer of the opposed letter, a very short letter, was identified, it is not clear why, as a Catholic columnist. Would such a specific identification have been made if the writer had been a Jewish, Muslim or Black American columnist? A fourteenth pro same-sex marriage appeared on August 14.

The strategy of The Times editorial page, in dealing with this extraordinarily important social issue (same-sex marriage) and certain other contentious issues is clear: After a sharp pro-same-sex marriage editorial has appeared, The Times, closing off discussion quickly in the letters column, published a brief selection (opposed in the minority or not printed at all) the very next day after the editorial's appearance so that only those persons who immediately wrote their letter and e-mailed or faxed it, preferably early in the day of the editorial's appearance could have even a chance of being considered for publication. On this issue and with this tactic the firm bias of those in charge is pellucidly clear.

Following Op-Ed Columnist Ross Douthat's ambiguous endorsement of opposite-sex marriage on 8/8 (The Marriage Ideal) seven letters were published, (8/16), none to be characterized as a substantive defense of opposite-sex marriage.

Further, in reporting the issue of clergy sexual abuse of minors, The Times has concentrated on allegations against Catholic clergy and omitted any coverage of non-Catholic religious and other personnel. In an editorial of 3/23/09, The Times specifically named the Catholic Church as worthy of punishment. On the other hand – for example, the paper did not give any coverage to two recent and notable cases of non-Catholic bishops in Pennsylvania – cases in the rabbinate and, especially, cases among public school teachers and other school staff.

That The Times has targeted the Catholic Church is beyond question. Moreover, The Times has repeatedly identified the clergy sex abuse of minors as pedophilia, a scientific term referring to the abuse of pre-pubescent children, whereas the overwhelming majority of the alleged abuse has been committed by adult males with post-pubescent males; namely, with teenage boys and young men, an abuse known as ephebophia. The latter (with minors) is a classic form of criminal homosexual behavior.

Finally, The Times while rebuking the Pope for his alleged failure to order bishops to report abusive clergy to the civil authorities (3/25/10) has failed to investigate why, in New York State, despite a proposed bill in the Legislature to require clergy and other human service persons to report sexual abuse of minors to the public authorities – a bill which has the full support of the Catholic Bishops and the Catholic Church in New York State – cannot be passed. Who are the groups opposed to this required reporting of the sexual abuse of minors to the public authorities? They should be required to explain their positions.

And The Times should be expected to address these issues.

December 3, 2010   What the Pope said in context

Editor: You state ("Advances on the AIDS Front," editorial, 12/3) that "last week... Pope Benedict XVI expressed the view that condoms could be used to prevent disease transmission."

In fact, the Pope, in a brief exchange with an interviewer, said only that a male prostitute might think that his using a condom would reduce the possibility of transmitting AIDS and that such a realization on the prostitute's part could represent an advance in his responsible use of his sexuality. The Pope was not addressing the basic issue of using condoms in respect to AIDS or otherwise.

But since his observations en passant have been and will be diversely interpreted and widely misinterpreted, we do deserve an authoritative clarification of this issue from the Pope's Congregation for the Doctrine of the Faith. The

Times would not want to mislead its readers nor would any teachers in the Catholic Church its members.

December 29, 2010   Difference is a basic principle

Editor: Your chastisement of Phoenix Catholic Bishop Thomas J. Olmsted and the U.S. Catholic bishops generally ("A Matter of Life or Death," editorial 12/23) emerges from irreducible differences of principle: The Times holds that it is morally acceptable to kill a new human being still in his or her mother's womb in order (among many reasons) to avert the possible death of the mother if she continues to carry the child.

The Catholic Church is convinced that no such direct slaying is morally acceptable, not even to avert the possible death of the mother, as is evident, by certainly and directly killing the child. It is never right to do evil that good may come of it.

The possible loss of the mother's life in this tragic scenario would be a physical not an intended or moral evil. In the actual case, the death of the one – the unborn child – is certainly and directly intended. The possible loss of the mother would result from natural causes and a death which all the resources of medical science would seek to prevent.

When The Times goes after Catholic hospitals for alleged failure to give "emergency reproductive care," a euphemism in this case for abortion, and for exercising religious freedom, it should lay all its cards on the table. What emerges is in this is not the old grey lady's compassion but her steely determination to value one innocent human life more than another.

SECTION IV: 2011—2014

February 14, 2011 A fundamental right if one qualifies

Editor: The Times (editorials "Marriage Equality in New York" 2/11, and "In Defense of Marriage, for All" 2/14) continues to fuel its engines for the race to end "blatant discrimination" and the "bigoted status quo" on same-sex marriage in New York State.

Objections to homosexual marriage, however, do not mask unjust discrimination or bigotry, but embody rather the rational certainty that the ability to perform the generative act is a basic constituent of marriage and always has been. Same-sex couples are constitutionally unable to do it.

Nature universally disqualifies same-sex persons from engaging in the generative or marital act. The "discrimination" charge is, in fact, a red herring. Nature has made man and woman sexually different.

Marriage is, indeed, a basic or fundamental right – if one qualifies. A father cannot marry his daughter or a mother her son. Brothers and sisters cannot marry. Same-sex persons even more radically do not qualify; they cannot in nature be the subject of a right to marry one another.

That's nature and natural moral law, which the civil law flouts at society's peril.

February 14, 2011   Bigoted, biased, discriminatory

Editor: Your 2/13 column "Race, Religion and Other Perilous Ground," giving a fair shake to the issue therein discussed, prompts me once again to address the Public Editor on what I judge to be The Times's biased editorial policy barring publication of any principled view opposed to its position on homosexual marriage. Previous letters to the former public editor met with no comment or response.

The objection: Over a period of 14 months (April 2009 to June 2010) when the issue of same-sex marriage (termed "marriage equality") was raging in various state legislatures, The Times ran at least 14 major editorials (list attached) vigorously supporting same-sex marriage, but at the same time admitted to publication no substantive letter or op-ed essay contesting the editorial board's view. (The Times's research service has confirmed my careful day-to-day scrutiny of the editorial pages during this period.) My complaint, of course, is not that any one of my letters (submitted after each editorial) or op-ed essay wasnot published but that NO substantive letter or op-ed essay – dealing with this proposed fundamental social change – was published during this period.

Now, with the issue being raised again (by Gov. Cuomo), two editorials (Feb. 11 and 14) have already appeared condemning the "blatant discrimination" and "bigoted status quo" that disallows homosexual marriage.

I conclude, at least for the 14-month period already cited and elapsed, that The Times has of deliberate purpose excluded from its opinion pages any principled expression of views conflicting with its own position on homosexual marriage and that this a violation of its avowed "liberal" character . What do you think?

February 14, 2011 - Op-Ed.   No basic civil right

Op-Ed Editor: When will The Times admit to publication a substantive op-ed essay that contests its view on same-sex marriage?

No Basic Civil Right

The Times contends – with at least fifteen major editorials within a two-year period, two already this month, that our nation must legalize same-sex "marriage" on pain of being discriminatory, unfair and bigoted and of denying to human beings a basic civil right.   State law now generally discriminates, it is maintained, by restricting marriage to two persons, one, male; the other, female. Such, however, has been the customary law of our civilization for millennia. Those who uphold this law are regularly characterized as "anti-gay," homophobic, ultra-right wing or religious fanatics. Arguments for the same-sex marriage position, however, are grievously deficient at their base in nature. Marriage exclusively between two persons of the opposite sex involves no unjust discrimination, no unfairness and no denial of a basic right – natural or civil. Why is that?

If a man and a woman can get married, why can't two men or two women? And, we might add, why not some other combination of men and of women? Why can't any kind of partnership be recognized as a marriage?

Why not? Here's why not: Nature says no. Marriage is the union of one man and one woman for a bonded and permanent life together that usually brings forth children and constitutes the family, the basis of society as we know it. Marriage is not a new invention. It is not merely a sentimental relationship which persons of either sex or of whatever age or familial ties can have with one another. Establishing the fundamental unit of society, man-woman marriage has been characteristic of virtually all societies from time immemorial. Nature's construction of man and woman shows that they are destined and fitted to be united with one another and to bear and raise children. Two persons of the same sex cannot do this. Giving to same-sex persons the right to marry is like giving a man the right to bear a child or nurse a child, or a woman of and by herself to conceive a child. He or she can't do it. And so he or she can't have the right to do it. Nature says no and nature says no to same-sex marriage.

Of course, sterile couples and elderly couples cannot conceive but they are not by nature itself disqualified for the conjugal union. Some other physical deficiency prevents its natural fruition. No same-sex union, however, can be a conjugal union.

What about equal rights? Indeed all persons have the same basic human rights and they should enjoy them except when nature itself universally disqualifies a certain class of persons for a particular right. Because two men or two women can't establish the sexual bond that ordinarily generates children, produces a family and gives children the required material and psychological support they need to grow up successfully, they cannot marry. Scientific studies show the benefits of having a mother and a father and the disadvantages suffered by children not so fortunate. How, then, can two men or two women marry or be supposed to have a right to do so?

We know that today families can be manufactured by various technological means. What natural science can do and should do are distinct and separate issues. We have yet to see over time the social effects of human manufacture compared with the nature's millennia of procreative marriage and the family. Same-sex marriages, duos or other combinations, like polygamy and polygyny, conflict with the natural moral law. What is the proof? It stares you in the face. Millennia of history re-enforce this truth. There can be no right to that which injures the person, the family or the social fabric.

Further, what about equal-rights' parallels? Same-sex marriage promoters regularly cite the woman's suffrage movement, the struggle against slavery and segregation, the battles to allow interracial marriages and achieve rights for the disabled and seniors as parallels for the effort to obtain equal rights for partners of the same-sex to marry. These comparisons have no relevancy. In no case has nature itself universally disqualified persons in the alleged parallels from enjoying and exercising the right they sought. Nature does issue a universal disqualification in the case of same-sex marriage.

Finally, legalizing same-sex marriage would over time be very harmful: 1)It would give legal and social approval to homosexual relations and put them on the same level as heterosexual conjugal relations; 2) It will promote those homosexual relations that are physically dangerous; 3) It will legitimize the view that there is no ethical difference between homosexual relations and the conjugal union; 4) It will reverse the immemorial judgment of our country and our civilization that homosexual relations are unnatural and immoral; 5) It will implicitly teach our youngsters that they have for marriage a range of sexual choices – heterosexual, homosexual, bi-sexual – and, if and when public opinion accepts it – polygamous, consensually incestuous and group marriage; 6) It will impair the psychological health and development of children (now perhaps manufactured), which, scientific studies show, need ideally the influence of a father (male) and a mother (female); 7) It will erode the understanding of the traditional family as the basic unit of our society; and 8) It will cause social service agencies whose ethical principles disallow same-sex "marriage" to be accused and convicted of discrimination and forced to end their public service.

This is the case against same-sex "marriage." It involves or relies upon nobody's particular religion, but rational reflection on the natural moral law ingrained in the consciences of all human beings because of their rational powers. True, all do not agree, but those who do are appalled to be summarily dismissed from the table of reasoned conviction and civil discourse.

April 12, 2011   **Parents' rights paramount**

Editor: Your editorial "Justice Kagan Dissents, 4-10, invokes Justice Kagan almost as a deity because she interprets the First Amendment Establishment Clause in a way that the Founding Fathers and their successors until recently would never have imagined.

What was originally enacted to insure religious freedom for individuals is now invoked to punish parents who exercise their natural and constitutional right to choose a religiously affiliated school for their children.

Such parents, like all other parents, must pay local, state and federal taxes, but are deprived of significant benefit from them if they chose a religiously affiliated elementary or secondary school for their children. Tax credits and vouchers are ways of easing a heavily burdened right, a penalty not imposed by the other Western democracies.

The Court's majority and decisive view, in upholding the Arizona Educational Tax Credit provision, while finding no violation of law also, in effect, safeguards and promotes not any religion but, like the First Amendment itself, religious freedom.

April 15, 2011   **Dangerous identifying of motives**

Editor: Gail Collins ("Behind the Abortion War, 4/14 column) obscures the main point of opposition to federal funding for Planned Parenthood (PP) by stating that doctrinaire (in her view) opinions against contraception actually motivated the opponents, who seek to defund all forms of artificial contraception.

Such opinions, however, are of little moment before the stark truth that PP performed 330,000 abortions in 2009, as the largest provider in the country, and that if, in truth, it doesn't use federal funds for that enterprise, such funding nonetheless frees up other funds to bolster its abortion industry.

These facts joined to the conviction that abortion is the (often savage) destruction of the innocent embryo or fetus – a human being in development– warrants cessation of funding, even when used only for non-abortion services, and awarding it to agencies in no way associated with this high-production abortion industry. That's the point.

May 2, 2011   **Close-minded journalists?**

Editor: In "A Tipping Point for Gay Marriage?" (The Week in Review, 5/1) Adam Liptak reports the views of some that "elite opinions generally and the legal culture in particular is racing ahead of popular opinion and shutting down a worthwhile debate." Still other critics cite the contemporary higher academic community as a bastion of such closed-minded elitism.

Missing from Staffer Liptak's report of censors is the journalistic elite. It is a fact – verified by The Times Research Bureau and its current public editor - that The Times's editorial pages have not admitted to publication any significant letter or op-ed essay opposed to same-sex marriage April '09 – April '11, despite its having published at least sixteen strongly pro-same-sex marriage editorials and sundry op-ed essays in that period.

The public editor says (2/15/11) it's true but he cannot effect change. Closed-mindedness at The Times? Yes, indeed.

May 16, 2011   **Right reasons for natural marriage**

Editor: Jaye Coe Whitehead ("The Wrong Reasons for Same-Sex Marriage," Op-Ed, 5/16) wisely rejects the "it will help us make more money" argument for legalizing homosexual marriage. But missing (understandably) from her essay but nowhere else on the editorial pages (anytime) is an essay with "The Right Reasons Against Same-Sex Marriage."

These center on the witness and judgment of our civilization, the self-evident truth that the one-man – one-woman relationship sealed by the sexual union open to life is normative. Nature itself universally disqualifies same-sex persons from marrying one another. No unjust discrimination, inequality or unfairness is involved. Psychological and sociological studies identify the several injurious effects that same-sex marriage will have on marriage, the family, religious freedom and the social fabric.

Are we fearful that some may be convinced by an exposition of the reasons against?

May 16, 2011 Op-Ed   **Bow down to the governor**

Op-Ed Editor: Governor Cuomo and some Albany legislators evidently think they are going to force a same-sex marriage law on many millions of fellow New Yorkers

207

very soon. They know what we want or should want and they are going to let us have it. They are just waiting for the proper moment – enough votes in the State Senate – to bestow their gift. Those who balk should be shunned.

The legislators in favor insist that this issue is one of "equal" rights. If a man and a woman can get married, why can't two men or two women? And, we might add, why not some other combination of men and of women? Why can't any kind of partnership be a marriage? Yes, they say, a partnership of two same-sex persons committed to one another and who promise to live with one another at least until they break up should be deemed a marriage.

Why not? Nature says no. Marriage is the union of one man and one woman for a bonded and permanent life together that usually brings forth children and constitutes the family, the basis of society as we know it. This definition needs no defense. It is a self-evident truth. Marriage is not a new invention. Establishing the fundamental unit of society, man-woman marriage has been characteristic of virtually all societies from time immemorial. Nature's construction of man and woman shows that they are destined and fitted to be united with one another and to bear and raise children. Two persons of the same sex cannot do this. Giving to same-sex persons the right to marry is like giving a man the right to bear a child. He can't do it. And so he can't have the right to do it. Nature says no and nature likewise says no to same-sex marriage.

Of course, sterile couples and elderly couples cannot conceive but they are not by nature itself disqualified for the conjugal union. No same-sex union can be a conjugal union.

But, again, what about equal rights? Indeed all persons have the same basic rights and they should enjoy them except when nature itself universally disqualifies a certain class of persons for a particular right. Because two men or two women can't establish the sexual bond that ordinarily generates children, produces a family and gives children the required material and psychological support they need to grow up successfully, they cannot marry. Scientific studies show the benefits of having a mother and a father and the disadvantages suffered by children not so fortunate. How, then, can two men or two women marry or be supposed to have a right to do so?

Oh, we know that today families can be manufactured by various scientific means. What science can do and should do are separate issues. We have yet to see over time the social effects of human manufacture compared with the nature's millennia of procreative marriage and the family. Same-sex marriages, duos or other combinations, like polygamy and polygyny, conflict with the natural moral law. What is the proof? It stares you in the face. Millennia of history re-enforce this truth.

Further, what about equal-rights parallels? Same-sex marriage promoters regularly cite the woman's suffrage movement, the struggle against slavery and segregation, the battle to allow interracial marriages and achieve rights for the disabled and seniors as parallels for the effort to obtain equal rights for partners of the same-sex to marry. These comparisons have no relevancy. In no case has nature itself universally disqualified persons in the alleged parallels from enjoying and exercising the right they sought. Nature does issue a universal disqualification in the case of same-sex marriage.

Finally, legalizing same-sex marriage would over time be very harmful: 1)It would give legal and social approval to homosexual relations and put them on the same level as heterosexual conjugal relations; 2) It will promote those homosexual relations that are physically dangerous; 3) It will legitimize the view that there is no ethical difference between homosexual relations and the conjugal union; 4) It will reverse the immemorial judgment of our country and our civilization that homosexual relations are unnatural and immoral; 5) It will implicitly teach our youngsters that they have for marriage a range of sexual choices – heterosexual, homosexual, bi-sexual – and, if and when public opinion accepts it – polygamous, consensually incestuous and group marriage; 6) It will impair the psychological health and development of children (now perhaps manufactured), which, scientific studies show, need ideally the influence of a father (male) and a mother (female); 7) It will erode the understanding of the traditional family as the basic unit of our society; and 8) It will cause social service agencies whose ethical principles disallow same-sex "marriage" to be accused and convicted of discrimination and forced to end their public service.

If the Governor and his friends in the Legislature insist on their goal, we need a referendum first to know where all New Yorkers stand.

May 18, 2011   **Isn't it called bribery?**

Editor: "If you want my bucks, vote my way," says billionaire Mayor Bloomberg (5/18), in effect to Albany legislators on the same-sex marriage issue. Another triumph for the rule of ethics politics!!

June 14, 2011   **Equality not the issue**

Editor: "They Need to Stand up for Equality" (editorial, 6/14) misidentifies the central issue on homosexual "marriage," which is the nature of marriage. It is a self-evident truth from time immemorial that marriage presents itself as the intended permanent bond of a man and a woman sealed by the sexual union open to life.

This heterosexual conjugal bond open to life and ordinarily productive of life constitutes the foundation of human society everywhere.

Two persons of the same sex cannot seal this conjugal union; nature universally disqualifies them. They can form other kinds of partnerships, but not marriage. Because nature universally disqualifies a man from bearing a child and a woman from generating new life by and of herself, man and woman are not therefore unequal but only different – by nature. So it is with marriage and "marriage a la mode." Equality is not the issue. The need to recognize and to stand up for marriage is.

June 24, 2011   **One-sided blitzkrieg**

Editor: "Politicians Who Fear the Public Light" (editorial, 6/24) bemoans the speck you find in the State Senate's eye for avoiding swift passage of a same-sex marriage bill – and choosing secret negotiations to break the impasse – while you ignore the beam in your own eye for printing some twenty forceful pro-homosexual marriage editorials over a two-year period without admitting to publication any significant letter or op-ed essay differing with your view.

The central issue in this - for The Times, non-existing – debate is not about equality but about the nature of marriage as a conjugal union open to life. Nature universally disqualifies same-sex persons from marrying one another. Like all other persons, they can form various kinds of partnerships, but not marriage. Editorial boards that fear debate certainly fear the public light.

June 27, 2011   **Just a matter of time**

Editor: Yes, it's time for The Times to crow. But your

page one 6/26 news story unabashedly tells how the homosexual marriage bill was actually passed: by the crazed idea that all consensual sex is good and equal; that "progressive" government must endorse this principle; that what's good for business makes good law and social policy; that bribes are ok if they advance one's goals; that emotional harangues are paths to the truth; and that bishops' letters and blogs are just a joke when it comes to educating and motivating citizens to act.

You say (editorials, 6/27) that the Constitution and state law protect religious entities from being hauled up on charges of "discrimination," "bigotry," and "violation of civil rights." Just wait and see. The inexorable logic of the homosexual agenda will brook no limit. It's already happened in the U.S. and in Britain. What are construed as "religious opinions" cannot prevail against what are construed as "civil rights."

August 22, 2011   A message that will change the world

Editor: Having read your editorials/opinion pages for both Saturday, 8/20 and Sunday, 8/21 (not a brief or pix in either edition reporting the Pope's visit to Spain), I can conclude only how valuable and transforming these premium pages would have been had they published, instead, with a few subheads and pix, the Pope's homilies to ca. 1.5 million youth and the rest of us.

Those who have listened to or read and assimilated his message: it is they who will change the world.

October 20, 2011   Just keep saying it

Editor: With "Another Test of Marriage Equality" (editorial, 10/18), The Times continues its relentless rhetorical crusade to dissociate the generation of children from the historic institution of marriage. Human nature, human sexuality and the human family loudly testify to this link which should be self-evident to all.

As that foreign army marched (1939) boldly into Poland as if that nation did not exist (but ultimately it prevailed), so also this effort to dissolve and extinguish by repeated assertion the evidence of reason and the testimony of history about marriage will ultimately fail. The various sciences of reason and the testimony of history belie the specious claim that nature itself violates equality and practices discrimination when it universally disqualifies same-sex persons from marrying one another.

October 21, 2011   **Abortion's aim is to kill**

Editor: In "Playing Politics with Women's Lives" (editorial, 10/21), you urge supporters of "women's reproductive rights" to defeat the Protect Life Act now pending in Congress which aims to protect hospitals that refuse on religious or moral grounds to perform emergency abortions "even if a woman's life was at stake."

Your premises and reasoning are confusing. No man and no woman has reproductive <u>rights</u>. We have a reproductive <u>power</u> which may rightly be exercised only in the context of marriage. It does not include the right for a father or mother to kill the new human life that may result from the exercise of that power.

In every abortion the life of the unborn child is at stake: the aim of the abortion is to kill the child. In how many instances the mother's life is <u>also</u> at stake needs demonstration. But we do not kill the one to save the other or vice versa. The medical first principle of "do no harm" deserves supreme confidence before such a challenge.

October 21, 2011
Compassion – Condemnation? A hard choice

Editor: "Accountability in Mission" (editorial, 10/21) posits Kansas City (MO) Bishop Robert Finn with knowledge of allegedly pornographic photos belonging to a diocesan priest last December but not turning them over to the police until May of this year.

The facts will show that in December Bishop Finn had knowledge of (he did not see) only one photo of an unclothed girl which, after consultation with a police officer and an attorney, was judged to be non-sexual, that is, not pornographic.

Unfortunately, Bishop Finn's pastoral and humane efforts to correct and rehabilitate the priest as a result of this incident and other complaints were unsuccessful; and more damaging evidence came to light, which was then reported to the police.

Let's not pile it on Bishop Finn.

October 27, 2011   Only ideologies, no truth!

Editor: Profs. John Santelli and Arik Marcell (letter, 10/26) think that public school sexuality education, because based on "scientific understanding and human rights," is ideology-free.

"Ideology" is the complex of principles with which one approaches an issue or solves a problem. To approach human sexuality in the context of the bonded love of a man and a wife ordinarily generative of children and establishing the family, to be guarded by chastity and modesty and used in no other context forms one basic "ideology."

To deal with human sexuality mainly as a powerful urge that can generate diseases and unwanted pregnancies that must be guarded against by devices and vaccines is another. In shorthand these are the ideologies of chastity and safe sex.

Both can stake a claim to being "scientific," one based on an authentic anthropology of man; the other, exclusively on experimental science and relativistic morals. As such, they are incompatible.

October 28, 2011
Science is clear when new human life begins

Editor: In "The 'Personhood' Initiative" (editorial, 10/28) you again cite "woman's reproductive rights." What about men's reproductive rights? In truth, neither men nor women have reproductive rights; they have a reproductive <u>power</u> which is rightly used only in the bond of marriage. Were it not so, men and women could establish at will breeding farms for the production of offspring.

In the bond of marriage, husband and wife have the right to those acts are ordinarily productive of children. But they cannot demand, as it were, from one another or of nature, the conception of a child. Most especially, neither has the right to effect the destruction of the offspring one conceived.

Describing the "personhood initiative" as a cell to grant legal personhood to a "fertilized human egg" sounds less fanciful and pointedly realistic when it is rephrased as a call to grant legal personhood to a new human being at his or her beginning.

It is an undeniable scientific fact that when fertilization takes place, a new human life begins, which, given its proper environment maintained, will develop through all stages before birth and after birth and wind up reading a letter like this, and not of set purpose be destroyed along the way, sometime savagely. This is the real issue, the issue that so many refuse to face.

October 31, 2011   **Chastity not fornication**

Editor: "For Their Own Good" (editorial, 10/29), as virtually all other Times' position statements on teenage sexuality, addresses the diseases to which teenage fornication gives rise, rather than the behavior patterns and underlying moral values that encourage promiscuity with its consequent serious diseases. Providing multiple "protections" (e.g. condoms, HPV vaccine for 11-12-year-old girls and boys) from the consequences of immoral conduct does little (nothing) to correct the immoral conduct itself.

How to do the latter? By parents and schools strongly emphasizing as a first principle of sexuality education that sexual intercourse belongs only in the context of faithful married love. Teenage fornication is morally wrong, physically and emotionally injurious and to be avoided at all costs. Adherence to this principle is "for their own good."

October 31, 2011   **Decency in ads cast off**

Editor: Shame on you! You admitted to publication in Sunday Styles (10/30) three graphically provocative sexual advertisements that transgress all bounds of decency.

The first, on page 13 (Nordstrom – Michael Kors) shows a nubile male clad only in shorts while a nubile female reaching over his shoulder is putting her hand into his shorts obviously reaching for his pubic area.

The second, on page 14 (Miranda for Miranda), shows a nubile female clad only in jeans with her back and face turned to the camera.

The third (Calvin Klein), page 20, shows another nubile female naked from the lower torso area up with a large pocket book covering her middle and chest area.

These advertisements transgress the bounds of decency and should not have been accepted for publication. You owe your readers an apology and a precise statement of your standards for ads of this nature.

November 3, 2011   **Where emphasis belongs**

Editor: Nicholas D. Kristof ("The Birth Control Solution" Op-Ed, 10/31), is right; family planning doesn't cause sex. The natural human urge, difficult to control, for sexual pleasure and sexual union is the cause.

But "family planning," an umbrella phrase that usually centers on the use of contraceptives, but also includes sterilizing, even abortifacient drugs and surgical abortion, does enable sex to be engaged in without concern for its natural consequences, conception and birth. Although it is impossible to determine scientifically to what extent the use or non-use of contraceptives affects the number of pregnancies, logic - admittedly a poor criterion in the context of passion – suggests that the availability of contraceptives facilitates and encourages non-marital sex.

The 'family planning/birth control solution' - in the sense of devices, gels, pills and even surgeries - will facilitate more illicit sex, if bring about fewer pregnancies, and may moderate the population crisis where it exists but will give no help to European countries pleading for at least replacement populations to pay for their social programs. Emphasis should be placed rather on general education, particularly of women, stimulating economic growth, eliminating government corruption, and on other all-important dimensions of this human crisis; namely, support of the dignity of the human person, of human sexuality, of marriage, of human life and of the natural family.

November 7, 2011   Employers have consciences, too

Editor: In "A New Battle Over Contraception" (editorial, 11/6), you endorse limiting religious freedom by forcing Catholic institutions serving the public to provide "contraceptive" insurance, which includes (your birth control article 11/5, A-17) sterilizing, abortifacient pills and devices.

You complain that many employees of these (mainly) Catholic institutions are deprived of medical aids they need and personally accept as ethically legitimate. You forget that the sponsors and leaders of institutions from which they have sought and received employment also are committed to ethical principles that bind them in conscience: in the provision of the services they give and in the implementation of policies toward their employees.

No person is forced to seek or accept employment from such institutions. When they are given such employment they accept it with the understanding that they accede to the institution's ethical principles insofar as they apply to employer-employee relationships.

We need no hacking away at the religious freedom clause of the First Amendment.

November 7, 2011   Socarides hit the nail on the head

Editor: The Times continues to level a tonnage of opprobrium ("Edging Toward Equality" editorial, 11/5) on those who defend the "deplorable", "atrocious" and "mean-spirited" Defense of Marriage Act (DOMA), together with the "shameful discrimination" it visits upon same-sex couples. Those who defend the <u>natural</u> institution of marriage and the intrinsic connection of this union of man and woman with the generation of children are portrayed as bigots and homophobes.

No state originally defined marriage and no state can re-define marriage. It is there, in nature, from time immemorial for all to see. Conceptually removing the generation of children from the concept of marriage makes it something different, another reality – some may call it a domestic partnership or civil union – but not marriage.

Indeed, achieving legalization of same-sex unions as marriage is secondary, implies homosexual activist Richard Socarides (letter printed 8/21): What's important is not the status of marriage but society's acceptance, approval and legalization of homosexual relationships and the equality of benefits.

For homosexual advocacy groups and supporting media, like The Times, confusing people by applying concepts of [in] "equality" and "discrimination" to the effect of a difference universally established in and by human nature for a specific purpose exemplifies the height of sophistry.

November 21, 2011   Imposing one ethical view on all

Editor: "Democrats who urge Obama…" (story, 11/20, p. 16) to enforce contraceptive coverage in health insurance plans miss two key points: 1) the so-called contraceptive coverage includes, as acknowledged in other Times stories, sterilization and potentially abortifacient pills and devices. No one should be forced to provide or to purchase insurance for such "preventive medicine."

2) The Catholic Church is mandated by its founder to help the sick, the poor, the needy and the aged; and it fulfills this mandate, in part, by a multiplicity of health-care institutions.

It is mandated also to teach the truth as it has received the same from its founder; and it implements this mandate through a multiplicity of educational institutions on various levels, all in service, (both health-care and education) to its own members and to American society as a whole.

In pursuing these ministries, the Church must act - as do all other similar institutions – in conformity with its own ethical/moral values, principles and norms. To be forced to do otherwise would violate one of the most precious and basic of citizens' rights, the right of religious freedom.

Is that what these Democrats want?

November 21, 2011   Make-believe world

Editor: Laura Abraham (NYT Magazine, 11/20) reports sex-education teacher Al Vernacchio as a "practicing Catholic" who characterizes himself as a partnered homosexual for 17 years, who approves, in individual cases, fornication, oral and anal sex for his high-school students.

Somebody is living in a make-believe world here, Al, the principal, or Laura, the (naïve) interviewer or both. For the Catholic Church, not a new entity on the horizon, human sexuality belongs exclusively in the context of the permanent, faithful bond of husband (man) and wife (woman) in the marital act open to the transmission of human life.

Editor: "Battling Over Birth Control" (editorial, 11/25) continues to blur basic facts in this debate over mandatory and free contraceptive insurance.

The first blur is the continuing failure to identify "birth control" insurance as including not only drugs and devices that prevent fertilization but also those that sterilize and act potentially as abortifacient. No one should be forced to provide or purchase such insurance.

The second blur is the failure to acknowledge that the sponsors of Church educational and health-care units have consciences, like all other citizens; and their consciences teach them that providing coverage for such drugs and devices is ethically and morally wrong. In the United States their decision is protected by the religious freedom clause of the First Amendment.

Those who seek employment or services from Church-sponsored units – which provide an immense benefit to the general public – do so freely. They must respect the ethical integrity of these institutions: the principles, norms and values that govern their employer-employee relations and the kinds of service they provide.

The third blur is the asserted principle of the "dime" which means we (the state) give you a relatively small grant to facilitate your public service, but for which we require you to renounce the ethical values and principles that govern your institutions and accept a different contemporary if widespread ethic the state has no title to impose.

Fortunately, in the United States the First Amendment disqualifies government from imposing such an ethic and gives wide berth to religious freedom.

Editor: The attached copy of a news story (with byline Douglas Dalby, published 12/9, A-6) in <u>The New York Times</u> states that the late Archbishop (d.1973) John Charles McQuaid of Dublin, Ireland (in office 1940-72) stands accused of serial child sexual abuse. Accused by whom? Ultimately in the published story, the accuser is Patsy McGarry, religious affairs correspondent for the Irish Times.

Basing himself, it appears, on a supplementary report (published July, 2011 to the state-sponsored Murphy Report released 2009 on sexual abuse of minors in Dublin Archdiocesan units) which refers (the supplement) to an unnamed cleric about whom two separate complaints had been made and a "letter of concern" from numerous persons had been received by the Archdiocese of Dublin (and presumably given to the Commission), Irish Times staffer Patsy McGarry categorically asserted that this unnamed cleric is the late Archbishop John Charles McQuaid.

It is startling that the original writer should have written and the NYTimes editor should have allowed this story to be published as it was with the sole authority for identifying the unnamed cleric being Patsy McGarry and he not offering or being required to give any credible public source for his designation of the unnamed cleric as Archbishop McQuaid.   By publishing the story as it appeared in the New York Times on 12/9, you have allowed the name of a distinguished and long-deceased Archbishop to be besmirched throughout the world.

Please give me an explanation of why this was done.

January 9, 2012 Baseless theory of reproduction rights

Editor; "Republicans Versus Reproductive Rights" (editorial, 1/9) delivers your familiar complaint about the current "assault" on women's reproductive rights, a veiled way of designating the claimed right of a woman to abort, eject and destroy the human life developing in her womb.

In truth, neither men nor women have reproductive rights; they have a reproductive power which is rightly used only in the bond of marriage. Were it not so, men and women could establish at will breeding farms for the production of offspring.

In the bond of marriage, husband and wife have the right to those acts that are ordinarily productive of children. But, even in marriage, they cannot demand, as it were, from one another or from nature, the conception of a child. Most especially, neither has the right to destroy the offspring one conceived.

The theory of "reproductive rights" belongs to the world-view that man and woman are a complete and total law unto themselves.

January 13, 2012 On the issue—careful study needed

Dear Sir: Prof. Sara Richey (For Priests' Wives, a Word of Caution," Op-Ed 1/13) identifies as a "religious tradition" the views on priests' wives of one medieval monk and Church official, Peter Damian (1007-72), With other officials of his time Peter – the Oxford Dictionary of the Christian Church tells us – confronted widespread "worldliness and simonical practices" among the clergy.

His remarks, admittedly extreme, must be placed, in their immediate context and, then, in the context of Church teaching from the New Testament through the ancient Fathers and councils down to our own day. The Eastern

Churches, Catholic and Orthodox, have from the earliest centuries had married priests, not to speak of the Reformation Church clergy from the 16th century to our own day.

One medieval Churchman's view does not constitute a "religious tradition." The II Vatican Council and modern-day bishops of Rome have spoken with deep respect for legitimately married priests and their families, while the same time teaching clearly and firmly that the celibacy of priests and bishops is modeled on the person of Christ and His mission and will find its total fulfillment when He comes in glory to present all of redeemed creation to his heavenly Father.

Prof. Richey needs to open her history books for a deeper and fuller appreciation of celibacy and marriage, including the marriage of priests. For the Church, it is the final state, the eschaton, which measures the now. For priests' wives, the word is not caution but welcome.

January 23, 2012   Obama imposes his ideology

Editor: By new HHS rules the Obama Administration (story, 1/21) has decided to force the very many Catholic non-parochial educational, health-service and social agencies to offer health-insurance to their employees that includes free coverage of various forms of contraception, sterilization and certain potentially abortifacient drugs.

This demand, if complied with, forces the sponsors and committed staffs of such units to act against their consciences and, moreover, represents a violation of the religious liberty guaranteed by the First Amendment to the Constitution.

Refusal by Church-related units to comply will result in the denial of any and all government assistance to these units that serve huge segments of the public, of all religions or none, who freely utilize these units. Shutting these down will irreparably damage the common good.

It is evident that these new regulations both on pragmatic and constitutional grounds must be withdrawn.

January 25, 2012   **He says it, so it must be so?**

Editor: New Jersey State Senator Stephen M. Sweeney asserts (story, Jan. 25, A-17) that same-sex marriage is a "civil right... already guaranteed in our Constitution" and cannot "be placed on the ballot." This is a pure and colossal begging of the question.

True, some states (and foreign nations) have declared or judged same-sex marriage a civil right. But that such a right appears in our Constitution is just plain false. Mr. Sweeney and his associates seem to have adopted Alice-in-Wonderland logic: I have said it; so it must be true.

Rights are founded on the dignity the human person and his or her needs. These natural-law rights may be confirmed or, at times, unfortunately denied by civil law. But civil law does not create basic human rights. Reason identifies them.

If men were to claim a right for their health insurance to cover ovarian cancer – or women to claim such a right for prostate cancer – wouldn't we laugh? Nature universally disqualifies these subjects from these rights. Likewise, nature universally disqualifies same-sex persons from marrying; they cannot beget children; and all generations, cultures and civilizations have recognized that the concept of marriage embraces that of children. It's a self-evident truth, there for all to see.

January 30, 2012
Man and woman are laws unto themselves?

Editor: Your editorials "Birth Control and Reproductive Rights" (1/30) and "Moving Ahead on Marriage Equality" (1/30) continue to illustrate the anthropological— philosophy of man – position that separates you by a vast chasm from that of the Catholic Church and of the Judeo-Christian tradition generally.

For The Times man and woman have an unspecified "right" to couple and to accept or refuse the effect on that coupling. That effect, if unplanned or unwanted, they can destroy. Indeed the woman alone may decide this. No law inherent in nature regulates these actions. Man or woman alone can determine what is advantageous to themselves. Moreover, their coupling has no necessary relationship to procreation. That may be exercised so that their coupling is not linked to man and woman but is open to same-sex relationships. This is called "equality."

For the Church, man and woman are intended by nature (and nature's God) for a unique covenant that necessarily includes the possibility of begetting, a power that must be respected and above all its effect be respected, the new unique human being.

These two anthropologies – these philosophies of man - are opposed and incompatible. Those who belong to the Church, work in its institutions or patronize them freely choose to do so. Why must The Times undemocratically seek to have imposed its philosophy of man on the Catholic Church?

February 8, 2012   **Equal ≠ Interchangeable**

Editor: "A Ruling for Equal Rights" (editorial 2/8) and "Another Victory for Marriage Equality" (editorial 2/10) plead without letup the same formalistic and positivistic reasoning of your many previous editorials on marriage "equality" and "equal rights," now unfortunately adopted by a federal appeals court in California.

What this thinking sets aside is <u>nature</u>: realities manifestly diverse are judged to be the same: oranges and walnuts are both edibles and can be served at table but they are radically different as juice-makers. One would have difficulty defending oranges and walnuts as equal juice-makers.

Thus if we chop away – as some members of our community wish to do – the possibility of begetting and raising children from our concept of marriage – then other models of marriage became possible. But if the self-evident truth of marriage in all cultures and civilizations is recognized as the institution that uniquely includes this begetting and raising of children, then we can't play the same-sex marriage tune. Marriage remains perpetually as it has been perennially. There is one marriage. It has no equal, no <u>a la mode.</u>

February 13, 2012   **One marriage, no <u>á la mode</u>**

Editor: "A Ruling for Equal Rights" (editorial 2/8) and "Another Victory for Marriage Equality" (editorial 2/10) plead without letup the same formalistic and positivistic reasoning of your many previous editorials on marriage "equality" and "equal rights," now unfortunately adopted by a federal appeals court in California.

What this thinking sets aside is <u>nature</u>: realities manifestly diverse are judged to be the same: oranges and walnuts are both edibles and can be served at table but they are radically different as juice-makers. One would have difficulty defending oranges and walnuts as equal juice-makers.

Thus if we chop away – as some members of our community wish to do – the possibility of begetting and raising children from our concept of marriage – then other models of marriage became possible. But if the self-evident truth of marriage in all cultures and civilizations is recognized as the institution that uniquely includes this begetting and raising of children, then we can't play the same-sex marriage tune.

Marriage is there in nature. It has not been defined nor can it be defined by the State. Marriage remains perpetually as it has been perennially. There is one marriage. It has no equal, no a la mode.

February 16, 2012
A phony crisis over religious liberty?

Is the dispute over requiring provision of free birth control insurance to women employees by religiously affiliated educational, health-service and charitable agencies a phony crisis over religious liberty as The Times (editorial, 2/11) maintained? Here are some considerations.

One: The phrase "birth control" inadequately describes the matter of the new policy on "preventive care" for pregnancy which includes, in fact, abortion-inducing drugs, sterilization, as well as those devices and applications usually referred to as contraceptives. Preventing life's beginning, suppressing one's life-giving power and ending a life once begun, it must be said, are radically distinct actions.

Two: The Catholic Church, the largest community of religious believers in the world, judges the use of these devices, procedures and drugs as wrongful, in one or more ways injurious to human dignity, human sexuality, marriage and the family. The Church deserves from the state respect, not legal coercion to change its teaching or to violate its teaching and its conscience in the operation of its public-service institutions. Ordinary citizens of various religions or none owe the same respect mutually to one another as persons and to the affiliated institutions they may collectively sponsor. Providing "birth control" insurance directly or indirectly would be for the Catholic Church implicitly to approve and promote what on the basis of natural moral law and religious belief it judges to be immoral. Individual believers, because their conviction is based on this widespread and long-held moral tradition, also deserve protection from being forced to violate their consciences by being compelled to purchase insurance that approves and facilitates what they judge as wrongful practices.

Three: It is often said that some Catholics themselves do not accept the Church's teaching on contraception or adhere to it in their own lives. This is more likely true with those (lapsed) Catholics not involved with the worshipping community. But even Catholics who may dissent from this teaching in their personal lives would not necessarily support state compulsion of Church authorities to violate their conscience by setting aside their authentic values and norms in the operation of Church public-service institutions. Polls are deceptive that do not distinguish between committed Catholics and Catholics in name only. In this country both are a huge number.

Just as the agents of government and the segments of society which disagree with Church teaching must respect the Church's values and norms, so must the Church respect, above all, the authority of the state exercising that authority within the limits imposed by the Federal Constitution. That Constitution forbids government to enact laws prohibiting the free exercise of religion, which "religion" includes the operation of educational, charitable and other humanitarian services. Religious liberty is exercised in the acts of conscience that determine the values and norms governing such services.

A growing tendency in our society today regards medicine or bio-medicine as <u>morally</u> – that is, whatever medical science can do is right - can be done, should be done and even must be done. This attitude toward medical science surely played a part in the disputes over human embryo destruction research to obtain stem cells and in efforts to support human cloning and assisted suicide that have arisen in recent years. The parameters of pure "medical" thinking, many observers would say, often neglect to consider, reflect upon and answer the great questions of philosophical anthropology and religion: In what does human dignity consist? What is the authentic meaning of human sexuality, of marriage and of family? What is the destiny of man? These are profound questions that the Church of its very nature must consider and answer in formulating its own position on "birth control," on human sexuality, marriage and the family. On what authority, for example, do some maintain that the "birth control" package in its entirety is an indispensable means to women's health?

<u>Four:</u> The question of religious liberty is one therefore that is instantly relevant. When the state tells the Church that it must provide free of charge directly or indirectly to female employees and patrons of its affiliated units a "birth control" package of abortion - inducing drugs, sterilization and contraception, it is forcing the Church to abandon its religiously based conviction on these matters and thus infringes on that right to religious freedom so prominent in our country's constitutional law, so precious in its heritage and present life. Moreover, those who work for the Church or who patronize its many public-service units do so by their own free choice. They cannot rightly demand that the Catholic Church scuttle the values and norms that inspire and govern these units.

Indeed, Mr. Obama's new rule – even with his "accommodations" - seeks to limit that religious liberty - with the right of conscience that exercises such liberty - guaranteed by the Constitution. There is nothing phony about this crisis at all. What will be the next step of government, many worried citizens ask, to force the Church to adapt its moral standards to those of an increasingly secularized society?

February 27, 2012   Civil liberty ≠ civil coercion

Editor: Dorothy Samuels (Sunday Observer, Feb. 25), editorial board member and former Executive Director for the NY Civil Liberties Union, makes several false assertions about the present flap between Catholic officials and the Obama Administration over the latter's new rule requiring free "birth control" insurance for women employees of all church-affiliated institutions. The chief, blatant falsehood is her assertion that the Church is seeking to impose its "religious views on millions of Americans who do not share them."

Potentially abortifacient drugs, chemical and surgical sterilization and the traditional contraceptive devices are now widely available to all men and women in our society. What Catholics and some others do oppose is to be forced (directly or indirectly) to provide free insurance for such drugs, services and devices and thus cooperate in their use and promote practices judged immoral.

Supporters of this new rule assume that these drugs, procedures and devices are necessary for women's health; namely, as preventive care for a newly recognized pathology or disease, pregnancy. Thus mandate their free access to all women. Any other view is deemed a kind of social blindness. Though currently widespread, such a view constitutes one ideological position. It reflects a philosophy of man radically different from that of the Catholic Church, whose values and norms are not those of some bizarre upstart sectaries but those of our civilization, of our Judaeo-Christian inheritance generally, subscribed to by all until very recently.

The Church does not want to be forced to abandon its own norms based on natural moral law and religious beliefs and to accept this current secular ideology with its norms and promote them in its specifically religious or religiously-affiliated institutions. The Church does not wish to be above the law but to have the respect of the law in accord with constitutional principles. Those who belong to the Church or accept employment from it or patronize its public-service institutions do so of their own free choice. They cannot demand that the Church act other than in accord with its own values and norms. In this country the First Amendment gives wide berth to religious freedom. Let's keep it that way.

February 29, 2012   Rhetoric cannot change nature

Editor: When you call for "equality" ("The Challenge to Marriage Equality," editorial, 2/29) between man-woman marriage and same-sex "marriage," you once again ignore and reject the basis of civil law in nature and the in natural moral law. Nature universally empowers and qualifies the one union to be marriage and disqualifies the other.

A man cannot assert or be given the right to insurance for ovarian cancer; a woman cannot do so in respect to prostate cancer. Nature has disqualified them for such rights.

In like manner, two persons of the same sex cannot assert or be given a right to marry. Nature universally disqualifies them, having established from the beginning the man-woman union – it's a self –evident truth – as the unique union for the continuance of the human race. No civil legislation originally defined marriage and no civil legislation can redefine it.

No amount of rhetoric can change nature.

March 2, 2012   **Spousal rights are coordinate**

Editor: Louise G. Troubek ("The Unfinished Fight Over Contraception, Op-Ed, 3/2) frames her comment in the current debate over President Obama's mandatory free "birth Control" (contraception, sterilization, potentially abortifacient drugs) insurance for women as a dispute over women's (apparently absolute) right to control their fertility and have comprehensive medical care (Read "birth control" package) necessary to support this right. That's her philosophical basis for her view.

Another philosophy of the human person would maintain that neither man nor woman has an absolute right over their fertility. Fertility is related to conception and conception is a moral possibility only within the marriage union. Marriage necessarily involves giving one's spouse the right to those acts that ordinarily bring about conception. If no such right is given, no real marriage exists. Conception, involving fertility, can be regulated only by mutual agreement within marriage. Women's and men's rights are coordinate. Neither is absolute.

Then, the question of means arises. Are any means to control fertility legitimate? The so-called fight over contraception is indeed a complex one.

233

March 7, 2012   Catholic bishops slandered

Editor: On the editorial page Feb. 25 (The Sunday Review, in a lengthy signed column entitled Sunday Observer) Dorothy Samuels, a Times editorial board member and former executive director of the New York Civil Liberties Union, wrote a scathing attack on the Catholic bishops by asserting among other things, that the Church is seeking to impose its "religious views on millions of Americans who do not share them."

As of this date (3/7), no letter has been admitted to print which takes issue with Ms. Samuels's utterly false charge. I cannot believe that no opposing letters have been received (since I know of at least one, my own). The Times continues to exhibit, as it did in it long series of editorials promoting same-sex marriage, to refuse to publish letters in substantial opposition to its view. A fine tight-locked negative policy for a supposedly "liberal" newspaper called to recognize the variety of opinions in the community in which it lives and serves.

Do you have a comment?

May 2, 2012   Look to the evidence

Editor: Reactions from Op-Ed Columnists Kristol and Dowd (4/20) and published letters from readers (5/1) attacking the Holy See's critical evaluation of the Leadership Conference of Women Religious display at most a cursory acquaintance with the document's content.

A few points to consider: Such an evaluation, when necessary, would be issued to any official church organization (LCWR is such) whether its membership were laymen, laywomen, religious women, religious men or clergy. The gender of the recipients is irrelevant. The basic question is: Does the membership - or more correctly, in this case, the LCWR leadership through the years - exhibit the objectionable characteristics cited. Membership in LCWR is by communities, not by individual Sisters. Rank-and-file Sisters have little to say about LCWR policies, programs and public statements.

The Holy See presents evidence for its critical comments. Think if departments of the federal government or official associations of federal employees were to lobby against the Administration. Contentious critics of government do not belong in government offices or in official associations.

The Sisters-Nuns of the Catholic Church in the USA deserve and receive enormous respect and gratitude from the clergy and the laity for their past and present extraordinary service. There is no doubt about this and nobody wants this relationship to change. Leadership persons in official Catholic organizations, however - whether of men, women, religious men, religious women or clergy - need to review their purposes, policies, programs, and public statements to test their harmony with those of the universal Church leadership, the College of Bishops and their unique primate and presider, the Bishop of Rome.

May 7, 2012   **Incredible discrimination**

Editor: "More Time for Justice" (editorial. 5/7) again backs a rank injustice by supporting Assemblywoman Margaret Markey's latest attempt to punish independent private, including religious, institutions, by lifting for one year the statute of limitations for civil suits involving child sex-abuse in such a manner as to exempt almost entirely all public institutions – including public schools and public childcare institutions – from such legislation's effects.

Several times in recent years Mrs. Markey has tried, but happily, failed to push through this discriminatory, divisive legislation. Even in her last attempt, when public pressure forced her to modify the text to include public institutions on an almost equal basis, her legislation failed.

Beyond the particular discriminating nature of the Markey Bill, statutes of limitations exist for very serious reasons and should not be modified unless even graver reasons argue for such a step.

Because the present version of Mrs. Markey's Bill has reverted to its original discriminatory nature, it is hard to avoid suspicion that a personal vendetta is at work. The Times has besmirched itself by backing rank discrimination against all private, independent and religious institutions in New York State.

May 8, 2012
Rank discrimination – not a peep from The Times

Editor: It is ironic that your 5/8 editorial "Monitoring Care for the Disabled" is in part negated by your 5/7 editorial "More Time for Justice" supporting Assemblywoman Markey's bill that would make it virtually impossible for children sex-abused in state facilities from later introducing civil suits for damages.

Were the place of treatment or care a private, including religious, facility, on the other hand, civil suits could be introduces ad libitum long after the alleged abuse had taken place.

Discrimination? The Markey bill reeks of it.

May 10, 2012   Choose: one nation under God

Editor: Now that Mr. Obama has clearly declared himself in support of same-sex marriage, the citizenry will, indeed, have a clear choice to make: the secularist path to abortion, sterilization, contraception, approval for homosexual activity, homosexual marriage, coercion for those who resist, assisted suicide, euthanasia, research destruction of human embryos OR the path of one nation under God affirming that man and his nature and his institutions are not autonomous but under the rule of God in His Creation. Reason and experience identify that rule: It is called the natural moral law.

May 11, 2012
Gross indecency: second try, Mr. Sulzberger, where are you?

Editor: On May 10, page A-11 The Times published a half-page, color advertisement for the Breast Cancer Awareness Campaign (apparently paid for by the Esteé Lauder Companies) that featured four young women – two black and two white, nubile, naked and beautiful, with only the lower part of their faces showing, gripping one another intimately at their breast, torso and buttocks levels.

Promoting support for the Breast Cancer Awareness Campaign is a laudable effort; but sexualizing the appeal, as this advertisement clearly does, only contributes to the degrading and debasing of women in our society as sexual objects. Moreover, breast cancer ordinarily attacks more mature women.

In any case, would you want your mother, wife, sister or daughter to appear in an ad of this kind? Modesty is a virtue that goes out the window with advertisements of this kind. Men also, less frequently, get breast cancer. Would they be similarly portrayed?

Please think on it.

May 25, 2012   The difference is in kind

Editor: Mae Kuykendall ("A Way Out of the Same-Sex

Marriage Mess," Op-Ed, 5/24) thinks that a Supreme Court ruling requiring each state to recognize same-sex marriages performed in any other state will gradually end the current confusion and contradiction over such marriages.

Such a legal tactic does not address the basic issue, which is the equal protection clause of the Constitution which same-sex marriage defenders understand as giving heterosexuals and homosexuals equal rights to marry one another. I maintain that it really doesn't or it shouldn't.

A heterosexual couple enters a union which by nature universally and from the beginning includes the intrinsic purpose of generating children. A homosexual couple enters a union which cannot generate children and of its nature excludes such generation. The two entities chosen are radically different.

Persons can be said to have equal rights with respect to the same entity or object; but, in this case, the entities which are the object of the right are not the same; they are radically different. The one is directed to an intrinsically generative union; the other, to an intrinsically non-generative union. The two deserve different names.

The accidental qualities that distinguish, for example, parties to an inter-racial, inter-ethnic, inter-tribal, inter-caste or inter-religious marriage do not impede their exercising their right to the same object; namely, the intrinsically generative union of marriage. The homosexual couple, on the other hand, seeks to exercise an entirely different right, the right to a homosexual union, a union which intrinsically excludes the possibility of generation. Thus having equal rights to marriage doesn't automatically entail having equal rights to a homosexual union.

To establish the equal rights of a person to a homosexual union, the first step would have to be to change the definition of marriage to: the union between two persons of the opposite-sex, or of the same-sex. In so doing society would make a change heretofore unheard of in the history of the human race and initiate an abrupt confrontation with nature. No state or society originally defined marriage; no state or society can claim any authority to re-define this irreversible and irreplaceable institution of nature.

What marriage has been (and is) is a self-evident truth immediately available to our experience. Such a redefinition would be equally (ir-) rational as would legislating that a woman will be called a man and a man, a woman, meaning they are the same. But they are not the same. Neither are marriage and homosexual union the same. And having a right to the one doesn't entail having a right to the other.

May 29, 2012   State forcing its dogma on the church

Editor: "The Politics of Religion" (editorial, 5/28) misrepresents the issue of the suits filed by many Catholic dioceses, health-care, educational and social-service agencies concerning the HHS mandate.

The original material element of the mandate was and is not simply contraception but, also, sterilization, chemical and surgical and potentially abortifacient drugs, all "neutral" elements advancing a "compelling" government interest only for those who have already adopted this view.

The formal point in contention, however, is something much broader; namely, limiting the concept of religious ministry to those institutions whose aim is to propagate the faith, by mainly employees of the same faith, to clients mainly of the same faith. The contrivances proposed by HHS, when challenged, to lift the insurance mandate for these "neutral" services from otherwise conscience-bound institutions suggest makeshift wizardry. They do not remove the necessary and morally objectionable cooperation required of these institutions with this "neutral" mandate.

Sadly, what you have called "phony" in an earlier editorial and, now, "bogus," is a grave concern to many millions of citizens whose Church is now portrayed as seeking to force its dogma on society, whereas, in fact, it is the State actually forcing its dogma on the Church.

June 1, 2012 **The child of rape is innocent**

Editor: "The Rights of Female Soldiers," (editorial, 6-1) presents the tragic and traumatic case of assaulted female soldiers now pregnant from this violent act. Shall the government pay for their abortions? Many will cry out, Yes, Yes?

But those will not even consider an abortion who hold uncompromisingly to the moral principle: Thou shalt not slay the innocent. The child conceived by violence is nonetheless from that moment a human being destined, without interference, to develop before and after birth to the adults we now are. Shall we brutalize and dismember this innocent child? All should cry out, No, No?

Government must, of course, provide all necessary care in this situation for both mother and child before and after birth, including assistance with adoption and every other moral option.

But - Neither men nor women have any reproductive rights. They have a reproductive power which is rightly exercised only in the love union of marriage. Though women pregnant by assault have endured a heinously violent act, one violent act does not justify another even more violent act, the slaying of an innocent human being in the womb.

June 4, 2012   **Equivocation is a blatant falsehood**

Editor: "In Defense of Marriage" (editorial, 6/4) subtly uses this title to denote both heterosexual and homosexual unions, to which, you hold, citizens should be able to choose as marriage under the equal protection clause of the 14th Amendment.

This reasoning is false. Why? The person choosing a heterosexual marriage and one choosing a homosexual union choose radically different objective realities.

The first enters a union which by nature universally and from time immemorial includes the intrinsic purpose and possibility of generating children. The second enters a union which cannot generate children and of its nature universally excludes such generation.

The equal protection of the law presumes the same or a rationally equivalent object. Between a heterosexual marriage and a homosexual union this is not the case.

The first step in advancing your goal would be to pass an amendment to the Constitution: "In the United States of America the word marriage shall be understood to mean a legally recognized heterosexual or homosexual union of two persons." Then those seeking either union would have equal protection.

The problem with such an amendment is that it defies nature, which universally and from time immemorial has disqualified homosexual persons from marrying one another.

June 11, 2012   **No value to the fertilized ovum**

Editor: "How Morning-After Pills Really Work" (editorial, 6/9) accepts current research that this pill does not impede implementation of the fertilized ovum in the womb but merely impedes ovulation.

But this is of little consequence since, as you say, besides approving early access to this pill without a doctor's prescription, you also approve RU-486, "which does abort an implanted embryo."

Decades ago your (then) editorial writer Soma Golden admitted on "this page" the scientific fact that a new human life begins at fertilization. The difference, she wrote, is over what value we attribute to this new human life.

Clearly "this page" accords no value to this new human life.

June 11, 2012
Marriage and the homosexual union: radically different

Editor: "In Defense of Marriage Act, Exposed" (editorial, 6/11) concludes apodictically with "the Defense of Marriage Act (heterosexual) clearly violates equal protection."

But is it so clear? The person choosing a heterosexual marriage and one choosing a homosexual union choose radically different objective realities.

The first enters a union which by nature universally and from time immemorial includes the intrinsic purpose and possibility of generating children. The second enters a union which cannot generate children and of its nature universally excludes such generation.

The equal protection of the law presumes the same or a rationally equivalent object to which the right is directed and its exercise protected. Between a heterosexual marriage and a homosexual union this is not the case.

How shall we make them the same? By giving the same name to both? That's an old philosophical heresy: nominalism.

June 15, 2012
Deliberate deception and discrimination

Editor: Your reports (6/13, 6/14) on legislative efforts to provide a "window" for persons alleging sexual abuse as minors several decades ago cites the Markey Bill repeatedly introduced, considered and then defeated in the NYS Legislature that would have targeted private institutions and left public schools and municipalities virtually exempt from such suits.

In the 2009 debate on this bill, its principal advocate was finally pressured to eliminate the outrageous discriminatory exemption for public institutions, but the bill was still defeated.

(In Colorado, Joan Fitz-Gerald and Marci Hamilton, mentioned in your reports, collaborated in the same maneuver: targeting the private institutions, being forced then to include the public, finally being blown away by the opposed public school interests.)

Now, in its current (Feb. 2012) version, the opposed Markey bill has let stay the discriminatory protections for public institutions and schools. Since the overwhelming majority of private institutions are Catholic, how can any fair-minded citizen fail to see this version of the bill as anything other than a continuance of a vendetta against the Catholic Church?

August 6, 2012
Pregnancy a disease to be prevented or ended?

Editor: The American Civil Liberties Union argues (letters printed 8/6) that the Obama contraception rule (add sterilization, abortifacient drugs) prevents employers from denying this "critical health care coverage" to those employees whose personal beliefs accept such devices and so the rule prevents discrimination. This is a deeply flawed argument.

It is based on the premise that pregnancy is a disease, like cancer, diabetes or heart disease, which it is not. Pregnancy is a natural human process, which nature itself tells us how simply and harmlessly to initiate or forbear.

Those whose personal beliefs permit them or even compel them to use the devices and procedures mentioned can easily do so; they are everywhere available like jelly beans and chewing gum; and more potent drugs may be just down the line. No one need seek employment with those whose conscience objects – and whose religion may teach them to object – and force them to join the assault on pregnancy by providing such coverage or cooperating in providing it to all their employees under the fallacious banner "critical preventive health care." The banner is false advertising.

This view is not that of a tiny sect with peculiar ideas but a widespread human community whose convictions are firmly rooted in the ethical tradition of our civilization.

August 28, 2012
Bashed for adhering to traditional moral views

Editor: You harshly rebuke Candidate Paul Ryan for his "social extremism" (editorial, 8/27) citing mainly, as the basis for your censure, his adherence to moral norms of our classic Judaeo-Christian civilization: respect for the right to life of the preborn child, which no man or woman has a right to kill; opposition to "birth control" that includes sterilization procedures and abortifacient drugs coercively provided for all; his firm support for the natural-law structure of marriage as the conjugal man-woman bond open to life; his opposition to equating homosexual orientation with homosexual activity leading to the so-called equal right of homosexuals to "marry" one another.

It's strange that a potential national leader should be so severely rebuked for his adherence to moral norms that have guided our civilization for centuries.

September 21, 2012
Hypocrisy at the highest and oldest level

Editor: You report (9/20 – A-22) that Governor Cuomo and Mayor Bloomberg are "upset" because two Republican state senators who provided key votes for homosexual "marriage" last year may now be defeated in their own primary bids for re-election.

But no one was upset (then or now) when Mr. Cuomo last year strong-armed these and other senators to vote "his way" on the issues and when Mr. Bloomberg offered (it was accepted), in effect, a $10,300 per-senator bribe for them to do the same thing. Not a peep. King Midas did even more later by hosting a high-dollar fundraiser for his liege men in the senate.

What if the archbishop of New York had offered (personally or through a lay proxy) a similar stipend to each of four state senators (party doesn't matter) to vote "his way" on homosexual "marriage". Opposed politicians, commentators, media people, homosexual activists and The Times editorial board would have descended on St. Patrick's Cathedral and reduced it figuratively to dust.

A bonfire generated by all the garbage in Naples (the Atlantis Naples) could not emit as sweet an aroma as that delivered by the "upsetment" of Messrs. Cuomo and Bloomberg when the democratic process does not go their way.

September 21, 2012   **Easy hypocrisy**

Editor: "Vox Pop Trumps the Parish Bulletin" (editorial, 9/20) reeks with hypocrisy for rebuking a Catholic parish bulletin that re-printed part of a public letter signed by seven former US ambassadors to the Holy See endorsing Mitt Romney for president. Over the last decade numerous Protestant and Jewish clergy in the pulpit or apart from it have publically endorsed candidates for president and other high offices. Not a peep from The Times.

Examples: In 2000 – A Queens minister and elected official Floyd Flake endorsed Democrat Al Gore; Rick Lazio and Hillary Clinton campaigned in a synagogue in the Hamptons; the Black Ministers Council of New Jersey endorsed Democrat Jon Corzine for governor.

In 2010 Minister Clinton M. Miller asked his Baptist congregation to vote for Democrat gubernatorial candidate Andrew Cuomo.

In African-American neighborhoods it has been common for some Baptist and AME pastors to make political endorsements in church. Our incumbent President recently called upon African-Americans "to go to your faith community" and organize "congregation captains" for his re-election.   Wife Michelle Obama recently told a Nashville AME congregation that there is "no better place" to talk about political issues than in church.

And do you remember when three major US Jewish organizations endorsed Democrat Walter Mondale for president?

How about it, friends? What's sauce for the goose is sauce for the gander.

October 4, 2012   **Huge begging of the question**

Editor: "Contraception and Religious Liberty" (editorial

10/4) praises Federal Judge Carol Jackson for dismissing a secular, for-profit mining company owner's suit against the contraception mandate as a violation of his religious freedom.

The content of the so-called contraception mandate is constantly blurred by omitting reference to its inclusion, beyond contraceptives, of sterilization procedures and drugs labeled by their manufacturers as potentially abortifacient. The mandated insurance, moreover, is not for curing illness but for inhibiting or ending pregnancy.

Judge Jackson maintains that the mandate is "neutral…expanding women's access to health care." This is a huge and ever-present begging of the question. The law actually imposes a particularist ideology on the nation.

Were the mandate further expanded to include "health care" benefits such as chemical and surgical abortion, assisted suicide and euthanasia, its so-called neutrality would be powerfully shorn away.

October 18, 2012   Natural science clinches the truth

Editor: Michael Peppard's Op-Ed "Paul Ryan, Catholic Dissident," 10/16, the printed responding letters and your editorial "If Roe v. Wade Goes," Oct.-17 miss several important distinctions in what appears as a political – religious debate on abortion.

First, as Fr. Orsi (letter) states, it is entirely consistent with Catholic moral teachings in the present circumstances of our country, where abortion is available virtually on demand with little prospect of ending it, to advocate and vote for a restriction of this huge evil to the three cases mentioned. One acts licitly to achieve such a practicable goal. Mr. Ryan is no dissident.

Second, the definition of abortion – the deliberate slaying of an innocent human being in his or her mother's womb - is not religion-originated, but a scientific fact. Abortion always entails brutality and death for the unborn child. Obscuring these truths is a ghastly deception.

Third, neither men nor women have a moral right to slay the innocent pre-born child. No human power, the state or the electorate, has or can confer such a right. Spouses have a conjugal right to those acts which ordinarily result in conception; but, from then on, their <u>duty</u> is to protect and nurture the new human being before and after birth.

Must the Catholic Church stand resolutely and compassionately for these truths? Yes, it must.

October 29, 2012   Twisting words and phrases

Editor: Thomas L. Friedman (The Week in Review, 10/28, "Why I am Pro-Life") cites several life-related issues he supports and regards such support as necessary to qualify a person as pro-life. He vehemently rebukes those "pro-lifers" whose only issue seems to be abortion and who may oppose these other issues.

At first the reader might think Columnist Friedman is backing Vatican II, Pope John Paul II and Cardinal Bernardin on what is called the consisted ethic of life. But read carefully, however, Mr. Friedman expresses his strong support for abortion on demand (described as the greatest of evils by the other sources just mentioned) and refers to this evil euphemistically as "women's personal choice over what happens in their own bodies."

He presents Mayor Bloomberg as the pro-life hero because, supporting many humanitarians life-related causes, he strongly backs abortion on demand.

Predictably, Columnist Friedman tells us that the traditional pro-lifers' starting point - human life begins at conception - is a "belief" acceptable as long as they go along with all the other "pro-life" causes on which even supporters of the same disagree as to a uniform solution.

The one thing you must avoid if you want to be qualified as pro-life is opposition to abortion on demand. Bio-medical science tells us authoritatively that a new human being begins at conception and, left undisturbed in its habitat and properly nourished, will develop before birth and after birth into the person writing or reading this letter. Abortion is deliberately destroying this new human life in the womb. Obscuring this scientific fact is at best ignorance and at worst hypocrisy.

November 1, 2012
Nature makes impossible same-sex unions

Editor: "Marriage is on the Ballot" (editorial, 10/31) sounds your familiar call for homosexuals to have the same right to marry one another as do heterosexuals; you dismiss the irreducible but complementary differences between man and woman that alone enable them to forge an authentic marital union. Finally you dismiss the serious legal and social consequences that homosexual "marriages" over time will bring to our society.

Nature from the beginning and universally has recognized only a man and a woman as candidates for the marital union, not because of any "inequality" with homosexual persons but because nature itself has universally disqualified persons of the same sex from marrying one another. They lack the inherent property to join their bodies in the marital union. Because of this radical disqualification, their union should be called by a name other than marriage. It may be an affectionate union but it cannot even in principle be procreative and therefore not marriage.

What citizens in some states are being asked to give approval legally and socially on the ballot is not marriage but homosexual union and the legal and social consequences for our society this approval will bring.

November 9, 2012   A leap over the cliff

Editor: "A Big Leap for Marriage Equality" (editorial, 11/8) continues to deny the radical difference between a heterosexual couple and a homosexual couple seeking to be recognized legally and socially as married. They are entering metaphysically different states of life – one, marriage; the other, a homosexual union. The law "leaping" to equate the two more likely will generate serious legal and social conflicts in decades to come.

From time immemorial, nature has been our guide for marriage: a man and a woman in a permanent union that in principle is procreative and ordinarily gives rise to a family, the foundation of human society everywhere. On the other hand, nature itself universally disqualifies two persons of the same sex from entering the marriage union. And where the same-sex union has been tried, serious legal and social conflicts have begun to emerge.

It's time for persons to set aside slogans such as marriage equality, freedom to marry, the so-called principle of fairness for homosexual persons, a stand against justice and proceed to a serious dialogue on philosophical anthropology to identify what nature tells us about the unique prerequisite for marriage. In short, that will show us that a homosexual union can never be a marriage.

December 4, 2012
Equivocation may be fun, but it's false

Editor: Columnist Frank Bruni ("Dear President Clinton," The Week in Review, 12/2) indicts former President Clinton and wife Hillary for their tepid support of same-sex

250

"marriage." He invokes the familiar slogan "marriage equality" and the legal principle "equal protection under the law" to buttress his complaint.

Though slogans and principles used as slogans may tend to educe a quick assent, they do not, in fact, support Frank Bruni's or any other advocate's brief for same-sex "marriage." Why?

Marriage is an institution of nature, based on the union of the two sexes for the consequent propagation in family units of the human race. No civil government eons ago set up marriage and no civil government now can re-fashion it and give it a broad-tent identity of polygamous or polyandrous, as well as monogamous heterosexual or homosexual unions.

Two persons seeking a homosexual union as a "marriage" and two persons seeking the heterosexual union of marriage seek radically different relationships. Nature makes universally impossible in the former the consummation of the potentially life-giving union constitutive of marriage. The two unions do not deserve the same name.

Since nature universally disqualifies same-sex partners from marrying, advocating the legalization of such unions constitutes (in this re-buff of nature) an abandonment of reason.

January 22, 2013   **Going all out for a failure**

Editor: "Stem Cell Gets a Reprieve" (editorial, 1/21) urges Congress to remove "virtually all restrictions on this promising area of [embryo stem cell] research."

While acknowledging that such research "kills" or "harms" the human embryo - the reason why large numbers of citizens vigorously oppose it - you do not refer to the scientific certainty that a new human being is launched at conception and thus, even in the case of a one-day-old human embryo, a human being is killed - a new human being, innocent and totally vulnerable, is destroyed in this research.

So it's OK deliberately to kill certain human beings because of their newness of age. Arguing that one-day-old or six-month-old pre-born human beings are not worthy of human and legal protection is a debatable philosophical opinion. What deserves acceptance is the universal judgment of natural science that a new human life begins at conception.

Adult stem cell research, involving no destruction of human life, has proved eminently successful for therapeutic purposes. On the other hand, human embryo stem cell research pursued for over a decade and a half has yielded virtually no reward for the support of this research touted so "promising" decades ago.

January 28, 2013   Balderdash too much to take

Editor: Frank Bruni's "Catholicism's Curse," (1/27) seems to adopt historian and author Garry Wills as his personal theologian and guide for his ultra-acerbic and, in part, woefully misinformed column of Jan. 27.

Well known as an intellectual and author, now somewhat disaffected Catholic, Wills presents himself as a practicing Catholic but has long distanced himself from key teachings of the Church and maintains a Catholic identity only on his own terms. Academics and journalists seeking comment on the Church should avoid consulting only such Catholics. Fully committed Catholics should be the first source for such information and comment.

One of Bruni's complaints has a recognized base: the clergy sexual abuse of minors. Though relatively only a small minority of the clergy were involved and only a relatively few bishops-ordinary (heads of diocese) in major misjudgments, the results were no less injurious to the victims and to the Church itself, which has learned a bitter lesson. Hindsight, of course, is advantageous: it gives added ammunition to the critics and causes greater embarrassment for those who seriously erred.

But on all the other "curses" cited by Bruni via Wills, close study will show that ignorance, personal disagreement and disaffection are at the basis of such charges: the Holy See as "gilded enclave," "frequently out-of-step" with the world, "relishing its roles, rituals, regulations and condemnations," insisting on the "invention of mortals," hounding the nuns. Take it from a priest with 55-years experience as parish priest, professor, journalist, editor and pastor: This indictment of Church leadership by Messrs. Wills and Bruni is balderdash. Pure balderdash.

January 28, 2013   Homosexual acts are always wrong

Editor: Your "The Boy Scouts Fall Short" (editorial, 1/30) once again bases itself on entirely different starting points from that of the Boy Scouts of America – and, we might add, that of the Catholic Church, the Eastern Orthodox Churches, Orthodox Judaism, Classical Protestantism and Islam.

Your starting points: Homosexual acts, as well as the homosexual condition, are natural, good and acceptable moral choices for all so inclined.

The other ethical starting point, supported by our entire Western civilization up to now and represented by the religions just mentioned (including Muslims) holds that homosexual <u>practice</u>, whatever its cause or origin, is always wrong and seriously so. The homosexual condition as such is ethically neutral, having nevertheless, an inherent tendency to wrongful acts. The diverse positions build on those diverse starting points.

Both are principled positions, the pro-homosexual being a very recent development, though homosexual persons have always been part of society.

The poet John Milton once said: '*Magna est veritas et praevalebit*" (Great is the truth and it shall prevail). May it be so.

January 28, 2013
Accidental quality <u>vs</u> fundamental difference

Editor: "Beyond Selma-to-Stonewall" (editorial 1/28) on "marriage equality" for homosexual persons perpetuates the philosophical fallacy that the concept of equality must ignore the radical diversity of nature.

Man and woman are equal but not the same. Nature has imposed their radical sexual diversity: A man cannot bear a child and cannot be given such a right. A woman cannot generate a child of herself and by herself. She cannot be given such a right. Nature has imposed this limitation on both.

Nature also established the remedy for this radical limitation in the equal marital bond. Inter-racial, inter-ethnic, inter-social (heterosexual) marriages are significantly different. The distinguishing difference here, however, is not the ability to procreate, but an accidental quality of the person.

Man and woman are equal but not the same. And this radical sexual diversity imposed by nature does not diminish their equality as persons by making it impossible for same-sex persons to marry.

Feb. 4, 2013   Pub. NYT Feb. 8, 2013
From phony to sensible?

Editor: "A Good Compromise on Contraception" (editorial, 2/2) calls the administration's latest revision of the HHS Mandate as "sensitive" and protecting "both religious liberties and women's access."

Your earlier editorial (2/11/12) at the beginning of this controversy labeled religious liberty a "phony crisis". If this latest revision suitably protects, as you say, this "phony crisis," your earlier judgment must have been a huge goof or a deliberate affront to those who protested its infringement on their religious freedom.

Moreover, the mandate required and requires free insurance not only for "contraception," but also for abortion-inducing drugs (as admitted by their manufacturers), chemical and surgical sterilizations and a broad range of FDA-approved contraceptives. None of these are "neutral" issues for the Catholic Church, which also had long advocated a broad new health-care law, which then, unfortunately, it had to oppose when the HHS mandate was included, forcing it to violate its moral principles. Claiming that the opposition was contrived to defeat Obama is a false if not nefarious claim.

The "sensitivity" you attribute to this latest revision (which calls for a careful evaluation) is that of the pragmatist: "Let's cut our losses, declare victory and move on."

February 4, 2013
Pay for what can be used only for a wrongful purpose?
No.

Editor: E. J. Dionne "An End to this church-state battle," (column, 2/4) soft-soaps the controversy, hopefully nearing an end, in which the Obama Administration – HHS sought to impose a mandate forcing the Catholic Church and other objecting religious groups to violate their moral principles, accept secularistic ones and give free in their manifold Church-sponsored institutions to women employees and other female clients for abortion-inducing drugs, sterilization and broad range of contraceptives.

Columnist Dionne makes it look like a great misunderstanding. Both sides sought to protect religious liberty: the liberty of the Church to act in accord with its moral principles and the liberty of its women employees to get these "birth control" instruments in free "health care" insurance. The authors of the mandate were mistaken: they thought the time was ripe to force the Church to capitulate and accept secular moral standards. They erred. But they'll try again, as Governor Cuomo is doing with his brazen support of ultra-liberal features in the proposed Reproductive Health Act.

Women and men can obtain all over this country the instruments which were to be provided by the mandate. There is no barrier to their access. But no one should expect that the Catholic Church will supply them.

February 14, 2013   Barking at the papal heels

Editor: Pope Benedict's decision, announced Feb.11 at almost age 86, to lay down his heavy burden as Bishop of Rome, Successor of Peter and primate of the universal Catholic Church has apparently encouraged some Pope-bashers to emerge to bark at the papal heels.

Among the first of these, the historian and author Gary Wills, a Catholic of sorts, arrived, as it were, in a chauffeured limousine on Feb. 13 to the Op-Ed page of The Times. While The Times news stories from Rome reported overwhelming outpourings of love and gratitude to this brilliant and humble Chief Shepherd of the Church, the op-ed page presented us with a bitterly acid portrayal of the papal office.

I comment here only on historian Wills's deceptive historical references: No popes, he says, and the majority ruled in the councils of the ancient Church. The term pope, it is true, was not commonly used for the Bishop of Rome until 500 AD. But the first great Councils: Nicaea, 325, acknowledged the existing broad geographical authority for Rome, as did Constantinople I (381), which acknowledged Rome's primacy and conferred secondary status on that See (Constantinople). At Ephesus (431) Celestine, Bishop of Rome, presided through Cyril (Bishop of Alexandria); and at Chalcedon (451), Leo the Great of Rome presided through his legates; and his doctrinal letter was accepted and hailed by all.

All the voting participants at these early general councils, save some Roman delegates, were bishops. Shades of Vatican II.

February 19, 2013   An academic way out of his field

Editor: Historian Garry Wills's new book Why Priests (Viking, 2013; reviewed 2/17), like his earlier Bare Ruined Choirs and Papal Sins, represents a demolition job on the Catholic Church and, though Wills does not acknowledge it, on the Eastern Orthodox Churches, the other ancient Eastern Churches and much of classical Reformation Church tradition. Randall Balmer, an Episcopal priest-chairman of the religion department at Dartmouth College, offers (in his review, 2/17) a fairly detailed summery of the book but a sparse evaluation, noting the similarity of Prof. Wills's views to those of Martin Luther and blandly approving Wills's sign-off: "There is one God and Jesus is one of his prophets... and I am one of his millions of followers." That's nice to know.

In fact, basing himself on personal study and reflecting conclusions reached long ago by some 18th-20th century mainly continental biblical critics, Wills tells us (and he is really sorry to have to tell millions of us naïve believers) that Jesus was no priest, offered no sacrifice, nor did his early followers consider themselves to be or to do such.

Such misunderstandings emerged, he tells us, in the 2nd – 3rd centuries, when based on the fuzzy New Testament Letter to the Hebrews, some followers of Jesus arrogantly attributed priestly functions and authoritative positions to themselves, giving rise to the "hierarchy" and the "papacy." All this, Wills contends, is a distortion of who Jesus was (a prophet)and what he wanted his followers to be, a community of brothers and sisters living together in peace and love with the Eucharist a symbolic meal reflecting that community spirit.

As one who taught biblical literature and early Church history for some years on the college level, I can say only that few if any scholars in this field - in the great Christian traditions cited above - will be able to educe more than a smile when reading this book. Is he kidding? No, Prof. Wills is not kidding. But those without scientific competence in this particular field of scholarship may be persuaded by this Pulitzer Prize winner's new book Why Priests? more aptly described as a fantasy on the New Testament and early Church history.

February 19, 2013
Let us bow down and worship Man

Editor: Frank Bruni (Op-Ed "Catholicism's Curses, 1/27 and "The Pope's Muffled Voice, 2/18) seems to evince both anger (1/20) at the Church and depression (2/18) over the papal transition. Too much publicity, he says, where is it? The Times could not hatch an editorial on the event that, Bruni tells us, has little real influence on people's lives, even Catholic lives. The Catholic Church's message, he says, in effect, is from the past to the past; it's on the wane.

Frank Bruni himself has made clear that he has long since passed from the Church flock to the religion of secularism: God is man, man is totally autonomous, his standards are his own, drawn from his own experiences, natural science and public opinion. Many from academia, the media and the government-in-place have in fact embraced this religion. Let us bow down and worship.

Does this present mise-en-scène discourage? We are used to the ups and downs in particular place at particular times. But the Catholic Church looks to its foundational promise: "Behold, I am with you all days even unto the end of the world" (Mt. 28:20).

February 20, 2013   Never too late to kill that intruder

Editor: "Reproductive Rights in New York" (editorial, 2/20) not surprisingly endorsed Gov. Cuomo's (not yet released in detail) abortion expansion program, officially the Reproductive Health Act, similar or identical to a bill already introduced in both houses of the Legislature. The Governor's final version is expected soon.

This new expansion of abortion "rights" will, if passed, designate abortion in state law as a fundamental right of women, to be accessible all through pregnancy, which is defined as beginning with implantation (not conception), able to be performed by non-physicians without any parental notification in cases of pregnant minors and with abortion becoming part of public health law rather than criminal law. If enacted, this proposed law will make New York the abortion capital of the world.

The basic deceptions underlying this continuing discussion over abortion are two: The first is the refusal of some – a great many – to accept the unanimous judgment of bio-medical science that from conception we have a new human being. Abortion is killing that new human being.

The second deception concerns reproductive "rights." Neither men nor women have any "right" to reproduction, to a child. They have a reproductive power, given them by nature, to place in marital love the actions that ordinarily result in the conception of a child. But they have no right to (demand) the child, but only to the complementary expression of love that ordinarily gives rise to the child, the gift of nature, to be nourished and cherished, never to be harmed in any way. Moreover, man and woman have a right to beget a child only within the marital bond, also a dictate of nature.

The discussion of abortion as one of "reproductive rights," omitting these considerations, is vastly misleading.

March 1, 2013   Kung: listen to me, he says. We have.

Editor: Prof. Hans Küng, 84, ("A Vatican Spring?" – How to Save the Church, Op-Ed, 2/28) has come out of retirement at Tubingin to deliver a missive with his new plan (actually, his old package of steps) to save the Church from self-destruction.

For the period 1966-79, after the II Vatican Council, Prof. Küng became the bull in the Catholic china shop demolishings, from his own personal theological island, many distinctive features of Church teaching and structure. Finally, in 1979, at the initiative of Pope John Paul II, Church authority withdrew his license to teach Catholic theology and he had to transfer to another department at Tubingin.

At the time many of us (see my letter published 1/7/80) still hoped that the question "How to Save Prof. Küng?" could be answered if the theological community, admiring, as we did, his extraordinary learning and creativity, could encourage him and persuade him to reconstitute himself within, rather than outside, the consensus of this world-wide community.

Alas, it was not to be so; and his now-proffered "spring" for the salvation of the Church is little more than a dust-off of that set forth forty years ago for reform of the Church: a free association of Christians, de-bureaucratization, the purge of various doctrines, accepting multiple marriages and divorces, married men and women clergy and a less stringent sexual ethic. Small reformist groups have adopted Prof. Küng's plan he now puts forward vehemently once again.

The Church leadership has consistently rejected Prof. Küng's package. All his admirers wish him a return to a peaceful, happy, healthful and productive retirement.

March 11, 2014 Pub. NYT March 13, 2014
The name is precious

Editor: Peter Manseau's essay reflects on the word "Catholic," which in ordinary sociological an doctrinal conversations identifies Christians, institutions and teachings in full communion or harmony with the bishop and the Church of Rome.

Belonging to a variety of rights (Roman [the largest], Greek, Maronite, Melkite, Syrian, Chaldrean, Ukrainian and even Anglican), these Christians have their distinguishing feature their full communion with the Church and the bishop of Rome.

The other classical Christian Church communities – canonical Orthodox, Anglican and Protestant – claim to be Catholic in some sense. But all through history, as today, small Christian groups – even individual congregations – have set themselves up as independent Christian churches, some including the word "Catholic" in their names.

The way to identify the authentically Catholic is to identify who is their bishop and ask whether he is in full communion with the Bishop of Rome. If yes, the congregation is Catholic. If no, they are not.

May 21, 2013   **Anything goes? Yes No**

Editor: Over the last few months Op-Ed Columnist Frank Bruni has been presenting himself as a "sensitive" critic of Catholic teachings and practices which he once adhered to as a believing and worshiping Catholic. His latest foray into mediatorship ("One School's Catholic Teaching," 5/21) concerns an Ohio female Catholic high school gym teacher who was asked to resign when school officials learned she had publicly taken up bed and board with another female. What's wrong with this choice? asks Frank. She was a great teacher.

Well, a public homosexual union (not just a homosexual inclination, which is nobody else's business) conflicts with the natural moral law and the teaching of the Catholic Church (and many other religions.) Those who staff Catholic institutions, such as elementary and secondary schools, are expected to at least avoid any public rejection of the Church's definitive teachings or a manner of life that publicly conflicts with that teaching. So the otherwise good gym teacher in a Catholic high school – having publicly entered a homosexual union - was asked to resign.

Another, perhaps clearer example: if all of a sudden it were discovered Governor Cuomo was teaching a First Communion class in one or other of the parishes where he may reside, the pastor would have to thank the Governor for his services and express the hope that he may qualify again sometime in the future.

June 18, 2013   **You learned journalism; you can learn theology, if you want to.**

Editor: Op-Ed Columnist and budding theologian Frank Bruni ("The Pope's Gay Panic," 6/16) has added a new chapter to his several months' bashing of the Catholic Church. His current whipping-post for offender is what he considers "obvious truths" is the Church's teaching on homosexuality and homosexual acts. For Bruni, the bird, whose nature is to fly, is being told, "Sorry, you can't fly"; and this, the Church should realize, is manifestly ridiculous.

For the Church, however, man's fallen nature as such or any of its particular realizations is not necessarily free from every deficiency, inherited or acquired, physical or emotional. Thus all human beings manifest some kind of physical or emotional deficiency or disorder in their lives.

The Church in its teaching tells us what the cause of this weakness is: sin entered the world through Adam, the head of the human race; and as a result of his originating sin, which is called a transgression, the evil of original sin has enveloped the whole of humanity, as has the redemption in Christ.

At a particular time we may not be able to explain by natural empirical science why a particular person suffers from a congenital disease, emotional or physical disorders and abnormalities in which general category the emotionally exclusive same-sex attractiveness may be included; but we don't, in that or in any other human disorder which can give rise to sinful action conclude that personal sin has taken place. As with every other kind of sin – this sin is imputed to the acting person only in so far as he or she maturely understands the wrongfulness involve in acting and gives sufficient consent to go ahead with the action.

It is not the state of experiencing the exclusive same-sex attractiveness that constitutes sin (though it is a condition that can lead to sin) but the actual choice of or implementing the homosexual action that constitutes sin (of course the case is radically different for those who seek lustful pleasure in either heterosexual or homosexual contact or both.)

Thus we must avoid a discussion of homosexuality and homosexual acts as related to Catholic teaching that is simplistic, shallow and misleading, hurtful both to those who experience same-sex attractiveness and to the Catholic Church teaching on this issue.

August 6, 2013 The premature infant struggling for life

Editor: "End of Life, at Birth" (Op-ed, 8/5) by Dr. April R. Dworetz presents the heart-rending dilemma facing parents and doctors when they must decide to save or allow to die many-weeks prematurely born infants, some with already pre-birth disabilities.

Clearly, a first step in this tragic matter should be directed to insuring the normal gestational period for mother and child. How can (especially very) premature deliveries be lessened and made rare? Is there a medical obligation to resuscitate one-pound already clinically dead infant? No. But the one-pound live or resuscitated infant is struggling to continue living. What help does he or she deserve to survive?

The premature infant struggling to live deserves every help current medical science can give him or her. Miracle, Dr. Dworetz's name for her one-pound premature infant example, was now likely to be discharged after extensive treatment but with chronic lung disease. Is that a reason to regret her survival? Will this disease be overcome by medical science in decades to come?

Who can say that marvelous medical advances will not take place in upcoming decades? Dr. Dworetz insists that Patrick Bouvier Kennedy, prematurely born at 34 weeks who lived for one day, would not have died today. We should not allow present infant deaths or present suffering to crush hope for the future.

Babies of Christian parents, our tiny brothers and sisters, if they cannot be saved, will be baptized and surrendered to a merciful God. But all such infants living and struggling to continue living deserves all the help we – parents, doctors, society – can give them.

October 24, 2013   Poor research; smearing the bishop

Editor: It is indeed unfortunate the Alison Smale in writing her story (Oct. 24, A-4) on German Bishop Van Elst's alleged "lavish spending" on himself contrasts the swift and decisive action of Pope Francis with that of the late Pope John Paul II who allegedly failed to take "public action when Bishop William Murphy of Rockville Centre, N.Y. drew criticism for a luxurious residential suite he had built in 2002, displacing 6 nuns."

Ms. Smale is dealing in poorly researched fantasy. The Cathedral Parish of St. Agnes, Rockville Centre renovated and converted an aged, three-story convent built to house about 60 nuns (six only, mainly seniors remaining) into: first floor – parish offices; second floor – youth center; third floor – residence for the diocesan bishop. The six nuns were offered another residence in accord with their needs.

The bishop's former residence (located a considerable distance from the cathedral parish property) was sold to provide, in part, funds for the renovation and conversion of the former convent's third floor to provide an up-to-date (2002) residence not only for the bishop (and his successors) but also for a full-time priest secretary, possible clergy guests and modest diocesan receptions.

That there was undue spending on a luxurious bishop's residence then is pure fantasy and its revival, now, also a smear.

December 2, 2013   Demolition expert

Editor: Bill Keller's half-page "Sex and the Single Priest" (Op-ed, 12/2) raises the hope, (vain, he knows) of dissident (and former, like himself) Catholics that the new Pope will adopt "their agenda": the priestly ordination of women, full acceptance of active homosexual practices (and therefore same-sex marriage) the consequent abolition of all sexual norms, including all norms concerning the conception and protection (before birth) of children, and an end to obligatory priestly celibacy in the Latin Church.

As always, we begin with a huge begging of the question: to what extent such changes are possible or desirable. The reformers or "progressives" have the idea, probably from their simple childhood catechism, that the Bishop of Rome, the Pope, is an absolute monarch who at the strike of the pen can change doctrines taught definitively in the past by pope and councils or policies and laws having grave reasons for their existence.

Can priestly celibacy be discussed? Of course. But it must be carefully and fully discussed. Anecdotal evidence or survey results from dissident or former Catholics (sorry, Bill) won't do. Please don't identify the experience of some with the experience of all. To Bill's friends who were unable to keep their solemn commitment, we say: God bless you; we hope you are happy. Let's work together to serve God's people until we meet at the Heavenly Banquet. But, in the meantime, Cheerio!

January 16, 2014   The new year: at odds forever?

Editor: "Abortion Restrictions in Texas and Beyond" (editorial, 1/8), "They Left a Good Ruling Alone" (editorial, 1/14) and "Abortion Rights before the Courts," (editorial, 1/15) build their case as always on two false premises – one, that women and men have "reproductive rights" that government cannot deny or intrude upon, the most basic example of which is the right to abortion.

What we have as human beings are reproductive powers which we can rightly use only in a specified context, namely, the bond of marriage between a man and a woman, nature's framework from which the family, the basic unit of society, emerges.

Who tells us this? Reason and the Judaeo-Christian ethic of our Western civilization and, increasingly, the ethic of our world civilization. Man and woman, husband and wife, parents and children: Nature stares us in the face. This framework is a self-evident truth.

If human beings had reproductive "rights," we could establish breeder farms and employ women and men to exercise their reproductive rights and provide babies as a business for those who want children but shun the reproductive process themselves.

267

It's laughable, preposterous and horrifying, isn't it? But that's where the logic of "reproductive rights" can take us.

The second premise: the refusal to acknowledge the indisputable scientific fact that in every case once conception has taken place – abortion kills a new and innocent human life: what is it worth?   Answer one: priceless, inviolable. Answer two: dispensable, disposable.

When we debate these two premises, we can at least have an intelligent dialogue on abortion and "problem" pregnancies. Without a common agreed standing point, we will be at odds forever.

January 6, 2014   Intellectual and legal solipsism

Editor: "New Victories for Marriage Equality" (editorial, 12/28) rejoices that same-sex "marriage" increasingly draws approval from judges, legislators and ordinary citizens. In fact, such persons show an increasing inability to grasp the radical difference and fundamental, unchangeable inequality between the heterosexual union – how ever qualified by racial, ethnic or social variations, all of which, in principle, admit of procreation – and the homosexual union, which absolutely excludes it.

The former union from time immemorial has borne the name marriage, which it owns by prescription; the latter does not qualify to be so named. Equal protection of the laws cannot apply in contexts where litigants seek protection or demand equality in respect to goods that are essentially diverse.

Judge Shelby's comments that "the individual's ability to make deeply held personal choices about love and family [must be] free from government intervention" and Judge Kennedy's earlier similar comments (the sodomy case, 2003) suggest that they both inhabit and invite us to join them in a solipsist intellectual world where all such decisions are made for oneself only by oneself. Abandon all reason, ye who enter here.

January 6, 2014   **Not so little in court**

Editor: To be exempt from the Obama Administration's HHS mandate to provide no-cost insurance to female employees for contraceptive devices, chemical and surgical sterilization and drugs labelled potentially abortifacient by their manufacturers, the Little Sisters of the Poor in Colorado must sign a self-certification stating that they object on religious grounds to providing insurance for such devices, procedures and drugs. This self-certification involves them, effectively, in delegating and authorizing a third party - a killergun, as it were - to provide in their stead what they hold to be immoral. Thus they become inevitably causal agents and accomplices in actions they deem evil.

The government and The Times describe the Sisters required action as merely signing a slip of paper which frees them from all responsibility, but which in reality makes them cooperators and accomplices, even if from a distance, in immoral acts. The Sisters are thus forced to violate their religious beliefs and go against what their consciences, based on their religious beliefs, tell them how to act in these circumstances.

This issue here is not government agreement with the religious, ethical or moral positions of the Little Sisters. The issue is whether the government can demand that the Sisters act in a way that violates their religious beliefs and their conscience decisions and as a result suffer this grievous spiritual burden. If non-compliant they suffer the heavy burden of financial ruin. They deserve exemptions from the HHS mandate.

January 23, 2014
Sexual orientation means sexual [homosexual] practice

Editor: The Federal Appeals Court judgment (1/21 in San Francisco, story 1/22, A-20) makes very clear a secondary but extremely important point in legal opinion: whenever in general discourse the phrase sexual orientation is used, it must now be taken to identify not only an exclusive same-sex attractiveness – homosexual attractiveness – but also homosexual activity. Homosexual attractiveness is nobody's business but a person's own, but homosexual activity brings the issue into a social context. Such activity is subject to evaluation.

Previous qualities identified and rejected as acceptable discriminatory principles – for example, race, ethnic origin, religious affiliation, age, economic or social background, disability – do not necessarily involve any activity. But sexual orientation necessarily in practice does.

The Federal Appeals Court now tells us that this activity has no morally objectionable quality before the law and therefore cannot be used as a criterion for any of such person from exercising and enjoying the same rights and privileges as other (heterosexual) citizens. That's a revolution for our civilization: Heterosexual (marital) and homosexual activity are on the same level. The Federal Appeals Court has delivered a new natural moral law for the country.

January 23, 2014
Solemn agreement just a piece of paper

Editor: Your 1/23 page-one story about the dismissal of a homosexual vice principal in a Seattle Catholic School because he "married" another man gives more prominence to the defense and promotion of homosexual activity than to the violation of the explicit or implicit contract he, other teachers and officials of Catholic institutions make in accepting their positions. If they find themselves in public conflict with the Church's doctrinal or moral teachings, they must resign.

Teenagers, inexperienced and with a strong and sincere emotional but, at most, minimal intellectual understanding of the issues at stake, can be easily maneuvered to support their former teacher. Nice photos, but intellectual sophistry in the message. On the same (continuing) page (17) the Washington March for Life got a small pix and no story. But the issue there was a witness by hundreds of thousands, including many young people, for innocent pre-born human life.

What a contrast between the values at stake: One man's trashing of a solemn commitment he had made; millions crying out: Let them live, our little brothers and sisters; let them live!

January 27, 2014 For the umpteenth time-why and how the HHS Mandate violates religious freedom

Editor: Your story (1/21) reporting the Supreme Court's extending its injunction blocking implementation of the so-called "contraception" mandate in the Affordable Care Act does not clearly show how and why this mandate violates religious freedom of the Little Sisters and other religious units with their beliefs.

First, the government "accommodation" requires them to sign a statement of their religious nature and authorizing and directing their insurance agent to provide in their stead the insurance specified by the mandate. In graphic terms, they have to engage a "killer gun" to do what they cannot morally do.

Thus they are involved causally in the whole procedure. They are made cooperators in the same action. They do not want to be involved in any way in providing or approving the use of the devices, procedures or drugs which the term "contraception" is used to denote; viz., contraception drugs, sterilization, chemical or surgical, or drugs labelled potentially abortifacients by their manufacturers. Furthermore, it is not clear what other drugs will be in the course of time approved for "contraception" but actually work in an abortifacient fashion and yet be able to be obtained through this insurance.

Thus those religious providers who judge the use of "contraceptives" chemical and surgical sterilization and abortifacient drugs morally and religiously objectionable rightly resist being forced to provide such insurance to their female employers.

January 29, 2014   **Important distinction**

Editor: "Contraception Before the Court" (editorial, 1/28) may mistakenly be read to say that the Supreme Court, in extending the injunction against inflicting the HHS mandate on the Little Sister of the Poor, modified the HHs rules and exempted the Little Sisters from the requirements making them accomplices or cooperators in providing the objectionable "contraception" service by delegation.

Carefully read, however, the court's stated requirements respect only the interim period before the Appeals Court issues its own decisions on the merits of the case.

The Supreme Court's modified rules, however, ironically, would seem to resolve the contested issue if the Appeals Court could order HHS to adopt them.

January 29, 2014   **False assumptions**

Editor: "A Formula for Repelling Women Voters" (editorial, 1/27) shows how several beggings of the question can create the appearance of proving that free "contraception" insurance for all and easy access to abortion for all can marvelously improve "women's health care" and honor their freedoms and "rights."

Premise One: Free contraception insurance for all female employees and easy access to abortion for all is a needed, substantial contribution to "women's health care and their freedoms." False. Contraception (devices, sterilization, drugs, including potential abortifacients) cure no illness. They are not "health care." They prevent or destroy pregnancy.

Premise Two: New, old or proposed legal restrictions on abortion deprive women of needed "health care." False. These services provide no cure for any illness. They are not health care. They are active or potential killers.

Premise Three: Tax credits for abortion are no more objectionable than tax credits or deductions for contributing to religious organizations! False. Equating upholding of human values in society with killing the innocent is an egregious distortion.

No. The formula for better women's "Health care" is respecting the dignity of women, supporting marriage, pregnancy, early childhood care, combatting poverty, improving education, providing through both government and private sources all the help needed to enable women to sustain what, for whatever reason, is a difficult pregnancy.

February 6, 2014

The philosophical basis – the third "religion"

Editor: "A Missing Argument on Contraceptives" (editorial, 2/6) refers to employers' "health plans" as covering "the full range of contraceptive services," phraseology used apparently to admit that far more than traditional contraception is involved; namely, contraceptive devices, plus surgical and chemical sterilization and drugs labelled by their manufacturers as potentially abortifacient.

Your grudging tolerance of the Religious Freedom Restoration Act of 1993 (evident in the editorial), as also your distain for the Hyde Amendment's prohibiting the use of federal monies for elective abortion, your egregious making equivalent of tax credits for abortion and contributions to religion and your fixed opposition to exempting any but "houses of worship," and consequently to the Little Sisters of the Poor Nursing Homes and, above all, to non-religious affiliated for-profit entrepreneurs – highlight your hard-based secularism, or secular humanistic, position.

Decades ago the late Supreme Court Justice William O. Douglas, no friend of religion, freely admitted that secular humanism - an intellectual amalgam based on opinions drawn from experimental science, sociology and rationalistic philosophy - was equivalently a religion.

It's this religion that some government leaders, some academics and other intellectuals today want to convince us is neutral and force upon the entire citizenry. Secular humanism – its metaphysics, ethics, bio-ethics- is not neutral and it deserves no more or less freedom in the civil order then all other religions. That's the missing argument re the First Amendment establishment clause on contraceptives.

February 24, 2014 A mistaken basis for a weighty right

Editor: Martin M. Beitler (letter 2/22) and Chicago Federal Judge Coleman (2/22 A-14) insist, rightly, that legislation and judicial decisions on "same-sex marriage" should not be based on changing public opinion but on the Constitution's equal protection clause, the true basis for the human and civil right of "marriage equality."

The difficulty with this thesis, however, is that traditional marriage and the legal homosexual union are radically diverse realities (the one including the procreative power; the other absolutely excluding it) never understood by legislators, jurists or society at large (until now) to qualify for the same name, marriage.

Equal protection of the law implies that citizens seek, univocally the same "right" from which some are currently inhibited from exercising by circumstances that in no way affect their ability to exercise that right. The homosexual couple cannot claim the right to marriage except by overturning the meaning of marriage and the equal protection of the law as applied to it as understood from time immemorial.

Neither the Constitution nor the natural moral law contains any basis for calling the homosexual union a marriage.

February 26, 2014   A faith-guided or religious life

Editor: In "License to Discriminate" (editorial, 2/25) you continue to view religious liberty only as freedom to worship or hold religious beliefs. Clinging tenaciously together in our pews and clenching our prayer and doctrine booklets, we dare not sniff outside this dog-house lest The

Times find we have transgressed proper bounds and be guilty of "discrimination."

Absent from The Times's ever-cramped view of religious freedom is any notion of the command to live one's whole life – to think, to speak, to write, to act, to vote – in harmony with the norms and values of one's religious beliefs.

Of course, all rights have limitations determined before the court of reason in a society where the common good, public order and the rights (sometimes conflicting) of all must be protected. But surely being coerced to cooperate in actions, celebrations or relationships one judges immoral is exactly one instance where religious freedom must trump the charge of discrimination.

"Sexual orientation" has come to mean now the acceptance, practice, promotion and depiction of all kinds of sexual activity by adults on a criterion of preference. There is no longer right or wrong but personal decision guided by preference or, as it may be, by legitimate "discrimination." The latter is the court of reason.

March 7, 2014 Op-Ed.   The claim of equal access

Op-Ed Editor: Some lawyers are currently trying to gain favorable judgments from the US court system, including the Supreme Court, for same-sex marriage by arguing that denying such recognition violates equal protection of the laws as guaranteed by the Fourteenth Amendment to our federal Constitution. A federal District Court Judge in San Antonio recently (Feb. 28) ruled in favor of same-sex marriage on that basis. Several New York Times editorials have also urged this approach. In this instance the alleged violation concerns access to marriage, denying this right to a certain class of persons because of their sexual orientation and practice; that is, because they engage in and can engage only in homosexual relations. Opposing such relations and marriage (same-sex marriage) based on them, it is held, violates equal protection guarantees and constitutes prejudice, invidious discrimination and a denial of "marriage equality." This reasoning is false.

Our understanding of marriage as an institution is one that has come down to us from time immemorial and from every corner of the earth. No state or society invented marriage; it was and is a basic relationship in nature and its purposes clear to all: A man and a woman enter a permanent partnership for companionship, love and life which, in principle, by their natural sexual union, gives rise to children, thus forming a natural family, the key element of society. Marriage was and is a sexual relationship, ruled by the complementary natural difference of male and female, even though individual spouses may fail to continue the sexual union or achieve its natural fruition by reason of age, injury or debility. Developing societies have gradually rejected polygamous unions.

People have understood this ordinance of nature and understand it now. The definition of marriage is lodged in human minds by human experience. When the contraceptive culture gradually evolved over the last two centuries, it became possible to remove the possibility of procreation, of having children, from the marital union. The premise for the complainants now is that the concept of marriage has (or should have) no necessary relationship whatsoever to the procreation of children. For the overwhelming majority of persons, however, this postulate removes, as it were, a central pillar from an overhanging roof. It is an essential change.

A new anthropological view

Is it not a grossly equivocal use of the term marriage to use it equally for the procreative marriage and the homosexual union? Should we now give the name and meaning of marriage to homosexual unions that by nature absolutely and universally exclude the possibility of procreation? If so, one can indeed hold that the present legal restrictions and social attitudes towards homosexual acts and homosexual (same-sex) marriages constitute not only the denial of equal protection of the laws but also prejudice, bigotry, unacceptable discrimination, a refusal to grant "marriage equality" and thus a violation of human and civil rights of homosexual persons who desire to marry one another.

To perceive the weakness of these assertions, let us first consider the US Supreme Court ruling on inter-racial marriage, given relatively recently (1967, Loving v. State of Virginia). The intending spouses, a man and a woman of two different races, sought marriage as it was universally understood - a permanent and potentially procreative union for one man and one woman. The only difference between the spouses was that of race, which was held by the State of Virginia at that time to prohibit marriage. Those opposed to inter-racial marriage relied on the racial difference – skin color, an accidental quality of a person - as the disqualifying circumstance. The Supreme Court's reasoning (1967) by analogy, however, makes clear that not only a racial difference but also all such other accidental qualities or differences – inter-racial, inter-tribal, inter-ethnic, inter-social class, inter-religious – entail no constitutional impediment to marriage. In fact, some such marriages already took place legally in other areas of the country or of the world. Indeed, however, opposition to such marriages, the Court said, was often based on a hidden prejudice that "such marriages just should not take place." The Virginia courts had truly denied the inter-racial couple equal protection of the law.

But, now, coming to the homosexual or same-sex marriage, a radically new element comes into play – a new view of the institution of marriage itself which removes an essential component, the (possible) procreation of children, always considered constitutive of the nature of the institution. They are not qualified to marry. The homosexual couple did not desire nor could they intend such a relationship. They could intend only an essentially diverse, alternative (and new) concept of marriage: a permanent loving partnership of two persons, characterized by a sexual relationship allowed by law but one from which procreation could not take place. (Even in this redefinition scenario, persons closely related by blood – e.g. - a mother and a daughter - could not marry.) But it is desired, claimed and demanded by such couples that this new, diverse relationship receive the name, legal and social status of marriage.

"Marriage" used equivocally

Should this redefinition, essentially contradictory, in part, to the received definition be accepted and the name marriage be equivocally used for them both? Those who say No maintain that this redefinition is an affront to (human) nature, to reason and to the experience of peoples all over the world from time immemorial. Moreover, it portends serious dangers for the family, the raising of children, the structures of society and the very continuance of the human race. A response to a relatively small group of complainants, this desired revision declares, in effect, the autonomy of man (the human person) over the institutions of (human) nature, after the fashion of some persons today who might say: "I was born a man (woman) but I now declare myself to be a woman (man) and demand to be treated legally and socially as such. Moreover, though I am aware of how marriage has been understood up to now in all civilizations, I demand my civil right to marry according to my own alternative concept of it. I demand that a homosexual union also be accorded the name, dignity and rights of marriage."

Two different – diverse realities

Equal protection by the laws for persons with the

requisite qualifications seeking the same object and alleging individual discrimination - for example, cases of acceptance for a particular job or type of job, job promotion, admission to a specific facility or school or exercise of a common civil right – is a key human - rights safeguard. In the case of marriage, however, one confronts the possibility of persons seeking radically diverse and contradictory understandings of marriage: traditional marriage, homosexual union or even a polygamous union. In fact, persons who testify to their experience of one or other degree of same-sex attraction do already have equal access to (traditional) marriage and therefore equal protection of the laws. They can and do legally marry. But they also want nature's institution of marriage to be changed.

Redefinition a step into darkness

Persons declaring themselves exclusively homosexual and seeking to marry a person only of the same sex are seeking a substantially different relationship, however, from that envisioned by the received laws and are manifestly demanding that the name, meaning, status, social and legal rights of that marriage be extended to the homosexual union. They are not vying with other persons for the same object, as is the case in examples mentioned earlier with persons seeking access to the same position or status. They do not want a union – marriage - which by nature universally includes the essential component of procreation or the potential thereof. Because they are not seeking that union defined in our history, laws and culture as marriage, they are not being unfairly excluded from marrying. They seek access to another status; viz. a homosexual union and have it given the name, dignity and rights of marriage. The concept of marriage which they now reject is not an arbitrary or particularist one, but one embedded in the mentality of civilizations of all time and entitled to be called <u>sui generis</u> marriage. According to our federal

Constitution, only the legislatures can change the definition of marriage.

On the other hand, this new, essentially diverse concept of marriage which society and the legal system are being asked to accept and to acknowledge as equal to the received definition manifestly offends (human) nature, reason and human experience. Together with the manufacture of children to which it will undoubtedly be linked, it poses serious dangers to the family, the raising of children, societal structures and the very continuance of the human race.

For all these reasons, no redefinition of marriage should be enacted to include homosexual unions, which could open the way to polygamous unions, homosexual or heterosexual. Should that redefinition occur, however, the Constitution or state laws would be in this instance defaced by the rule of unreason, the clear affront to nature. The immemorial understanding and definition of marriage, or action on its basis, however, provides no foundation for claiming violation of equal protection of the law in the case of homosexual partners barred from marriage because they are not seeking marriage as understood by the law, but an incompatible alternative. Same-sex marriage is not marriage.

July 2, 2014   **Shoe on the wrong foot**

Editor: "The justices endorse imposing religion on employees" (editorial, 7/1) misidentifies the party imposing something and the one being imposed upon.

The U.S Government is imposing on certain employers the requirement to provide their female employees with insurance that includes all FDA-approved contraceptives, oral and surgical sterilizations and drugs labeled by their manufacturers as potentially abortifacient.

The employers are being forced to violate their conscientious convictions, based on natural moral law or on religion or on both to provide materials or procedures they judge to be evil.

July 10, 2014   **Starting-point crucial**

Editor: "Hobby Lobby's Disturbing Sequel" (editorial 7/9) disturbs only those who with the Obama Administration and The Times support the imposition upon American citizens of the so-called neutral requirement to provide free-of-charge insurance for all FDA-approved contraceptives, chemical and surgical sterilization and drugs labelled potentially abortifacient by their manufacturers, the object of which is to prevent or end the disease of pregnancy.

Those who, on the other hand, maintain that such forced provision violates their consciences and religious liberty will be happy that the opt-out process is made bluntly simple for all and requires no one to designate, in effect, a surrogate to provide his or her compliance.

What government judges "morally neutral" in its religion of secularism is judged ethically and religiously offensive by other religions of this land. What The Times formerly labelled (editorial 5/27/12) as a "dramatic stunt" "built on air" now seems to contain a more challenging substance.

September 5, 2014   **Court legislating advances**

Editor: "A Blunt Defense of Marriage Equality," (editorial, 9/5/14) praises the Seventh Circuit Federal Court of Appeals (8/28) effectively declaring "unconstitutional" laws barring practicing homosexuals from marrying one another and identified such legislation as violating equal protection and due process guarantees of federal law.

Actually, the reasoning used to defend bi-sexual marriage rejected by the judges, is irrelevant or at most of secondary importance. Writers, jurists, scholars and legislators of earlier generations had no idea that the word marriage would be extended to include the homosexual union and that the denial of the name and legal privileges of marriage for such unions would be construed as a denial of equal protection of the laws. The two are so radically different; the attempt to equate them is rank equivocation.

Those seeking marriage and those seeking the homosexual union are seeking two radically different relationships – one including, in principle, and the other absolutely excluding the possibility of generating children. Until each state of the union, to which marriage laws belong, declare (arbitrarily and falsely) that marital marriage and the homosexual union are the same reality and deserve the same name and legal rights, claims about denial of equal protection are baseless.

September 15, 2014   Pub. NYT Sept. 22 (shortened)
This Is What an Abortion Looks Like

Editor: Merritt Tierce ("This Is What an Abortion Looks Like," Op-ed, 9/13), in commenting on the Wendy Davis case in Texas and praising her forthrightness, describes her own tangled, excruciatingly painful emotional struggle in reaching her own final decision to abort (again). What an abortion looks like is relegated to the brief reference that an early abortion is merely a "five-to 15 minute procedure."

Yes, we must sympathize with Merritt for her suffering, in her case caused mainly by the promiscuous life she led after her divorce. Merritt tells us it's OK. It's our job so say it's OK each woman has the right (a man, too) to make [the decision] and do with his/her body what she/he will. Sad. In the case of a pregnant woman, moreover, there is more than one body - two bodies, two lives, not merely one. No recognition that a developing human life has been destroyed and I have done it. No recognition of the terrible wrongdoing, no sorrow, no repentance, no desire to make amends. It's OK, Ok. Sad.

September 25, 2014   No ultimatum from Frank Bruni

Editor: Op-Ed Columnist Frank Bruni ("I Do Means You're Done, 9/25) puts on his theologian's robe once again to tell Pope Francis and his successors that if they don't change the Church's teaching on sexual morality - especially the teaching on homosexual relations – as several "enlightened" countries around the world have done - the Church is going down the tubes.

Bruni's readers must understand that everything he says is based his personal conviction that homosexual relations are morally legitimate, as is therefore same-sex marriage. His view contradicts the sexual morality of the Old and the New Testaments, of our Savior Jesus Christ, of the Catholic Church which speaks us in His name, of Eastern Orthodox, Orthodox Lutheranism, Orthodox Judaism and Islam.

The Catholic Church does not condemn anyone; but it must correct those Catholics who in a public act reject its teaching. So the two senior gentlemen in Montana did that and could not avoid the consequences. How could they have been unaware for thirty years of the biblical/Church teaching on homosexual relations? The Catholic Church cannot admit change in its definitive teaching, which the principles of sexual morality are.

Public rejection of the Church's definitive teaching brings consequences for clergy, religious and laity regarding sacramental participation and holding church offices. What these two senior gentlemen from Montana need is a friendly sit-down with Church representatives who will help these would-be faithful Catholics understand and willingly take the steps needed to straighten out this unfortunate squabble.

September 30, 2014   Politics a species of fashion?

Editor: "The Tide of the Culture War Shifts" (editorial, 9/29) provides new evidence that politics should be re-classified under the broader heading FASHION. The Times delivers it in daily and special-issue advertising: the design, the message, the bodily pose, facial expressions and assorted accoutrements on a relatively youthful body draped in a fast-changing couture seeking the fullest visual-emotional response indicating a buyer has been won. So it is with political couturiers seeking to put a more inviting face on all "birth control," sterilization and abortifacients approved by the FDA and all paid for by "preventive health care" insurance. The tide is in, these advocates tell us and the "right-wing" bigots, supporters of discrimination and foes of women's reproductive rights and of marriage equality are flattened.

But the latest Pew Trust polls point out that the direction of the shifting tide is not certain. The tide that carried out all the flotsam-jetsam and brought in all these paid-for gifts will move out again. The tide is a kind of fashion as is the politics and public opinion of the day.

October 7, 2014   A columnist free to dump

Editor: Frank Bruni's column (10/5) for the Times' Sunday Review section mentions his previous columns (9/25/14,

6/16, 2/18/13) in which he slanders, assaults and condemns the Catholic Church for the Church's biblical teachings on sexual morality, concerning which no response, including my own, was admitted to print. Now, he has added a fourth (10/5) column, no less gratuitous, insulting and misinformed than the previous three.

Although the assertions in this column and the previous ones amount to, as it were, an indictment in a court of law by an uncredentialed and uninformed person, and no response of the accustomed or required letter's length could possibly deal with the charges – even if it were admitted (past expertise suggests it would not be printed.)

Thus I have a suggestion for you. If you wish to maintain journalistic fairness, that you invite a Catholic journalist also competent in Church teaching and concerned for fairness and courage and give him/her the same space to respond to Frank Bruni.

If no one is invited or admitted, prepare to join the chorus of the already large company of those who are convinced that you can't get a fair hand from the editorial management of The Times. For a candidate I recommend William A. Donohue, president of the Catholic League for Religious and Civil Rights. His competence in this field is well known and widely appreciated.

October 17, 2014   **Precise labels are important**

Editor: "Reproductive Rights on the Ballot," (editorial, 10/4) and "The Supreme Court Acts for Texas Women (editorial, 10/16) continue to use the term <u>reproductive</u> mistakenly. Because reproduction has already taken place when the sperm and ovum meet, the right being sought or supported is to expel or destroy the developing fertilized ovum - an abortion.

All scientists agree that a new human life begins with fertilization. The fertilized ovum, apart from accident or assault, is well on its way to becoming an embryo, a fetus and a neo-nate once reproduction has occurred. Advocates often use a change of words to minimize or maximize perceived evil. Very common in recent years has been the use of <u>pedophilia</u> to designate mature males who molest teenage males, whereas <u>pedophile</u> properly designates adults molesting young children, not teenage males. Ephebophilia is mature males molesting teenage males. The overwhelming majority of perpetrators in the recent-years sex scandals has been homosexual ephebophiles not pedophiles.

October 22, 2014   Reviewing from the balcony

Editor: Pope Francis must be chuckling as he reads Columnist Thomas L. Friedman's "Putin and the Pope," (10/22) where he finds himself compared, much to his own advantage, with Vladimir Putin, currently of Moscow and world political fame.

The Pope gets A+ for pushing his flock "to be more inclusive of gays and divorced people" for his general empathy with the world's troubled, whereas Putin gets an F for "hostility" and being a "thug." We're happy for the good P.R. Pope Francis gets for the welcoming language found actually in the interim and final reports of the recent synod (10/5-18). A caution must be had, however, in drawing too much from specific words.

A person is not defined by reference to his or her sexual orientation and practice. Great (and ordinary) men and women have been and are homosexually oriented. Welcoming, respectful language can be found in the doctrinal congregation's 1986 Declaration, even long before that in a pastoral letter of the late Bishop Mugavero of Brooklyn some forty years ago, in letters of the USCCB and, above all, in the universal Catholic Catechism (1992).

The reason why some people in the Church are wary of unqualified positive welcoming language on this issue is the conclusion that many will draw, even some more insistently: Now your next step is to welcome homosexual practices as equally acceptable with heterosexual marital love. Not so. A welcome is not a license to do wrong.

October 27, 2014
Reserve judgment for the Synod Part II

Editor: Ross Douthat's "The Pope and the Precipice" (Sunday Review, 10/26) can be called only astonishing in the alarmist deeply concerned insight – if true – he provides into the significance of the Synod on the Family (Part I) recently held in Rome. I detect a soul-stirring not usual for a Times Op-Ed familiar.

Does his account show a Church, certain leaders of which - including the Bishop of Rome - on the "precipice" seeking to change some basic Church teachings? For those of us not intimately conversant with the workings, transcripts and memos of the synod, however, there are too many ifs, buts, seems, suggests, perhaps, etc., even for Ross Douthat himself, to arrive at any categorical answer. But as a journalist dedicated to accuracy and completeness, Douthat's account deserves careful discussion.

Delegates to the Synod, it must be recalled, entered the council long prepared with a working document, which they then discussed avidly, from which an interim summary draft was provided, then vigorously debated, and a finalized summary document issued – which is for discussion throughout the Church during the coming year. Part II of the Synod takes place a year from now. Precipice or wide-open plain is a year ahead.

EPILOGUE

Dear Readers: Having mulled over these 300+ letters to the editor of The New York Times dealing chiefly with religion-related editorials from over a 50-year plus period, you can recognize that The Times editorial board is no friend of religion, particularly of the classic Judaeo-Christian religion inextricably bound up with the heritage of our civilization and our nation. Rather, it is fair to say that this newspaper has been and continues to be a firm and powerful voice for the demolition of this religious heritage, most notably respecting the ethical norms endorsed by its tenets concerning the inviolability of innocent human life, human sexuality, marriage, the family and religious freedom.

The most recent expression of this editorial trend has been, in the first decades of this century, an almost frenzied campaign to gain for the homosexual union universal legal and social acceptance as marriage. And, high on the heels of this effort is a similar push for special civil rights by claimants of gender dysphoria, the claim by persons conceived and born in one sex to belong now to the other.

As a great granddaughter of the 18th-century European Enlightenment and its celebrated protagonist Voltaire - "écrasez l'infame," the Judaeo-Christian religion known to him in his day or, more simply, dogmatic religion - The Times still confronts this sparring partner in the intellectual arena. This ancient foe, religion, however, is itself somewhat weakened by a continuously evolving public-opinion-regulated a la mode form of the traditional faith. Against this less stalwart barrier, The Times still must engage Orthodox Judaism and the Catholic and Orthodox forms of Christianity.

For The Times, the proper venues for religion's activities are their worship halls, instructional annexes, if any, and space for services to fellow believers. God is a rather vague entity, privately acknowledged and worshipped, very diversified in his requirements for diverse adherents and, above all, not to be dragged into the public forum as a participant for his reflections on public issues.

From that kind of intellectual environment, a secularist atmosphere wedded to Cartesian reason and tangible scientific evidence alone, it is easy to lay down inhibiting, restricting rules such as the Jeffersonian metaphor "the wall of separation between Church and State," which was meant as a caution and a protection for the freedom of both sides of the great divide, but became enshrined much later as the first unassailable interpretive principle used by Voltaire's intellectual descendants as a hammer to keep religion in its place.

The resistance of The Times and other secularist bastions in the thought world, notably the public-school establishment, to consider additional relevant principles in identifying forms of permissible aid to religiously affiliated schools, their students and their tax-paying parents was telling. The latter also clearly have natural, parental and civil rights to a practicable school choice, guaranteed by Pierce vs. Society of Sisters (1925) and the UN Universal Declaration of Human Rights (1948). But such a cause was and is a loser at The Times.

The gradual loss, too, distinct from specific religious tenets, of the concept of the natural moral law in the legal philosophy of Western civilization but evident in our nation's foundation documents, entailed lessened support for basic ethical norms protecting the inviolability of innocent human life, human dignity, traditional marriage and equality in human relationships. But from a world recognized as subjects to the dominion of a Creator God a transition has been taking place to the total dominion of man over man and man's world. Thus the ethical anomalies of which The Times has found itself not the origin but a strong editorial supporter in the intellectual world and for change in societal structure.

In this slide to a different worldview, fairly described as secularist and relativist, where man is sovereign, the lessening influence of the Judaeo-Christian religion is undoubtedly, also, as mentioned, a significant factor. The Times religion-related editorials are witness to and an active agent in this trend. Readers must be alert to this development and not be passive onlookers but active opponents of the slide and cogent proponents of the Judaeo-Christian worldview.

Destroying human life in the womb by surgical dissection or lethal drugs, manufacturing children, deliberately sterilizing persons, directly intervening to help people die, other life-destroying procedures such as human embryo experimentation and human cloning pose instant challenges. Happily both worldviews reject capital punishment, even when inflicted in accord with law, and the ever-present savagery of war. Sexual partnership between persons of the same-sex proclaimed as "marriages," including logically, if not in fact, multiple spouses of the same or diverse sexes, transgendering of persons from one sex to the other – all these excepting the firmly rejected capital punishment and savagery of war – are justified as man seeking and achieving in freedom his personal self-identity.

Truly, each new tinkering with human nature, even those proclaimed as life-enhancing, contribute to the building of the Tower of Babel – man overreaching himself in seeking to be sole master of himself and of his world. Arbitrary human choice has replaced the natural moral law discoverable by reason in man himself and his own experience. This natural moral law, confirmed and buttressed, to be sure, by the Judaeo-Christian religion, is the clarifying and determining rule for his developing and enhancing his life in this world.

Who is sovereign? As we travel along this path to greater and greater human control, who is sovereign? Are there limits to the autonomy the Creator God has given his vicar, man, in developing God's creation? Yes there are. The natural moral law provides the rule and the limit.
God the Creator is still sovereign.

INDEX

N.B. The bulk of the material in this volume is made up of Letters to the Editor of The New York Times. The subject of each letter is coordinate to the editorial (or op-ed. essay) on which it comments, and which is identified in the first sentence of the letter. The number of letters on a particular subject is thus determined by the number of editorials on that particular issue. The index here is that of these issues with a reference to the letters (page) sent in response.

210, 210-211, 211, 211-212, 212-213, 214, 225, 237-239, 242-243, 249-250, 250-251, 253-254, 254, 270, 270-271.

- equal access constitutional clause alleged to guarantee such a homosexual marriage right: pp. 226-227, 227-228, 276, 276-281.

- state-mandated imposition of ethically disputed norms for certain kinds of morally neutral "contraceptive" health-care insurance to be provided free to all female employees in various Church-associated institutions: pp. 233, 282, 282-283.

- Catholic teaching not understood: pp. 26-27, 33-35, 61-62, 78-79, 81, 89-90, 100-101, 102, 112-113, 114-115, 128-129, 145-146, 158-159, 185-187, 198-199, 199, 212, 220-221, 222-223, 223-224, 228-229, 252, 253, 256-257, 257-258, 261-262, 284, 285-286, 287.

- conferral of priestly/episcopal ordination on men only: pp. 41-42, 64-66, 266-267.

- public law, policy and religious convictions: pp. 91-92, 92-93, 255.

- art and bigotry: pp. 98- 99.

- Church and state: pp. 122, 139, 140, 171-172, 174, 231-232, 234, 234-235, 239, 269.

- natural marriage: pp. 207.

- compassion – condemnation: pp. 214.

- publishing only one point of view: pp. 161, 162, 164, 175-176, 177-178, 201-202, 206-207, 244.

Made in the USA
Middletown, DE
25 January 2015